Undocumented Migration to the United States

IRCA and the Experience of the 1980s

Edited by

FRANK D. BEAN
BARRY EDMONSTON
JEFFREY S. PASSEL

RAND CORPORATION
Santa Monica, CA

THE URBAN INSTITUTE
Washington, DC

Library of Congress Cataloging in Publication Data

Undocumented Migration to the United States: IRCA and the Experience of the 1980s/edited by Frank D. Bean, Barry Edmonston, and Jeffrey S. Passel.

1. Aliens, Illegal—United States. 2. United States—Emigration and immigration. 3. United States. Immigration Reform and Control Act of 1986. I. Bean, Frank D. II. Edmonston, Barry. III. Passel, Jeffrey. S.

JV6493U53   1990   353.0081'7'09048—dc20   90-12967
                                                                                          CIP
ISBN 0-87766-490-0 (alk. paper)
ISBN 0-87766-489-7 (alk. paper; casebound)

Urban Institute books are printed on acid-free paper whenever possible.

Printed in the United States of America.

9   8   7   6   5   4   3   2   1

Distributed by:
          University Press of America
4720 Boston Way   3 Henrietta Street
Lanham, MD 20706   London WC2E 8LU ENGLAND

The RAND Corporation was chartered in 1948 as a nonprofit institution to "further and promote scientific, educational, and charitable purposes, all for the public welfare and security of the United States of America." To meet these objectives, RAND conducts rigorous analyses of significant national problems to provide decisionmakers and the public with a better understanding of the policy issues involved.

RAND's research is analytic, objective, and interdisciplinary. National security programs focus on the planning, development, acquisition, deployment, support, and protection of military forces, and include international matters that may affect U.S. defense policy and strategy. Domestic programs include civil and criminal justice, education and human resources, health sciences, international economic studies, labor and population, and regulatory policies.

THE URBAN INSTITUTE is a nonprofit policy research and educational organization established in Washington, D.C., in 1968. Its staff investigates the social and economic problems confronting the nation and government policies and programs designed to alleviate such problems. The Institute disseminates significant findings of its research through the publications program of its Press. The Institute has two goals for work in each of its research areas: to help shape thinking about societal problems and efforts to solve them, and to improve government decisions and performance by providing better information and analytic tools.

Through work that ranges from broad conceptual studies to administrative and technical assistance, Institute researchers contribute to the stock of knowledge available to public officials and private individuals and groups concerned with formulating and implementing more efficient and effective government policy.

Conclusions or opinions expressed in Institute publications are those of the authors and do not necessarily reflect the views of other staff members, officers or trustees of the Institute, advisory groups, or any organizations that provide financial support to the Institute.

ACKNOWLEDGMENTS

Financial support for the Program for Research on Immigration Policy is provided by The Ford Foundation, and a special debt of gratitude is owed not only to the Foundation in general, but also to Paul Balaran, William Diaz, Mary McClymont, and Steve Cox in particular, all of whom have provided helpful guidance and assistance to the Program and its activities.

Many of these chapters are revisions of papers initially presented at a conference sponsored by the Program and held at The Urban Institute. Several persons deserve particular thanks for helping to make the conference and resulting book possible. They include William Gorham and Steven B. Hitchner at The Urban Institute for their unfailing support of immigration policy research; LaVonia Proctor for organizing the conference and helping with the word processing on several of the chapters; Sheila Lopez for coordinating the process of chapter revisions undertaken by authors from around the country; three anonymous reviewers for making numerous helpful suggestions for revising all or parts of the manuscript; and the conference participants for their insightful comments on the papers during the conference discussions.

CONTENTS

Foreword   xix

Introduction   *Frank D. Bean, Barry Edmonston, and
Jeffrey S. Passel*   1
   Types of Undocumented Immigrants   3
     Degree of Commitment to Living in the United
      States   4
     Legal Status   5
   Assessments of Undocumented Migration   6

**1 Perceptions and Estimates of Undocumented
Migration to the United States**   *Barry Edmonston,
Jeffrey S. Passel, and Frank D. Bean*   11
   Perceptions of Illegal Immigration   12
     Historical Background   12
     Speculative Assessments   15
   The Need for Analytical Estimates   19
   Conceptualization and Measurement of Illegal
     Immigration   22

**2 Post-IRCA Undocumented Immigration to the
United States: An Assessment Based on the June
1988 CPS**   *Karen A. Woodrow and Jeffrey S. Passel*   33
   Has IRCA Worked?   33
     Size of the Undocumented Population   34
     Flow of Undocumented Immigrants   34
     Outline of the Chapter   35
   June 1988 Current Population Survey   35
   Estimated Legally Resident Foreign-Born
     Population   38

Characteristics of the Foreign-Born Population
    Included in the June 1988 CPS   42
    Country of Birth and Period of Entry   42
    Changes over Time   45
Estimates of the Undocumented Immigrant
    Population and the Impact of IRCA   46
    Undocumented Immigrants in the June 1988 CPS
        and June 1986 CPS   47
    Change in the Undocumented Population   50
    Pre-IRCA Undocumented Immigrants Who Did
        Not Legalize   54
    Post-IRCA Undocumented Immigration   56
    Effect of SAWs on the Estimates of
        Undocumented Immigrants   59
Discussion and Conclusion   65
    Methodological Issues and Future Research   67
Appendix   73

**3 Annual Estimates of Nonimmigrant Overstays in
the United States: 1985 to 1988**   Robert Warren   77
Definitions   78
Estimation Procedure   79
    Estimates of System Error   79
    Estimates of Overstays   80
    Assumptions and Limitations   81
Results   82
    Continent of Origin   83
    Country of Origin   83
    Trends in Overstays by Country   84
    State of Destination   85
    Age   86
Additional Analysis   87
    Departure Statistics   88
    Other Analyses   94
    Summary   97
Appendix   101

**4 Post-IRCA Changes in the Volume and Composition
of Undocumented Migration to the United States: An
Assessment Based on Apprehensions Data**   Frank D.
Bean, Thomas J. Espenshade, Michael J. White, and
Robert F. Dymowski   111

Purpose and Rationale   112
Kinds of Apprehensions Statistics   114
Developing a Model of the Process   118
   The Model   118
   Variables and Data   120
Empirical Results   125
   Descriptive Results   125
   Regression Estimates   133
   Components of Change in Apprehensions   139
Discussion   143
Conclusion   152

5 Undocumented Migration to the United States:
Evidence from a Repeated Trials Model   *Thomas J.*
Espenshade   159
   Repeated Trials Model   160
      The Social Process of Illegal Alien Apprehension   161
      A Formal Model of the Apprehension Process   162
      A Preliminary Examination of IRCA's Effects   168
   Determinants of the Undocumented Migrant Flow   170
   IRCA's Impact on the Undocumented Flow   172
   Discussion   175

6 Effects of the Immigration Reform and Control Act
of 1986: Preliminary Data from Mexico   *Douglas S.*
Massey, Katherine M. Donato, and Zai Liang   183
   Data Sources   185
   Short-Term Impact on Undocumented Migration   189
   Long-Term Impact on Use of Social Services   198
   Summary and Conclusion   207

7 Undocumented Migration from Mexico to the
United States: Preliminary Findings of the Zapata
Canyon Project   *Jorge A. Bustamante*   211
   Reform of U.S. Immigration Laws   211
   A Paradox   213
   The Measurement of Migrant Flows Across the
      Border   214
   Some Preliminary Findings   216
   Conclusions   222

8 Impacts of the 1986 U.S. Immigration Law on Emigration from Rural Mexican Sending Communities   *Wayne A. Cornelius*   227
  Methodology   227
    Knowledge and Perceptions of IRCA   230
  Propensity to Migrate   232
  Effects of Legalization Programs   235
  Settlement Patterns in the United States   238
  The Economies of Migrant Families   241
  Conclusion   243

9 Undocumented Migration Since IRCA: An Overall Assessment   *Jeffrey S. Passel, Frank D. Bean, and Barry Edmonston*   251
  Flow of Migrants Across the U.S.-Mexico Border   252
    Relationship between INS Apprehensions and Migration Flows   253
    Review of Research Studies   254
    Research Findings   257
    Other Evidence   258
  Stock of Undocumented Immigrants in the United States and Additions to the Permanent Resident Population   259
    Visa Overstayers   260
  Conclusion   262

About the Editors   267

About the Contributors   269

Tables

2.1 Construction of Estimated Legally Resident Foreign-Born Population, by Area of Country of Birth: June 1988   39
2.2 Foreign-Born Population by Area or Country of Birth and Period of Immigration: June 1988 Current Population Survey   43
2.3 Foreign-Born Population by Area or Country of Birth and Period of Immigration: June 1988, June 1986, and November 1979 Current Population Surveys and 1980 Census   44

2.4 Foreign-Born Population in the Current
     Population Survey, Estimated Legal Foreign-
     Born Residents, and Estimated Undocumented
     Population in the CPS, by Area or Country of
     Birth and Period of Immigration: June 1986
     and June 1988   48
2.5 Estimates of Undocumented Immigrants Included
     in the June 1988 Current Population Survey
     and Undocumented Immigrants "Not Expected
     to Legalize" in the June 1986 Current
     Population Survey, by Area or Country of Birth
     and Period of Immigration   52
2.6 Estimated Annual Change in Undocumented
     Immigrant Population Based on Comparison of
     June 1988 Current Population Survey, Earlier
     Current Population Surveys, and the 1980
     Census, by Area or Country of Birth: 1986–88,
     1979–88, and 1980–88   53
2.7 Foreign-Born Population from the June 1988 and
     June 1986 Current Population Surveys and
     Estimated Legal Foreign-Born Entrants: January
     1987–June 1988 and January 1985–June 1986   58
2.8 Estimates of the Undocumented Population
     Included in the June 1988 Current Population
     Survey Based on Alternative Assumptions
     About Inclusion of Special Agricultural
     Workers (SAWs)   63
2A.1 Approximate Standard Errors and Confidence
     Intervals for Foreign-Born Populations: June
     1988 Current Population
     Survey   75
3.1 Computation of System Error for Nonimmigrants
     Arriving October 1986 to March 1987   80
3.2 Selected Nonimmigrant Statistics: 1985–88   83
3.3 Estimated Nonimmigrant Overstays, Expected
     Departures, and System Error: Fiscal Years
     1985–88   84
3.4 Estimated Overstays by Area of Origin: 1985–88   86
3.5 Estimated Nonimmigrant Overstays, by Continent
     of Origin and Class of Admission: Fiscal Years
     1985–88   87
3.6 Top 10 Countries of Overstays: Fiscal Year 1988   88

3.7 Estimated Nonimmigrant Overstays, by Area and
    Selected Country of Citizenship: 1985–88   89
3.8 Countries with Large Changes in Overstays:
    1985–88   92
3.9 Top Six States of Destination of Overstays: Fiscal
    Years 1986–88   92
3.10 Estimated Nonimmigrant Overstays, by State or
    Area of Destination: Fiscal Years 1986–1988   93
3.11 Estimated Nonimmigrant Overstays, by Age and
    Class of Admission: Fiscal Years 1987 and
    1988   95
3.12 Estimated Overstays by Age: Fiscal Year 1988   97
3.13 Provisional Estimates of Net Overstays: Fiscal
    Year 1988   98
3A.1 Nonimmigrant Classes of Admission and
    Variables Included in Nonimmigrant
    Information System   103
3A.2 Illustration of Procedure for Estimating
    Overstays: B2 (Tourist) Arrivals, by Air,
    October 1986 to March 1987   104
3A.3 Expected Departures by Country of Citizenship:
    Fiscal Years 1985–88   108
4.1 Type of Apprehension by Length of Time Illegally
    in the United States: All Sectors, January
    1977–September 1989   116
4.2 Variable Names, Definitions, Sources of Data, and
    Expected Signs of Estimated Coefficients   122
4.3 Average Annual Linewatch and Non-linewatch
    Apprehensions, Enforcement Hours, and
    Apprehensions per Hour: Fiscal Years 1977–89   130
4.4 Average Annual Apprehensions (Mexican Males,
    Mexican Females and Children, and Non-
    Mexicans), Enforcement Hours, and
    Apprehensions per Hour: Fiscal Years 1977–89   132
4.5 Regression Results for the Logarithm of Monthly
    Linewatch and Non-linewatch Apprehensions,
    1977–89   134
4.6 Regression Results for the Logarithm of Monthly
    Apprehensions of Mexican Males and Females
    and Children, 1977–89   140

4.7 Reduction in Linewatch Apprehensions Due to
     IRCA's Provisions, Including Changes in INS
     Enforcement, SAWs Legalization, and
     Remaining IRCA Effects   144

4.8 Reduction in Non-linewatch Apprehensions Due
     to IRCA's Provisions, Including Changes in
     INS Enforcement, SAWs Legalization, and
     Remaining IRCA Effects   146

4.9 Components of Post-IRCA Changes in the
     Apprehensions of Mexican Males and of
     Mexican Females and Children   148

5.1 Repeated Trials Model   163

5.2 Average Monthly Values of the Undocumented
     Flow in Pre-IRCA and Post-IRCA Periods   169

5.3 Variable Names, Definitions, Sources of Data, and
     Expected Signs of Estimated Coefficients   171

5.4 Regression Coefficients for the Logarithm of the
     Monthly Flow of Undocumented Immigrants,
     1977–88   173

5.5 Impact of IRCA on the Flow of Undocumented
     Migrants to the United States   174

6.1 Age-period Analysis of the Probability that Males
     will Leave San Francisco del Rincón,
     Guanajuato, on a First Trip to the United
     States   192

6.2 Age-period Analysis of the Probability that Males
     will Leave Either San Francisco del Rincón or
     León, Guanajuato, on a First Trip to the United
     States   194

6.3 Predicted Probabilities that a 20–24-Year-Old
     Male Will Migrate Illegally to the United States
     and that a Male will Migrate Illegally by Age
     40 Given Period Rates: San Francisco del
     Rincón and León, Guanajuato, 1975–88   195

6.4 Method that Undocumented Migrants Used to
     Cross the U.S.-Mexico Border, the Number of
     Apprehensions they Experienced, and the Fee
     Paid to Coyotes, by Period, 1975–88: Migrants
     from San Francisco del Rincón and León,
     Guanajuato   197

6.5 Logistic Regression Analysis of the Probability of
     Ever Using Selected Social Services: Migrants
     from Four Mexican Communities, 1982   200
6.6 Logistic Regression Analysis of the Probability of
     Having Children in U.S. Schools: Migrants
     from Four Mexican Communities, 1982   203
6.7 Logistic Regression Analysis of the Probability of
     Having Taxes Withheld from Paycheck:
     Migrants from Four Mexican Communities,
     1982   204
6.8 Predicted Probability of Using Selected Social
     Services by Years of U.S. Experience and Years
     Since Receiving Documents: Migrants from
     Four Mexican Communities, 1982–83   206
8.1 Knowledge and Perceptions of IRCA   231
8.2 Propensity to Migrate   233
8.3 Legal Status of Emigrants from Research
     Communities, by Period of Migration to the
     United States (Pre- and Post-IRCA)   239

Figures

4.1 Total Apprehensions at Border   126
4.2 Linewatch Apprehensions at Border   127
4.3 Non-linewatch Apprehensions at Border   128
4.4 Comparison of Apprehensions at Border   131
5.1 Probability of Being Apprehended on Each
     Attempt: All Southern Border Sectors   166
5.2 Monthly Flow of Undocumented Immigrants: All
     Southern Border Sectors   167
7.1 Zapata Canyon Project: Greatest Number of
     Undocumented Immigrants per Day, a
     Comparison of December 1986–88 (Women
     Only)   216
7.2 Zapata Canyon Project: Greatest Number of
     Undocumented Immigrants per Day, a
     Comparison of December 1986–88 (Men Only)   217
7.3 Monthly Averages of the Greatest Number of
     Undocumented Immigrants per Day in the
     Zapata Canyon (Men Only)   218

7.4 Monthly Averages of the Greatest Number of
    Undocumented Immigrants per Day in the
    Zapata Canyon (Women Only)   218
7.5 Immigrants' Total Expenses from their Regions of
    Origin to the Border (Tijuana)   219
7.6 Immigrants' Total Expenses from their Regions of
    Origin to the Border (Ciudad Juárez)   220
7.7 Immigrants' Total Expenses from their Regions of
    Origin to the Border (Nuevo Laredo and
    Matamoros)   221
7.8 Education Level of Undocumented Immigrants
    who Crossed through Tijuana from October
    1987 to September 1988 (Women Only)   222
7.9 Education Level of Undocumented Immigrants
    who Crossed through Tijuana from October
    1987 to September 1988 (Men Only)   223
7.10 Education Level of Undocumented Immigrants
    who Crossed through Nuevo Laredo from
    October 1987 to September 1988 (Men Only)   224

FOREWORD

The 1986 Immigration Reform and Control Act is the most sweeping revision of U.S. immigration policy since the national quota system was abolished in 1965. Its major objective is to reduce illegal immigration through two strategies—legalizing immigrants already in the country and reducing future flows to the country through imposing penalties on employers who hire illegal aliens. The success of the legislation will, therefore, be measured at least in part by whether the flow of illegal immigrants to the United States has been reduced. This book uses a variety of data sources and methodologies to address that important but complex question.

The book is one of a series of products of the Program for Research on Immigration Policy. The Program, with funding from The Ford Foundation, was established by The RAND Corporation and The Urban Institute to study important domestic and international issues raised by IRCA, to address the larger continuing questions and problems of immigration and immigrant policies, and to disseminate and exchange information about IRCA and immigration through publications, working groups, and conferences.

Initial drafts of many of the chapters by the contributing authors were presented at a Program-sponsored conference held at the Institute on July 21, 1989, and revised to take into account points made in the conference discussions. The chapters by Thomas Espenshade and Wayne Cornelius were specially commissioned because each of them adds important supplementary information to the analyses contained in the conference papers. The chapters by the volume editors provide context and coherence by reviewing the background literature on the issues raised by the problem of measuring and interpreting undocumented immigration and providing an overall review and synthesis of the results presented in the chapters and related research.

The Institute is pleased to publish this volume as part of its long-standing interest in population issues generally, and immigration questions particularly. The size, growth, and impact of the illegal immigrant population in the United States were hotly debated in the period culminating in the passage of IRCA. That debate is still going on, fueled by uncertainty about the effects of IRCA on the illegal immigrant flow. This book presents the most up-to-date evidence on the issue, in the hope of improving the information base underlying the debate and the policies that will result from it.

William Gorham
President

INTRODUCTION

Frank D. Bean, Barry Edmonston, and Jeffrey S. Passel

Since the mid-1960s, immigration to the United States has undergone three important changes (Bean, Vernez, and Keely, 1989). The first has involved increases in legal immigration brought about by the passage of the 1965 Amendments to the Immigration and Nationality Act of 1952. By abolishing the national origins quotas that had been in operation since the early 1920s and by giving priority to family reunification as a basis for immigrant admission, the amendments have led to levels of immigration that by historical standards are quite high. For example, during the 1980s, nearly 600,000 immigrants per year were granted lawful permanent residence in the United States, levels that were surpassed only in the peak immigration years early in the 20th century.

The second major change has consisted of a shift in the national origin composition of immigrants. During the 1950s, nearly 70 percent of immigrants came from European countries or Canada. This figure dropped to about 20 percent during the 1970s and then to about 15 percent during the 1980s. The percentage coming from Asian, Latin American, or Caribbean countries increased from about 30 percent during the 1950s to about 75 percent during the 1970s, and then to over 80 percent during the 1980s (U.S. Immigration and Naturalization Service, 1989). The Hispanic and Asian components in the recent immigration flows have also included sizable numbers of refugees from Cuba and Southeast Asia, persons who subsequently have changed their status to that of permanent resident alien. Thus, immigrants have not only become more numerous than at any time in decades, but they also have perhaps become more visible (Bean and Sullivan, 1985).

The third important shift has involved an increase in illegal immigration, which began in 1964 after the end of the Bracero Program (an agreement operated jointly by the United States and Mexico for temporary workers in agriculture). At that time, the number of illegal labor migrants coming from Mexico started to rise. The immigration of persons who entered the country legally and then stayed beyond their visa expiration dates also increased. Partly in response to these trends, the Select Commission on Immigration and Refugee Policy was established in 1978 with a mandate to study all aspects of U.S. immigration policy. The commission concluded in its final report that "one issue has emerged as most pressing—that of undocu- mented/illegal immigration" (U.S. Select Commission on Immigra- tion and Refugee Policy, 1981: 35). This perception also came to be shared by the general public. For example, 87 percent of respondents in an early 1980s survey in southern California thought that "the illegal immigration situation" was currently either "somewhat se- rious" or "very serious" (Muller and Espenshade, 1985: 201).

All of these changes contributed to a movement to reform U.S. immigration policy. To many lawmakers and citizens during the late 1970s and the early 1980s, the country seemed to have "lost control of its borders," and the costs of immigration appeared increasingly to outweigh the benefits. Even worse to some observers, the nation's immigration policies appeared ineffective in preventing illegal entry into the country at a time when tens of thousands of legal petitioners were waiting to obtain entry visas. These concerns combined to cre- ate a strong push to curtail illegal immigration. After several false starts reflecting continuing debate and controversy over immigration policy, the U.S. Congress passed the Immigration Reform and Control Act (IRCA) in October 1986, and the legislation was signed into law the following month.

IRCA constitutes the most sweeping revision of U.S. immigration policy since the national origins quota system was abolished in 1965. Although the legislation contains several major provisions, its major objective is to reduce illegal immigration. It was expected that this would be accomplished in two ways: first, by legalizing illegal im- migrants already in the country (through both a regular legalization program and a legalization program for special agricultural workers [SAWs]); and, second, by reducing future flows to the country through the imposition of penalties on employers who hire illegal workers (Bean et al. 1989). The litmus test by which the legislation will be judged is the extent to which these aims have been accomplished. Based on numbers, the legalization programs have been quite suc- cessful, enrolling 1.8 million and 1.3 million applications in the regular and SAWs legalization programs, respectively (González Baker and Bean, 1990). But to determine whether IRCA has changed the flow of illegal immigrants coming to the country is a more difficult matter.

This book addresses this issue of whether IRCA has succeeded in reducing illegal immigration. The chapters following present the most up-to-date evidence available on the size of the illegal population in the United States and its changes during the 1980s, a topic of considerable public policy significance (e.g., see Bean et al., 1989; Passel, 1986). Issues pertaining to the size, growth, and impact of the illegal population in the United States were debated vociferously before the enactment of IRCA (Bean, Telles, and Lowell, 1987). They will continue to be important policy issues for years to come, if for no other reason than that it is impossible to evaluate whether IRCA has been successful without knowing the size of the illegal population in the years after IRCA's passage.

TYPES OF UNDOCUMENTED IMMIGRANTS

Meaningful assessments of the volume and impact of undocumented migration must distinguish among several different kinds of entrants. One classification comes from the government, which makes a distinction between (1) persons who enter without any sort of legal visa (called "EWIs" because they "enter without inspection") and (2) persons who enter with legal visas but remain beyond the authorized time limit (called "visa overstayers"). Similar to visa overstayers are other foreign-born persons who enter the United States legally but violate the terms of their temporary visas by taking a job (for example, persons who hold tourist visas but work). The distinction between EWIs and visa overstayers is useful to the degree that it facilitates the measurement of an important underlying reality in undocumented immigration. In the case of EWIs and visa overstayers, almost all EWIs are from Mexico and most visa overstayers are from non-Mexican countries (see chapter three). The distinction does not provide much insight, however, into two dimensions of variation that are important for understanding the results of studies of the size and impact of the undocumented population. These dimensions are the degree of commitment to living in the United States and legal status.

Degree of Commitment to Living in the United States

Undocumented migrants come to the United States with varying degrees of commitment to reside in the country. Those intending to stay permanently are often called "settlers," and those intending to return to their countries of origin "sojourners" (Chavez, 1988). In the case of undocumented Mexicans and Canadians, some observers would add still a third category—"commuters," or persons who "do not actually live in the United States, but rather cross the U.S.-Mexican or U.S.-Canadian borders on a daily or almost daily basis to work in the United States" (Passel, 1986: 183). This typology should be kept in mind when attempting to sort through the evidence on illegal immigration, particularly that relating to labor migration from Mexico. As noted later, the distinctions are also relevant to discussions of "stocks" (or populations) of undocumented aliens versus "flows" across the border (Bean et al., 1989).

Although it is common to think of sojourners as consisting of Mexican undocumented immigrants, there are also sojourners from other countries, as well as sojourners who are legal immigrants. Indeed, the high rates of emigration from the United States by legal immigrants from Caribbean countries (Warren and Kraly, 1985) suggest that many are actually sojourners. Sojourners from countries other than Mexico and Canada probably have longer durations of residence in the United States.

The distinction between sojourners and settlers is often a matter of degree. Massey and others have documented that migration between Mexico and the United States is a process occurring over a period of time, rather than a single event (Massey et al., 1987; Portes and Bach, 1985). Many individuals start as sojourners. Over time, as their ties to the United States become stronger and those to Mexico weaker, they extend their stays in this country to the point where they consider their residence to be the United States.

IRCA may have changed this settlement process in several ways. For a large segment of the sojourner population, IRCA has made crossing the border easier through the SAWs legalization program (Bean et al., 1989), which may hasten the settlement process, thereby converting many sojourners into settlers. On the other hand, for many formerly undocumented immigrants, the general legalization program, having regularized immigrants' status in the United States, will permit them to travel to Mexico more frequently. Some proportion of this settled population may ultimately return to Mexico and become sojourners or commuters as a result of the legislation.

Legal Status

The various legal statuses of foreign-born persons living in the United States correspond fairly well with the ideal types of settlers, sojourners, and commuters. Permanent resident aliens represent the group usually thought of as "legal immigrants." The vast majority of this group consists of settlers, although significant proportions of permanent resident aliens return to their countries of origin within 10 years (e.g., Warren and Peck, 1980). Refugees consist mainly of settlers also, although if conditions change in the country of origin, significant numbers of refugees could emigrate. Asylees are similarly situated.

The groups of aliens legalized under IRCA, as conceived of in the law, also correspond to the settler and sojourner ideal types. Those granted legal status under the general legalization program are settlers, since legalization required at least five years continuous residence in the United States. SAWs, on the other hand, were generally conceived of as sojourners who returned to the United States every year to participate in seasonal agricultural activities. Undoubtedly, however, some of the SAWs were settlers. And even the SAWs who were really sojourners are entitled to settle in the United States under the terms of IRCA. At this point, the proportion of the SAWs population that has settled in the United States is not known.

Nonimmigrants can enter the United States in a large number of different visa categories. Some nonimmigrants are entitled to stay in the United States for considerable lengths of time. However, the category of nonimmigrant should, by definition, include mostly sojourners, since the conditions of admission imply departure. The principal exception is the refugee category, which the U.S. Immigration and Naturalization Service (INS) classifies in the nonimmigrant group.

Undocumented immigrants fall into all three categories. Lack of clear demarcation between the settler/sojourner categories is partly responsible for the exaggeratedly large numbers sometimes used to describe the size of this population (Passel, 1986). Large flows of sojourners or commuters across the U.S.-Mexico border (as suggested by INS apprehensions) have been interpreted by many observers as indicating growth in the settled undocumented population that is as large as that in the labor migration flows. However, empirical work over the last decade has failed to find evidence for annual growth of 1 million or more persons in the undocumented population, as would be implied by annual INS apprehensions exceeding this amount.

ASSESSMENTS OF UNDOCUMENTED MIGRATION

In analyzing undocumented immigration to the United States, it is particularly important to distinguish between "stock" and "flow." The former term refers to the number of illegal aliens residing in the country at a particular time. The latter term refers to the number entering (or exiting) the country during a specific time interval. Failure to distinguish between these categories has contributed to confusion about the size of this population. Stated differently, because the number of illegal migrants (especially Mexicans) coming into the country has often appeared to be quite high, observers have sometimes assumed the number residing here was equally high. This view overlooks the fact that the majority of illegal migrants return to the country of origin. In short, commuters and sojourners have often been mistaken for settlers.

Two useful ways to classify efforts to estimate illegal immigration are, first, according to whether they provide estimates of the stock or the flow of illegal aliens, or both; and, second, according to whether they provide estimates of Mexican or non-Mexican illegal immigration, or both. These distinctions are vital because estimating such different segments of illegal stocks and flows requires different data sources. Moreover, different data sources are not equally useful for estimating numbers of Mexicans and non-Mexican stocks and flows. Current Population Survey (CPS) data, for example, are more useful for estimating the number of Mexicans than the number from other countries, because the latter are spread over so many different countries of origin that the individual country estimates are unreliable. Apprehensions data, when used to assess changes in flows, yield valuable information only on Mexican flows because the vast majority of apprehensions are of Mexicans.

Estimates of stocks and flows from individual non-Mexican countries must therefore rely on other data sources. Fortunately, illegal aliens from non-Mexican countries differ from Mexicans in important ways that make this possible. For example, illegal aliens from other countries appear largely to have initially come to the United States legally and then to have over-stayed their visas. Data on visa overstayers thus provide one way to estimate changes in illegal flows involving persons from particular countries other than Mexico. CPS data are also useful for assessing non-Mexican stocks and flows, although, as noted, the sample size in these surveys is not large enough to yield reliable information for individual non-Mexican countries.

The various authors in this book rely on different data sources to tackle the problem of estimating whether IRCA has had an impact on illegal immigration to the United States. It should be noted that some of the chapters present results based on data collected in Mexico, the single most important source country for illegal immigration to the United States. Examining Mexican, as well as U.S., data is especially important to round out the picture of changing patterns of illegal immigration, because IRCA could have the effect of reducing both the stock of illegal Mexicans in the country (through legalization) and the flow coming into the country (by creating disincentives for sojourners already in the country to continue going back and forth) without deterring the initiation of new illegal migration.

Chapter one, by Barry Edmonston, Jeffrey S. Passel, and Frank D. Bean, examines the recent history of efforts to estimate the size of the U.S. undocumented population. The authors note that controversy over the definition and measurement of various U.S. subpopulations is not a new phenomenon, especially when these subpopulations have involved racial and ethnic groups. Moreover, public policy debates revolving around questions of the size of population subgroups have frequently led to the reporting of distorted numbers in the public media. The authors document, for example, exaggerated press reports concerning the size of the U.S. illegal population, and show how research results have contributed over time to the development of greater consensus about these numbers and more accurate media accounts.

Chapter two, by Karen A. Woodrow and Jeffrey S. Passel, examines 1980 U.S. Bureau of the Census data and a series of CPS data sources from the 1980s to estimate the size of the illegal population included in these data sources and its change over time. The authors use a residual methodology that involves subtracting an estimate of the legal population from the census or CPS estimate of the foreign-born population to obtain an indication of the size of the undocumented component. They also examine changes during the 1980s in the size of this component. When disaggregated by country of origin, the results are more useful for Mexico than for other countries.

In chapter three, Robert Warren develops and presents estimates of visa overstayers in the United States, including data for two years before and two years after IRCA. This is the first time such estimates have been calculated. Because the CPS data reported by Woodrow and Passel in chapter two cannot reliably be disaggregated by country of origin, Warren's data provide the only information available on the possible effects of IRCA on illegal migration from *individual* non-Mexican countries.

Chapter four, by Frank D. Bean, Thomas J. Espenshade, Michael J. White, and Robert F. Dymowski, analyzes monthly tallies of INS apprehensions data at the U.S.-Mexican border using time-series methods to assess changes in apprehensions patterns since IRCA's passage. Their analysis endeavors to remove statistically the influence of demographic, economic, and seasonal factors that affect the flow of undocumented Mexican migrants (and thus the number of apprehensions). The result is a more systematic basis for assessing whether apprehensions may have been affected by IRCA. The authors also present for the first time separate results for men and for women and children, thus enabling an examination of the hypothesis that IRCA may exert a differential impact on these two components of the undocumented flow at the southern border.

Chapter five, by Thomas J. Espenshade, is a companion piece to chapter four. It provides an illustration of the importance of taking into account multiple apprehensions of the same individual in interpreting changes in apprehensions levels over time. Apprehensions data overstate the number of individual *persons* who are caught crossing the border illegally, because some individuals are caught more than once. Models that consider this factor represent an improvement over those that assume an isomorphic correspondence between apprehensions and crossers.

The sixth chapter, by Douglas S. Massey, Katherine M. Donato, and Zai Liang, is the first of three chapters to present data collected in Mexico. Massey and his colleagues examine survey data collected in two Mexican communities in 1987–88 as well as findings from an earlier survey of four communities collected in 1982–83. The authors use age-period-cohort analysis to estimate the probabilities, by year, of making a first trip to the United States. Although their number of post-IRCA observations is very small, the analysis serves to focus our attention on first-time migration. This is crucial, because first-time and repeat migration may be different phenomena and may rise or fall depending upon different factors.

Chapter seven, by Jorge A. Bustamante, presents the findings of a unique data collection project that has been monitoring the number and kind of undocumented persons crossing the U.S.-Mexican border at one of its highest traffic points—Zapata Canyon, just outside Tijuana. In addition to monitoring the flow through regular, periodic photographic observations, Bustamante has conducted interviews of crossers both before and after IRCA to survey their migration experiences. His results are thus not only relevant to the question of changes in the volume of flow, but they also shed light on shifts in the composition, degree of difficulty, and financial expense associated with undocumented migration.

Chapter eight, by Wayne A. Cornelius, draws upon 945 interviews conducted in 1988–89 in three communities in the traditional sending states of Jalisco, Michoacán, and Zacatecas. His research examines how IRCA has affected perceptions of the U.S. labor market, the propensity to migrate, settlement patterns in the United States, and the economies of migrant families and their home communities. The research also provides a basis for assessing how the legalization programs of IRCA may be changing the nature of both the legal and undocumented migrant flows to the United States.

In chapter nine, the editors of this volume examine these and related results as a basis for drawing conclusions about IRCA's impact on undocumented migration three years after passage of the legislation. The conclusions pertain more to Mexican undocumented migration than to migration from other countries, simply because most of the available data are for Mexicans. But as the work of Warren and Passel (1987) has shown, Mexican illegal migration constitutes a majority of illegal migration to this country.

References

Baker, Susan González, and Frank D. Bean. 1990. "The Legalization Programs of the 1986 Immigration Reform and Control Act: Moving Beyond the First Phase." In In Defense of the Alien, edited by Lydio F. Tomasi, 3–11. New York: Center for Migration Studies.

Bean, Frank D., and Teresa Sullivan. 1985. "Immigration and Its Consequences: Confronting the Problem." Society 22 (May/June): 67–73.

Bean, Frank D., Edward Telles, and Lindsay Lowell. 1987. "Undocumented Migration to the United States: Perception and Evidence." Population and Development Review 13 (4, Dec.): 671–90.

Bean, Frank D., Georges Vernez, and Charles B. Keely. 1989. Opening and Closing the Doors: Evaluating Immigration Reform and Control. Santa Monica, Calif, and Washington, D.C.: The RAND Corporation and The Urban Institute.

Chavez, Leo. 1988. "Settlers and Sojourners: The Case of Mexicans in the United States." Human Organization 47 (2, Summer): 95–107.

Massey, Douglas S., Rafael Alarcón, Jorge Durand, and Humberto González. 1987. *Return to Aztlan: The Social Process of International Migration from Western Mexico.* Berkeley and Lost Angeles: University of California Press.

Muller, Thomas, and Thomas J. Espenshade. 1985. *The Fourth Wave: California's Newest Immigrants.* Washington, D.C.: Urban Institute Press.

Passel, Jeffrey. 1986. "Undocumented Immigration." *Annals, American Academy for Political and Social Sciences,* 487 (Sept.): 181–200.

Portes, Alejandro, and Robert Bach. 1985. Latin Journey: *Cuban and Mexican Immigrants in the United States.* Berkeley and Los Angeles: University of California Press.

U.S. Immigration and Naturalization Service. 1989. *Immigration Statistics: Fiscal Year 1988.* Washington, D.C.: Statistics Division, U.S. Immigration and Naturalization Service, April.

U.S. Select Commission on Immigration and Refugee Policy. 1981. *U.S. Immigration Policy and the National Interest: the Staff Report of the Select Commission on Immigration and Refugee Policy.* Washington, D.C.: U.S. Government Printing Office.

Warren, Robert, and Ellen Percy Kraly. 1985. *The Elusive Exodus: Emigration from the United States.* Population Trends and Public Policy Occasional Paper No. 8. Washington, D.C.: Population Reference Bureau.

Warren, Robert, and Jeffrey S. Passel. 1987. "A Count of the Uncountable: Estimates of Undocumented Aliens Counted in the 1980 U.S. Census." *Demography* 24 (3, Aug.): 375–96.

Warren, Robert, and Jennifer M. Peck. 1980. "Foreign-born Emigration to the U.S.: 1960–1970." *Demography* 17 (1, Feb.): 71–84.

Chapter One

PERCEPTIONS AND ESTIMATES OF UNDOCUMENTED MIGRATION TO THE UNITED STATES

Barry Edmonston, Jeffrey S. Passel, and Frank D. Bean

Assessments of the success of the 1986 Immigration Reform and Control Act (IRCA), as well as estimates of the social and economic effects of illegal immigration, depend upon the development of estimates of the number of illegal aliens residing in the country at a particular time (the "stock" of illegal aliens) and upon gauging the number coming into the country each year (the annual "flow" of illegal immigrants). Public policy debates about the size and impact of the illegal alien population must be based, in other words, on a clear understanding of the demographic conditions of this population: its size, dynamics, and structure. Because of the policy significance of these questions, it is important to obtain some historical perspective on how illegal immigration has been perceived, as well as some grasp of the important methodological issues involved in trying to assess the size of the undocumented population in the United States. Thus, the purposes of this chapter are: (1) to examine perceptions and conjectures about the size of the illegal alien population in the United States in the decades preceding the passage of IRCA; (2) to discuss the reasons why these assessments came to be viewed with skepticism; and (3) to present a conceptualization of the illegal alien population that serves as a guide for interpreting estimates of the size of this population, together with the data sources, research approaches, and empirical results of some of the analytical assessments on population size.

It should be noted at the outset that we use the terms *illegal alien, undocumented migrant,* and *illegal immigrant* interchangeably. Although there are subtle differences in connotation among these terms, there has been little consensus in the research literature as to which is the superior label for this population. Actually, none of these terms is entirely satisfactory. A person who enters without documents and intends to stay only a short time and then return home might best be called an *undocumented migrant.* A long-term resident who enters as a visitor and then stays permanently might best be called an *illegal immigrant*. For official purposes, an *illegal alien* is defined as someone who is physically present in the United States and who either entered the country illegally, has not regularized his or her immigration status, or has violated his or her terms of entry. This definition includes those who enter without documents or with false documents, as well as several categories of individuals who entered the country legally but subsequently came to reside in the United States in an illegal immigration status. As we note later, this definition makes no distinctions among more temporary and more permanent immigrants, nor among immigrants who come for different reasons.

In discussing estimates of the illegal migration to the United States, it is also important to distinguish the gross inflow from the net flow of illegal migrants. The gross inflow represents the number of new illegal entrants to the United States in a given time period. The net flow, or net change in the illegal migrant population, represents the difference between the number of new illegal entrants and departures from the illegal alien population. In this case, we take departures to include death, emigration (through either deportations or voluntary and undetected exits), and conversion to legal residence. The gross inflow of illegal migrants always exceeds the net flow and, hence, the observed inflows for a particular time period cannot be interpreted as an indication of the size of the net flow without taking into account departures. Later sections in this chapter offer a more detailed exposition of the relationship between gross and net flows for the the illegal migration population.

PERCEPTIONS OF ILLEGAL IMMIGRATION

Official statistics and demographic estimates both shape and are shaped by social and economic policies (Duncan, 1984). Interest in statistics on race and ethnicity and estimates of illegal immigration are no exception.

Historical Background

A brief historical review demonstrates that interest in ethnicity and immigration is not a recent phenomenon in the United States. In the 1890s, Francis Walker, who was then director of the Census, cited census data in support of the argument that the United States was being overrun by "less desirable" immigrants. Describing immigrants from southern and eastern Europe as "beaten men from beaten races" (in Conk, 1987: 162), he suggested that newer immigrants constituted poorer stock compared to earlier immigrants. While Horace Greeley was stating "Go West, young man," Walker noted that the new immigrants did not have the resources to leave the large cities of the East and hence were not helping to continue the progress of the United States in the West (in Conk, 1987: 167). These "undesirable" immigrants were therefore viewed as a burden on the nation. Walker's arguments contributed to the development of an intellectual foundation for the later enactments of national origin quotas. Thus, even in early immigration studies, data on immigrants, examined by ethnicity and social and economic characteristics, were used to support immigration restriction and a realignment of immigration national origins.

In the decades following, the United States considered literacy tests and medical examinations as bases for exclusion, and finally realized that the "new" immigrants from southern and eastern Europe could be effectively excluded using national origin quotas. These national origin quotas were developed in conjunction with Bureau of the Census studies that showed that the fastest growing immigrant groups were primarily ones that were relatively small in the earlier censuses (Conk, 1987: 164). Two successive pieces of immigration legislation, in 1921 and 1924, changed the national origin quotas for U.S. immigration. The 1921 act introduced the first quotas for U.S. immigration, setting national origin limits at 3 percent of the number of foreign-born of that group enumerated in the 1910 Census. This act became law at a time when immigration had been at levels of 880,000 persons per year from 1900 to 1910 and 574,000 per year from 1910 to 1920. Yet the 1921 act effectively limited immigration to about 358,000 persons per year. The act also effectively weighted the ethnicity composition of immigrants toward the "old" ethnic groups of northern and western Europe, but did allow for some southern and eastern European immigrants. Even this mix of immigrants, however, was considered by some Americans to allow entry to too many of the "new immigrants."

The 1924 act, called the Immigration Act of 1924, immediately limited immigration for national origin groups to 2 percent of that nationality as enumerated in the 1890 Census. If 2 percent yielded less than 100 people, then 100 was set as the quota. The effect of this act was to set an overall limit for quota immigration at about 162,000 persons per year. Then, as of July 1, 1927, the 1924 act specified that the national origin quotas were to be based on the proportion of that national origin group enumerated in the 1920 Census times 150,000, yielding a total limit on quota immigration of 150,000. However, the act permitted selected categories of non-quota immigration, so the actual number of immigrants could exceed 150,000. The second phase of quotas was postponed twice before becoming effective on July 1, 1929. The 1924 quotas for immigrants thus based the national origins on the ethnicity of the native-born, who were predominantly of northern and western European origin, and of the foreign-born population, which included many who entered the United States several decades prior to the massive flow of immigrants from southern and eastern Europe. The country-of-origin quotas established in 1924 effectively brought about a dramatic restriction in immigration, as well as national quotas that persisted for 40 years.

Restrictions on Asian immigration have a more complicated history. The Chinese Exclusion Act of 1882 effectively ended immigration of Chinese to the United States and was the first proscription of an ethnic group in this country (Lee, 1989). Additional Asian groups were restricted through legislation in 1917 that created "barred zones" for Asian immigration. Japanese immigration was restricted by the Gentleman's Agreement of 1907, and their immigration was effectively ended by the Immigration act of 1924. Finally, Filipinos, who continued to immigrate since the United States governed the Commonwealth of the Philippines, found their movement curtailed by the Congressional Act of 1934. Thus, immigration legislation enacted in the 1920s, in association with additional restrictions for Asians, substantially realigned ethnic quotas, addressing the "problem" of the "new" immigrants by the procedure of establishing ethnic quotas based on the "old" ethnicity of the native-born and the established foreign-born population.

A recurrent issue in the study of immigrants involves the definition of ethnicity. Debates about ethnicity in the United States as embodied in Census definitions arose in the context of two issues: controversy over the place of blacks in United States society and debate about the need to change immigration policies. The differences between natives and immigrants have often overlapped with other discussions about how to define and measure ethnic status (Petersen, 1987: 194). National origin quotas in the 1924 legislation were deplored by Robert Park, a leading sociologist at the University of Chicago, who argued that studies of assimilation showed the eventual assimilation of newer immigrant groups (in Petersen, 1987: 195). These questions about ethnicity and assimilation have underlain census data collection efforts, with questions asked at various times on the place of birth of one's parents, the number of years elapsed since immigration to the United States, and whether the person was a naturalized citizen or had applied for naturalization. After the restrictive policies of the 1920s, interest in ethnicity waned somewhat, but later underwent a resurgence because of social changes in three periods: expanded immigration after World War II, increased refugee numbers, and increasing immigration from Asia and Latin America after 1970.

Policymakers in the United States have long been concerned about changing ethnicity and about the social and economic characteristics of immigrants and the United States population. The terms *illegal* and *undocumented*, while having a dramatic quality, have earlier precedents in phrases such as "new" and "undesirable" immigrants. The social and political issue of illegal immigrants, and the desire for data on their numbers, is immersed in a historical pattern of public policy concerns about changing immigration flows.

Speculative Assessments

Over the past 20 years media reports have frequently referred to a "flood" of illegal immigrants to the United States or a "vast sea" of illegal aliens residing in the country. Most of these media accounts have been based on speculative assessments or conjectures, some cited so frequently that they became accepted facts in the public imagination. Initial speculative assessments of the illegal alien population were developed "out of the blue," to use the words of a recent observer (Hill, 1985). These speculative figures included national totals aggregated from educated guesses by U.S. Immigration and Naturalization Service (INS) regional directors around the United States and unsubstantiated opinions provided by unnamed persons in Delphi surveys in which a group of experts were queried about their opinions. These assessments were reported, often uncritically, by the press, and exaggerated figures were perpetuated by later press reports that quoted the earlier accounts. We now know that the initial conjectures on the size of the population were much too high, and early critics (e.g., Keely, 1977; Siegel, Passel, and Robinson, 1980; and Bean and King, 1982) questioned the accuracy of "high" illegal immigration numbers. However, it took several years before an accumulation of empirical estimates began to cast widespread, serious doubt on the validity of the early speculations (Bean, Vernez, and Keely, 1989; Passel, 1986).

To shed light on trends in press reports about the illegal population, we collected the information reported here in two ways. First, we reviewed the several dozen research articles in the scholarly literature for citations of any press accounts. Second, we systematically surveyed articles in five national newspapers: the *Christian Science Monitor*, the *Los Angeles Times*, the *New York Times*, the *Wall Street Journal*, and the *Washington Post*. We located articles published between January 1975 and April 1990 that contained either the phrase "illegal aliens" or "illegal immigrants," and either the words "quantity" or "number" in the text. We then examined the article to see whether a specific numerical estimate was cited and, if so, the specific estimate and justification for the estimate. We report on trends in press reports through 1985, when the National Academy of Sciences released its report on immigration statistics. This report argued that the numbers of illegal aliens in the United States were substantially fewer than generally reported in the press. Moreover, by 1985, researchers had published a number of estimates that, at least within the scholarly community, provided convincing indication that the size of the population was lower than the speculative assessments.

Estimates of the size of the illegal alien population have varied greatly over the past two decades. One of the earliest entries into the policy debates was that of INS Commissioner Raymond Farrell, who conjectured in 1972 that there were one million illegal aliens then in the population (in Hill, 1985: 226). Although Farrell's assessment was apparently unsupported by empirical research, subsequent research (Warren and Passel, 1987) suggests that this assessment may have been reasonable. The escalation of estimates seems to have occurred after Commissioner Farrell's term. For example, in 1976, General Leonard J. Chapman (1976a), then commissioner of the INS, testified before a congressional subcommittee that there were 4 million to 12 million undocumented aliens in the United States in 1975. Chapman was a noted advocate of the perspective that high illegal immigration was a threat to United States borders, and that massive increases were needed in funding and in INS Border Patrol personnel to curb the problem. Chapman's estimates, which were significantly higher than previous figures, were not derived from empirical work.

Also in the mid-1970s, the Immigration and Naturalization Service commissioned Lesko Associates to prepare assessments of the size of the illegal alien population in the United States. Although the specific universe for the Lesko group's assessments was poorly defined, the firm concluded that there were 8.2 million undocumented aliens in the country in 1975, of which 5.2 million were undocumented aliens of Mexican birth (Lesko Associates, 1975). Although Lesko Associates claimed that their results were based on empirical work, their method, in fact, relied on a survey of individual speculative assessments using the Delphi technique. Their assessments were subsequently criticized as an inappropriate use of this technique (Siegel et al., 1980), and the study has also been faulted by scholars and researchers on other grounds (for a detailed assessment, see Roberts et al., 1978).

The Immigration and Naturalization Service gradually lowered its estimate to about 6 million illegal aliens in the United States, while admitting to a variation of several million persons around this number. For example, an INS staffperson estimated, in a 1977 periodical published for INS employees, that there were 6 million illegal aliens in the United States in 1976 (Guss, 1977). Commissioner Chapman (1976b) also narrowed his range for the number of illegal aliens, suggesting that there were 6–8 million in the country in 1976. Although these figures represented a lowering of earlier figures, they entailed no firmer basis in empirical research. In 1978, INS Commissioner Leonard Castillo (1978), although offering no rationale for his estimates, lowered Chapman's earlier assessments by several million, noting that there were 3–6 million illegal aliens in the United States in 1978.

Few speculations about the number of illegal aliens in the country appeared after about 1978. In the early 1980s, INS commissioners became noticeably reluctant to cite single numbers or even a numerical range. Criticisms of unsubstantiated speculations were joined by new research results suggesting that the number of illegal aliens was considerably below the figures publicly stated by the INS leadership. Nevertheless, a few speculative assessments continued to surface in the public debate. For example, in 1985 Corwin noted that there were 8 million to 10 million undocumented aliens in the United States in 1981. His conjecture was an aggregate of speculative assessments of the illegal alien population from various countries of origin for specific areas in the United States.

Speculative assessments about the annual flow of illegal aliens into the United States have been very infrequent. Commissioner Chapman (1976a) provided an early assessment in testimony to the U.S. Senate Subcommittee on Immigration and Naturalization, suggesting that a 500,000 net annual increase in the illegal alien population was occurring in the 1970s. At about the same time, Secretary of Labor Ray Marshall (Los Angeles Times, 1977) argued that 2 million to 3 million undocumented migrants entered the United States each year in the mid-1970s. Although this figure was outlandishly high as an estimate of the net flow to the United States, even given the large estimates on the size of the illegal alien population put forth in the mid-1970s, the number was picked up and subsequently reported by the Wall Street Journal (1977). Immigration officials were also quoted as saying that about 700,000 apprehensions of illegal aliens attempting to enter or already in the country occurred annually. For every apprehension, they speculated there were two to three successful entries by illegal aliens. Such figures often were interpreted as indicating that more than 2 million persons entered the country each year. However, none of these interpretations took into account multiple apprehensions of the same individual or return migration of the seasonal illegal migrants. Nor did observers try to reconcile 2 million illegal entrants each year with the INS assessment of a total of 6 million illegal aliens residing in the United States.

By the early 1980s, research had revealed that there were several categories of illegal immigrants coming to the United States and that a substantial proportion of illegal aliens returned to their countries of origin following seasonal or short work periods. This research suggested that perhaps 200,000 or 300,000 illegal aliens, at most, were being added annually to the United States population (Passel, 1985). The results of this and other analytical research on illegal immigration were reviewed and evaluated in a report issued by the National Research Council (Hill, and Warren, 1985), the research arm of the National Academy of Sciences (NAS), in June 1985. This study also included an assessment of the size of the illegal population, which was estimated to range from 2 million to 4 million persons, figures substantially below previously cited figures in the press. Also, the report concluded that the population of illegal aliens had not been growing rapidly in recent years.

Three out of the five earlier cited national newspapers covered the results of the NAS study: the Wall Street Journal (1985), the New York Times, (1985) and the Los Angeles Times (1985). The New York Times (1985), in particular, noted that prior estimates reported by the press were often made with woefully inadequate data and that the speculative conjectures had almost invariably been too high.

Our review of press reports from 1985 to the present indicates that the major United States newspapers are now somewhat more cautious about reporting data on the number and flow of illegal aliens into the United States. We located only four press reports during the period from 1985 to 1989, three in the *Washington Post* (1985, 1987, 1989) and one (aside from the 1985 article on the NAS study) in the *New York Times* (1987). In the *Washington Post* (1985) article, INS Commissioner Alan Nelson stated that the INS had no precise figures on the numbers of illegal aliens entering the United States each year, but that the "median belief" was that the number was about 6 million. In support of this, he noted that 1.3 million illegal aliens were apprehended in 1985, which was a slight increase compared with the numbers apprehended in the two previous years. In 1987 the *Washington Post* published an editorial referring to "the millions of undocumented workers" in the country, but did not give a specific numerical estimate, and the New York Times (1987) ran a front-page article noting that the United States was enforcing laws on employers who hire illegal aliens, but the story did not cite any specific estimate of the number of illegal aliens in the country. Recently, the *Washington Post* (1989), in an editorial on the large number of illegal immigrants who seek asylum, argued that the number of illegal aliens entering the country has diminished since 1986. The editorial also stated: "No one has an exact figure on those who sneak across the border. . . ."

THE NEED FOR ANALYTICAL ESTIMATES

The wide differences in the initial speculative assessments of the size of the illegal alien population, in conjunction with strong criticisms of these numbers by demographic researchers, provided an impetus to develop analytical estimates that were more empirically based. Several questions were raised in the first criticisms, which provided a working agenda. In particular, demographers offered specific criticisms of speculative assessments. First and foremost, researchers were suspicious of the conjectural basis of the assessments, which had wide numerical ranges and changed constantly. Second, scarce and poor data existed on illegal immigrant flows, and demographers were wary of early work that extrapolated from unrelated data or generalized from data bearing no explicit relationship to illegal alien flows. Third, in the late 1970s, methods for the study of illegal immigration were not yet well-developed. Although researchers could see that many illegal immigrants were in the United States and that more were arriving every year, they concluded that speculative assessments needed a firmer empirical and analytical basis.

These criticisms provided a focus for early research. By the late 1970s, researchers had identified the following key tasks: (1) the need to develop methods for estimating illegal aliens residing in the country; (2) the need to review the quality of available data that could be used for studying the illegal alien population; and (3) the need for independent estimates of the number of resident illegal aliens and the annual flows. A number of reviews of available empirical estimates of the size of the illegal alien population became available. Siegel et al. (1980) offered the first, relatively complete review of empirical studies. Later, Hill (1985) reviewed a similar selection of the best studies, adding his own estimates, and Bean, King, and Passel (1986) discussed empirical studies that focused on the size of the illegal immigrant population of Mexican origin.

Siegel et al. (1980: 18) concluded their review of analytic studies available by 1980 by noting that "there are currently no reliable estimates of the number of illegal aliens in the country or of the net volume of illegal immigration to the United States in any recent past period." Their review disregarded, of course, speculative assessments with no grounding in data. But they were also uncomfortable in accepting the then available empirical studies. Specifically, they indicated several criticisms: first, that available studies typically depended upon broad untested assumptions about the data; second, that alternative reasonable assumptions often could be used, and these alternatives produced major differences in the estimates; and third, that some studies were biased in their data and methods in ways that affected the final estimates.

Hill's (1985: 227) review of available studies offered the following summary:

(a) for those studies that produced estimates of upper and lower population limits, the range between the limits is typically large; (b) variations from method to method are large; (c) the estimates do not show a clear trend over time, although no estimates are available for the period since 1980; (d) only two estimates, the maxima of Lancaster and Scheuren for 1973 and Bean, King, and Passel for 1980, are consistent with an illegal population in the range of 6–12 million.

Hill criticized many of the same studies discussed by Siegel et al. in 1980, but also reviewed several more recent empirical studies. Although analytical studies had improved markedly during the early 1980s, Hill concluded that many studies continued to rely on untested assumptions [in fact, key assumptions of several important studies cannot be tested with available data] and that, furthermore, the final estimates are sensitive to these assumptions. Hill suggested the reasonableness of a population figure of about 1.5 million to 3.5 million illegal aliens in the United States in 1980, although he quickly noted that there was no compelling evidence for the upper and lower bounds of this estimate. Finally, Hill argued that no firm empirical basis existed for conclusions about increases or decreases in the size of the illegal alien population during the late 1970s and early 1980s.

Bean et al. (1986) reviewed substantially the same set of studies summarized by Siegel et al. (1980) and Hill (1985). They included a few more recent studies and a more detailed evaluation of estimates of illegal aliens at the subnational level, and emphasized in their conclusions that available analytical studies estimated the illegal alien population for one specific time. Like the two previous reviews, Bean, et al. (1986) noted the sensitivity of estimates to data assumptions and that analytical research had not established conclusive lower and upper limits for the size of the illegal alien population. However, they differed from Hill in concluding that available evidence suggested that the undocumented Mexican population grew during the late 1970s.

By the early 1980s, some measure of consensus had emerged about the state of available information on the illegal population in the United States. General agreement existed on several key points. First, there were no entirely satisfactory estimates of the number of illegal aliens residing in the United States. Not only were the speculative assessments merely conjectures "out of the blue," but the available empirical estimates typically relied on untested assumptions or had major data limitations. Second, most of the empirical work had been carried out on immigrants from Mexico, and these estimates thus neglected the unknown number of illegal aliens from other parts of the world. Estimates of illegal aliens from Mexico were often multiplied by a "correction factor," which had little empirical basis, to achieve an estimate of the total number of illegal aliens. Third, even given the major problems with available empirical estimates, the estimates were usually significantly below the speculations often cited. Speculations of 6 million to 12 million or more illegal aliens in the United States did not receive support from empirical studies, which found substantially lower numbers, perhaps of 3 million to 5 million at most. Fourth, it was clear that the very high speculations about the number of undocumented Mexican nationals in the United States were confusing the high number of apprehensions of short-term migrants with permanent, long-term illegal immigrants. This issue needed greater attention in empirical studies. Fifth, available empirical work suggested the need for new and possibly novel data collection and analysis, from independent data sources, to provide testable, specific estimates of the illegal alien population.

CONCEPTUALIZATION AND MEASUREMENT OF ILLEGAL IMMIGRATION

Illegal aliens are often treated as though they constitute a homogeneous category. This confounds discussion and makes it difficult to analyze the pathways of individuals into and out of the illegal alien population. Passel (1986: 183-84) distinguished between three types of undocumented immigrants: "settlers," "sojourners," and "commuters." These three types of immigrants can be identified by their length of residence in the United States and, in a related fashion, by their frequency of travel to the United States. This distinction is important because it determines the number of persons residing in the United States per illegally entered immigrant. "Settlers" immigrate to the United States with the intention of establishing permanent residence. This type of immigrant is more likely to involve family members, including children, and to be from countries not contiguous to the United States. Because settlers stay year-round and for a long period of time, they tend to make use of a broader range of social services than short-term residents. However, it is important to note that the distribution of settlers by duration of stay depends upon past annual flows and the rates of departure from the illegal alien population. The illegal alien population becomes generally more recent in their length of stay in the United States during periods of high entry and becomes generally longer-resident during times of low entry. The distribution of the average length of stay in the illegal alien population is critical for discussion of legalization programs that are based on demonstrated length of stay in the country, since the proportion of aliens who can meet such a criterion will depend in large part upon the nature of past in- and out-flows.

"Sojourners" are persons who enter the United States for a specific purpose, usually to seek employment, and who return to their home country after a brief stay. The duration of their stay may vary, but they differ from settlers primarily in that they return after a brief period in the destination country. The bulk of the United States sojourner population comes from countries close to the United States, especially Mexico, and is often seasonal in nature. The sojourner population has consisted predominantly of males and overwhelmingly of young adults. Most of this population comes to the United States for work-related reasons.

"Commuters" cross the border into the United States on a daily or weekly basis, working in the United States but residing across the border. This is a relatively small group, estimated to be in the tens of thousands (Passel, 1986: 183), with most of the illegal commuters crossing the Mexico-United States border. This group currently makes few demands on social services and related institutions in the country, since its members and their families continue to reside outside the United States.

Differences between settlers, sojourners, and commuters are difficult to ascertain at the time of migration, since the original intentions of migrants do not predict the eventual length of stay in the United States. Experience in the United States interacts with original intentions, and intentions may change over time. A young male might enter the country as a sojourner and, while working seasonally here, find good prospects for longer-term employment. He might then bring his family, with the intention of staying only a year or so, but eventually become a long-term settler. Or a family may come with the intention of settling here, but return to their home country after experiencing poorer employment prospects than anticipated. So the boundaries between settlers, sojourners, and commuters are in fact fuzzy and, moreover, may change over time for the same individual.

Entrance and exit from the illegal alien population vary considerably. Understanding the processes by which an individual enters this population, and may subsequently leave it, has important implications for the types of illegal aliens being assessed and for public policy options to deal with these groups. There are three primary routes by which one becomes an illegal alien in the United States: illegal entry into the country, legal entry but staying beyond the authorization period, and legal entry but violating the terms of entry. Illegal entry can occur when an individual enters the United States without inspection. These entries without inspection (EWIs) represent the most common type of illegal entry and principally occur through the United States border with Mexico, although entry through the Canadian border (including entry by non-Canadians) is not uncommon. Many settlers from Mexico enter by this route, and it is the main form of entrance for sojourners and commuters. Increasingly, however, the INS also apprehends non-Mexicans entering from

Mexico, although they still represent only a small proportion of INS apprehensions. An individual can also enter illegally by using false documents. This entry path is less commonly used but may occur at any port of entry.

Individuals who legally enter the country can also become illegal aliens. There are two main types within this category. One consists of individuals who overstay their authorized period of residence. For example, a foreign student may legally enter the United States with an F-1 (academic students) or J-1 (exchange visitors) visa, may subsequently and legally receive an H-1 (temporary workers and trainees) visa for six months of employment off-campus, but then may illegally continue to reside and work in the United States after the six-month term of employment ends. This person has violated the terms of entry by illegally staying after the authorized period. Another group consists of individuals who illegally work, even though they legally entered the United States. A tourist who enters the United States on a B-2 (tourist) visa, for example, would be illegally employed if he or she worked for pay while on the B-2 visa.

Individuals may leave the illegal alien population in three ways: departure from the United States, death, or by regularizing their status. An individual may continue for many years as an illegal alien, although eventually he or she must leave the population, if only by death, assuming the person did not depart the country or regularize status.

Three types of departure from the United States are possible. First, the INS may deport the person. This type of exit does not account for a great number of departures. Deportation is a formal, judicial process and occupies a disproportionate amount of administrative effort on the part of the INS. Second, apprehension by the INS followed by "voluntary" departure results in the bulk of departures by illegal migrants. In this case, the INS apprehends the person, who is typically found trying to enter the country at the border, and provides him or her with transportation back to the closest point of entrance. No formal hearings are held and the apprehended person agrees "voluntarily" to return to the country of origin. It should be emphasized that individuals who exit in this way have been in the United States for only a short period. Third, an individual may leave the United States without having come to the notice of the INS.

The second kind of exit from the illegal alien population occurs by the death of individuals in the United States. Older illegal aliens may live and work for many years in the United States without detection and eventually die in this country. The fact that United

States mortality registration is almost complete has given rise to several demographic methods for estimating the size of the illegal alien population based on registered numbers of deaths (Borjas, Freeman, and Lang, 1987; Robinson, 1980).

The third kind of exit from the illegal alien population is by regularization of status. Three legalization routes are used. First, a person obtains a valid immigrant or nonimmigrant visa. An immigrant visa may be obtained because the undocumented person is sponsored by a relative by blood or marriage or because of a skill or job offer. A nonimmigrant visa may or may not authorize employment but does allow the person to remain in the United States for a set period. Second, the person may qualify for an "amnesty" or legalization program, specifically those authorized by the 1986 Immigration Reform and Control act (IRCA). Other, technical provisions of immigration law permit an equivalent of legalization in some special cases but involve small numbers of cases each year. Third, special congressional bills have been rare in the last quarter of a century, but also can lead to regularization.

For accurate estimates of the number of illegal aliens in the United States, and changes in their population size, information would ideally be available on the stock of illegal migrants, the annual number of entrants and exits of illegal migrants, the annual number who regularized their migration status, and the mortality of the resident illegal migrant population. With this information, it would be possible to calculate the population size from year to year and the net changes from all components. Unfortunately, such information does not exist nor is likely to be available in the future.

In the absence of reliable counts, several types of data have been used to estimate the size of the illegal alien population, including indirect approaches, direct surveys, direct census approaches, and subnational approaches. Indirect approaches cover a wide variety of procedures by relating independent data sources. Rather than attempt a direct accounting of illegal aliens through a population census, indirect procedures amass independent data sources and use them to infer a plausible range of estimates, consistent with the demographic relationships among the data sources. For example, a finding of implausibly high mortality rates for young adult males could imply that reasonably high illegal young adult male migration exists in the population, and that these individuals were not included in the census count used to calculate the implausible rate (Robinson, 1980). Several key datasets have been used by demographers to make indirect estimates: (1) apprehensions data that classify the apprehended person by duration of residence in the United States; (2) the Alien Address Reporting system (I-53) information from the INS; (3) mortality data for the United States, with the assumption that deaths of illegal aliens would be reported in the national vital registration system's death data; and (4) monthly Current Population Survey information.

Direct survey approaches have been used on several occasions (North and Houston, 1976; J. A. Reyes Associates, 1977; see also Keely, 1977, for discussion), many involving surveys of samples of illegal aliens in the United States. Survey researchers remain skeptical, however, of the validity of direct surveys, since respondents who are illegal aliens may have an understandable hesitancy to report their immigration status. The representativeness of these samples is also a major and acknowledged problem in all competent direct surveys. On the other hand, useful information has been provided by surveys in Mexico (CENIET, 1982) that asked Mexican respondents about their prior residence in the United States.

Several researchers have provided useful estimates based on census data from the United States and Mexico (Bean et al., 1983; Warren and Passel, 1987). With Mexican data, one examines census material for evidence about those who left Mexico, presumably mainly to come the United States. With United States census data, Warren and Passel (1987) take INS data to estimate the expected population of legal aliens. Then, the number of illegal aliens is the difference between the census count of aliens and the estimate of legal aliens.

Subnational estimates have sometimes been developed with residual techniques. One distinct advantage with residual methods using United States decennial census data is that, when done properly, estimates can be made for groups by country of origin, age and sex, and for subnational areas. Several researchers have been active in working on this type of estimate, and have provided estimates of the number of illegal aliens for states and metropolitan areas (Bean, Lowell, and Taylor, 1988; Passel, 1986; Passel and Woodrow, 1984). On occasion, residual and survey techniques have been combined for subnational areas (Heer and Passel, 1987).

Specific other demographic research approaches depend on particular types of data, and their estimates vary with the availability and quality of key basic data. For example, because of the demise of the alien registration system after 1981, it will be more difficult to make some types of estimates using 1990 Census data. The Alien Address Reporting program provided counts of aliens by period of entry, age, sex, immigrant status, country of birth, and place of residence. Although there is considerable uncertainty about the completeness of reporting in the I-53 database, these data did provide a specific basis for developing estimates of the number of legal aliens resulting in the United States. No replacement for these data has been developed.

The current best estimates of the size of the illegal alien population come from a limited number of studies. Although a large number of competent, large-scale empirical studies have not been conducted, it should be emphasized that current studies are adequate for addressing many of the important policy questions about this population. These studies suggest a range lower and narrower than ranges given by conjectures and speculations in the mid-1970s. At that time some speculations ran as high as 12 million illegal aliens in the United States with several hundred thousand (if not millions of) undocumented migrants being added annually to the United States population.

A range of 2 million to 4 million illegal migrants in the United States in 1980 has now been generally accepted. This range is consistent with Hill's (1985) range of 1.5 to 3.5 million, it is the same as the National Research Council's (Levine et al., 1985) assessment, and is slightly wider than Passel's (1985) estimate of 2.5 to 3.5 million. The 1.7 million illegal aliens who registered for IRCA's general amnesty program also lends credence to this range of estimates. Thus, as more research has accumulated, the estimates of the illegal alien population in the United States have become smaller and the range has become narrower.

Empirical work from 1980 to 1986 has generally found that the net population growth from illegal migration was in the range of 100,000 to 300,000 per year (Woodrow, Passel, and Warren, 1987). This amount of growth would have led to a 1990 undocumented population in the range of 3 million to 6 million. However, 1.7 million illegal aliens were legalized under IRCA's general amnesty, thereby reducing the potential numbers in 1990. In addition, some part of the 1.3 million who sought legalization under the SAW (special agricultural worker) provisions of IRCA would have been included in the 1990 figure. Other effects on the potential figure for 1990 included possible reductions in illegal immigration and emigration flows induced by IRCA. All of these figures are consistent with the INS (1989: 30) conjecture that "an estimated 1.7 to 2.9 million persons resided illegally in the United States at the beginning of 1989."

A more definitive assessment of the size of the illegal alien population is probably not possible at this time with available data.

Chapters two and three in this volume report assessments using the most up-to-date measures possible from sound, empirical techniques. Further research and potential confirmation of these estimates must await the results of the 1990 Census of Population, additional surveys, and the accumulation of additional data by the INS.

References

Bean, Frank D. and Allan G. King. 1982. *Estimates of the Number of Illegal Migrants to the United States*. Research Report. Austin: Governor's Task Force on Illegal Aliens.

Bean, Frank D., Allan G. King, and Jeffrey S. Passel. 1983. "The Number of Illegal Migrants of Mexican Origin in the United States: Sex Ratio-Based Estimates for 1980." *Demography* 20 (1): 99–110.

————. 1986. "Estimates of the Size of the Illegal Migrant Population of Mexican Origin in the United States: An Assessment, Review, and Proposal." In *Mexican Immigrants and Mexican Americans: An Evolving Relation*, edited by H. Browning and R. de la Garza, 13–16. Austin: CMAS Publications, University of Texas Press.

Bean, Frank D., B. Lindsay Lowell, and Lowell J. Taylor. 1988. "Undocumented Mexican Immigrants and the Earnings of Other Workers in the United States." *Demography* 25 (1, Feb.): 35–52.

Bean, Frank D., Georges Vernez, and Charles B. Keely. 1989. *Opening and Closing the Doors: Evaluating Immigration Reform and Control*. Santa Monica, Calif., and Washington, D.C.: RAND and Urban Institute.

Borjas, George J., Richard Freeman, and Kevin Lang. 1987. "Undocumented Mexican-Born Workers in the United States: How Many, How Permanent?" Cambridge, Mass.: National Bureau for Economic Research.

Castillo, Leonard. 1978. "Statement before the House Select Committee on Population." U.S. House of Representatives. 95th Cong., 2d sess., Apr. 6, 497–515. Washington, D.C.: U.S. Government Printing Office.

CENIET. 1982. *Informe Final: Los Trabajadores Mexicanos en los Estados Unidos (Encueta Nacional de Emigracion a la Frontera Norte del Pais y a los Estados Unidos—ENEFNEU)*. Secretaria del Trabajo y Prevision Social. Mexico City: Centro Nacional de Informacion y Estadisticas del Trabajo.

Chapman, Leonard J. 1976a. "Statement of Leonard J. Chapman." U.S. Senate, Committee on the Judiciary, Subcommittee on Immigration and Naturalization, 94th Cong., 2nd sess., Mar. 17. Washington, D.C.: U.S. Government Printing Office.

————. 1976b. Address before the Michigan Associated Press Editorial Association, Gaylord, Mich., June 11.

Conk, Margo A. 1987. "The 1980 Census in Historical Perspective." In *The Politics of Numbers*, edited by William Alonso and Paul Starr, 155–86. New York: Russell Sage Foundation.

Corwin, Arthur F. 1985. "Numbers Game." In Illegal Immigration: Job Displacement and Social Costs, edited by Donald J. Huddle, Arthur F. Corwin, and Gordon J. MacDonald, 61–83. Alexandria, Va.: American Immigration Control Foundation.

Duncan, Otis Dudley. 1984. *Notes of Social Measurement: Historical and Critical.* New York: Russell Sage Foundation.

Guss, E.J. 1977. "Even if You're on the Right Track, You'll Get Run Over if You Just Sit There." *I and N Reporter* (U.S. Immigration and Naturalization Service) 25:52.

Heer, David M., and Jeffrey S. Passel. 1987. "Comparison of Two Different Methods for Computing the Number of Undocumented Mexican Adults in the Los Angeles County." *International Migration Review* 21 (Winter): 1446–1473.

Hill, Kenneth. 1985. "Illegal Aliens: An Assessment." In *Immigration Statistics: A Story of Neglect*, edited by Daniel B. Levine, Kenneth Hill, and Robert Warren, 225–50. Washington, D.C.: National Academy Press.

J.A. Reyes Associates. 1977. "The Survey Design for a Residential Survey of Illegal Aliens." Report submitted to the U.S. Immigration and Naturalization Service. Washington, D.C.: J.A. Reyes Associates.

Keely, Charles. 1977. "Counting the Uncountable: Estimates of Undocumented Aliens in the United States." *Population and Development Review* 3 (Dec.): 473–481.

————. 1982. "Illegal Migration." *Scientific American* 246 (Mar.): 41–47.

Lee, Sharon M. 1989. "Asian Immigration and American Race-Relations: From Exclusion to Acceptance?" *Ethnic and Racial Studies* 12 (July): 368–390.

Lesko Associates. 1975. *Final Report: Basic Data and Guidance Required to Implement a Major Illegal Alien Study during Fiscal Year 1976.* Washington, D.C.: U.S. Immigration and Naturalization Service.

Levine, Daniel B, Kenneth Hill, and Robert Warren, eds. 1985. *Immigration Statistics: A Story of Neglect.* Washington, D.C.: National Academy Press.

Los Angeles Times. 1977. "Marshall Warns on Illegal Aliens." *Los Angeles Times* Sept. 23: A19.

————. 1985. "Number of Illegal Aliens in U.S. May Be as Low as 2 Million, New Study Contends," *Los Angeles Times* June 25: Sec. I, 4.

New York Times. 1985. "Low Number Given for Illegal Aliens: Report Says Their Population Has Probably Not Gone Up Sharply in Recent Years." *New York Times* 134, sec. A (June 25): 14.

————. 1987. "United States Now Enforcing Law on Employers of Illegal Aliens." *New York Times* 136, sec. A (Aug. 24): 1, 17.

North, D., and M.F. Houston. 1976. *The Characteristics and Role of Illegal Aliens in the U.S. Labor Market: An Exploratory Study.* Washington, D.C.: Linton.

Passel, Jeffrey S. 1985. "Undocumented Immigrants: How Many?" In *Proceedings of the Social Statistics Section of the American Statistical Association, 1985,* 65–81. Washington, D.C.: American Statistical Association.

————. 1986. "Undocumented Immigration." *Annals, American Academy for Political and Social Sciences* 487 (Sept.): 181–200.

Passel, Jeffrey S., and Karen A. Woodrow. 1984. "Geographic Distribution of Undocumented Immigrants: Estimates of Undocumented Aliens Counted in the 1980 Census by State." Paper presented at the annual meeting of Population Association of America, Minneapolis. Also in International Migration Review 18 (Fall): 642–671.

Petersen, William. 1987. "Politics and the Measurement of Ethnicity." In *The Politics of Numbers,* edited by William Alonso and Paul Starr. New York: Russell Sage Foundation.

Roberts, Kenneth B., Michael E. Conroy, Allan G. King, and Jorge Rizo-Patron. 1978. *The Mexican Numbers Game: An Analysis of the Lesko Estimate of Undocumented Migration from Mexico to the United States.* Austin: Bureau of Business Research, University of Texas.

Robinson, J.G. 1980. "Estimating the Approximate Size of the Illegal Alien Population in the United States by the Comparative Trend Analysis of Age-Specific Death Rates." *Demography* 17 (2): 159–76.

Siegel, J.S., J.S. Passel, and J.G. Robinson. 1980. "Preliminary Review of Existing Studies of the Number of Illegal Residents in the United States." Report to the U.S. Commission on Immigration and Refugee Policy. Washington, D.C.: United States Bureau of the Census. Reprinted in 1981 in *U.S. Immigration Policy and the National Interest: The Staff Report of the Select Commission on Immigration and Refugee Policy.* Washington, D.C.: U.S. Government Printing Office.

U.S. Immigration and Naturalization Service. 1989. *Statistical Yearbook of the Immigration and Naturalization Service.* Washington, D.C.: U.S. Government Printing Office.

Wall Street Journal. 1977. "Rising Tide." *Wall Street Journal* Sept. 17: 3.

————. 1985. "Number of Illegal Aliens Steady in U.S. Despite More Bids to Enter." *Wall Street Journal* June 25: 62, 64.

Warren, Robert, and Jeffrey S. Passel. 1987. "A Count of the Uncountable:

Estimates of Undocumented Aliens Counted in the 1980 United States Census." *Demography* 24 (3, Aug.): 375–94.

Washington Post. 1985. "Record Numbers of Illegal Aliens Seized." *Washington Post* 108, sec. A (Oct. 15): 21.

_____. 1987. "The Amnesty Numbers." *Washington Post* 110, sec. A (June 10): 16.

_____. 1989. "A Crisis on the Border?" *Washington Post* 112, sec. A (Jan. 28): 20.

Woodrow, Karen, Jeffrey S. Passel, and Robert Warren. 1987. "Preliminary Estimates of Undocumented Immigration to the United States, 1980–1986: Analysis of the June 1986 Current Population Survey." In *Proceedings of the Social Statistics Section of the American Statistical Association, 1987.* Washington, D.C.: American Statistical Association.

POST-IRCA UNDOCUMENTED IMMIGRATION TO THE UNITED STATES: AN ASSESSMENT BASED ON THE JUNE 1988 CPS

Karen A. Woodrow and Jeffrey S. Passel

The Immigration Reform and Control Act of 1986 (IRCA) changed the context of undocumented immigration to the United States. Over 1.7 million formerly undocumented immigrants who had been in the country since 1982 or before were granted legal status, which could eventually lead to citizenship. Another 1.3 million undocumented aliens applied for legal status as special agricultural workers (SAWs). IRCA funded increased border enforcement activities to stem the flow of undocumented immigrants. It also made hiring undocumented immigrants illegal in an effort to prevent these individuals from finding employment in the United States. This provision had the twofold intention of reducing the attractiveness of the country to persons considering immigrating illegally and of forcing post-1982 undocumented immigrants to leave the country by eliminating their means of making a living. IRCA has numerous other provisions, but these are the major ones dealing with undocumented immigration.

HAS IRCA WORKED?

Obviously, it is not easy to answer the question of whether IRCA has worked in terms of reducing the number of undocumented immigrants in the United States and the number who continue to come to the country. A particular difficulty is the absence of definitive data on the number and flow of undocumented aliens before and after the passage of IRCA. This chapter attempts to address some aspects of IRCA's effectiveness in dealing with the undocumented population by drawing on data from the 1980 Census and various Current Population Survey (CPS) supplements on the foreign-born population.

Size of the Undocumented Population

Warren and Passel (1987) used a residual methodology to estimate that 2.1 million undocumented aliens were included in the 1980 Census. The estimate was derived as the difference between the census figure for the foreign-born population and an independent estimate of the legally resident foreign-born population in 1980. Data on the foreign-born population collected in CPS supplements for November 1979, April 1983, and June 1986 have been crucial for estimating the size of the undocumented population since the 1980 census (Passel and Woodrow, 1987; Woodrow, Passel, and Warren, 1987). The June 1986 CPS, the last pre-IRCA measurement, included an estimated 3.2 million undocumented immigrants (Woodrow, Passel, and Warren, 1987).

This chapter uses the same residual methodology to produce a post-IRCA measurement of the number of undocumented immigrants included in the June 1988 CPS. In constructing this estimate, it is necessary to derive an independent estimate of the legally resident foreign-born population in the country in June 1988. This figure is based on an estimate for 1980 (Warren and Passel, 1987) and components of change between 1980 and 1988, including aliens admitted for permanent residence, certain classes of nonimmigrants, and estimates of mortality and emigration. The nonimmigrants, such as refugees, asylees, and students, are included because they are considered U.S. residents by census and survey residence rules. Another large category is aliens receiving temporary resident status under Section 245A of the Immigration and Nationality Act (INA) pursuant to IRCA; we denote this group as "legalizing aliens" under IRCA's "general amnesty." This chapter also discusses the effect of SAWs on the undocumented population and their potential impact on our estimates.

Our assessment of IRCA's effect on the undocumented population focuses on whether undocumented immigrants have been eliminated from the population, or their numbers substantially reduced, by June 1988. In addition, with data from the June 1988 CPS, we attempt to classify the remaining undocumented population in 1988 as: pre-1982 entrants who did not legalize under IRCA, post-1982 entrants who were not eligible, or post-1986 entrants who came after IRCA was enacted.

Flow of Undocumented Immigrants

In addition to presenting estimates of the undocumented population as of June 1988, this chapter examines the flow of undocumented immigrants to the United States. Previous analyses found that undo-cumented immigration added an average of between 100,000 and 300,000 persons per year to the population of the United States for 1980–86 (Woodrow et al., 1987). The current study investigates in two ways whether IRCA has had an impact on the flow of undocumented im-migrants. The first assessment estimates the average annual population change attributable to undocumented immigration by comparing the undocumented population in June 1988 with estimates for previous dates.[1] The second focuses directly on the inflow of immigrants for the 1987–88 period. The CPS data for 1987–88 entrants are compared directly with estimates of legal entrants based on administrative data. Although the numbers are small and sampling variability represents a serious impediment to drawing firm conclusions, the data do produce some useful indications of post-IRCA flows, particularly when com-pared with similar estimates for 1985–86 entrants.

Outline of the Chapter

The next two sections of this chapter, respectively, describe the June 1988 CPS supplement on the foreign-born population and enumerate the various corrections and modifications to the raw CPS data. The principal adjustments include allocation of nonresponse to the coun-try-of-birth question and a small correction for misreporting of na-tivity. The methodology used to construct the various estimates of the legally resident foreign-born population in June 1988 is described briefly. More detailed descriptions of the methodology can be found in earlier papers (Warren and Passel, 1987; Passel and Woodrow, 1987; Woodrow et al., 1987).

These sections are followed by several analytic sections. The first is a general description of the major characteristics of the foreign-born population in the June 1988 CPS. The next section focuses on the estimated size of the undocumented population in June 1988 and their countries of origin. The third section attempts to assess the flow of undocumented immigrants in the post-IRCA era and includes several illustrative calculations based on different assumptions about the presence of SAWs in the June 1988 and earlier Current Population Surveys. The chapter concludes with a discussion of the implications of the results and suggestions for further analysis and research.

JUNE 1988 CURRENT POPULATION SURVEY

The June 1988 Current Population Survey[2] included supplemental questions on country of birth, citizenship, year of immigration, and country of birth of parents, which were asked of all respondents. (See appendix table 2A.1.) The foreign-born population from the survey includes all persons born in foreign countries except persons "born abroad of American parents." The CPS universe (i.e., the civilian non-institutional population) encompasses foreign-born persons who are permanent residents of the United States, including undocumented immigrants as well as certain types of temporary foreign-born residents who satisfy the Census Bureau's "usual residence" definition (e.g., students). Foreign-born visitors and travelers are not included in the CPS universe. Before analyzing the June 1988 CPS data, we corrected the data for certain known deficiencies.

NONRESPONSE

About 8 million persons failed to report nativity in the June 1988 CPS. Their nativity status was therefore allocated on a pro rata basis, with about 10 percent being allocated as foreign-born. Foreign-born persons with unknown country of birth (about 1.4 million persons), or citizenship, or year of immigration were allocated pro rata to specific categories.

MISREPORTING OF NATIVITY

Previous analyses of the 1980 Census and CPS data have revealed a noticeable amount of misreporting of the United States as the place of birth by persons actually born in Mexico (Warren and Passel, 1987; Passel and Woodrow, 1987; Woodrow et al., 1987). The amount of misreporting in the 1980 Census was estimated to be 205,000 persons, or about 5 percent of the native-born population of Mexican origin. In the November 1979 CPS, misreporting was higher, about 406,000 persons; it was 463,000 persons aged 14 and over in April 1983 and 610,000 persons of all ages in the June 1986 CPS. In every case, the degree of misreporting was higher in the CPS than in the 1980 Census.

To assess the level of misreporting as native-born by foreign-born persons of Mexican origin in the June 1988 CPS, we compared the survey estimate of the native-born population of Mexican origin to an independent estimate for June 1988. This estimate was developed by surviving the 1980 estimate of native-born persons of Mexican origin (Warren and Passel, 1987) to June 1988 using life table survival rates and data on births to Mexican origin women for 1980 to 1988.

The independent estimate of the native-born population of Mexican origin for June 1988 was only 218,000 higher than the CPS figure. This difference, amounting to only 2.7 percent of the estimated 8.3

million natives of Mexican origin, is not statistically significant. Thus, there is no evidence of misreporting of nativity among the Mexican population in the June 1988 CPS. However, to make the estimates of undocumented immigrants for June 1988 consistent with earlier estimates, the 218,000 excess in the native-born category was distributed on a pro rata basis by period of entry to the population born in Mexico.[3] This adjustment increased the foreign-born population in the June 1988 CPS by about 1 percent and the Mexican-born population by almost 6 percent.

COMPARABILITY WITH PAST CPS DATA

Because the sample design and weighting procedures for the CPS were changed several times between April 1984 and January 1986 (Creighton and Wilkinson, 1984; Passel, 1986), data collected in June 1986 and June 1988 are not strictly comparable to figures for April 1983 and November 1979, as collected and published in Census Bureau reports. However, all figures shown here for April 1983 and November 1979 have been reweighted to conform to current weighting practices (Passel and Woodrow, 1987). The reweighting increases survey figures for persons of "Other" race and Hispanic origin.

COMPARABILITY OF 1980 CENSUS DATA AND CPS DATA

Weighting procedures used in the CPS are designed to achieve comparability with the previous census for age-sex-race groups and for age-sex-Hispanic groups (Creighton and Wilkinson, 1984; Passel, 1986). In spite of the weighting, some groups are covered less well in the final CPS estimates than in the census. The foreign-born population appears to be such a group (Passel and Woodrow, 1987). Thus, comparisons of the 1980 Census with post-1980 CPS data seem to understate growth in the foreign-born population.

Another source of inconsistency between 1980 Census and CPS data is misreporting of citizenship status by persons who are "born abroad of American parents." Many such persons erroneously report that they are naturalized citizens. The CPS data are edited to correct for misreporting by persons who are born in a foreign country and who report at least one U.S.-born parent. Because the 1980 Census did not include questions on country of birth of parents, editing of citizenship responses in the census could not be as extensive as in the CPS. The CPS editing improves the quality of the data, and so the foreign-born population in the census may be overstated relative to the CPS estimates because of the more extensive editing in the latter.[4] Thus, measures of growth in the foreign-born population derived from comparing the 1980 Census and a CPS would tend to be understated. Growth figures derived by comparing data from different CPSs are not affected by this problem.

ESTIMATED LEGALLY RESIDENT FOREIGN-BORN POPULATION

There is no *current* data source on the size of the legally resident foreign-born population, or for legal aliens or naturalized citizens separately. The annual Alien Registration Program, conducted by the INS prior to 1982, served as the basis for estimating the legally resident alien population in 1980. Warren and Passel (1987) evaluated the 1980 registration data and corrected them for underregistration. At the same time, these authors also developed an independent estimate of the naturalized citizen population for 1980.

Similar methods cannot be used for 1988 because the Alien Registration Program no longer exists. Instead, we have used demographic components of change to develop an analytic estimate of the legally resident foreign-born population in 1988. The base population for this independent estimate is the 1980 estimate of legally resident aliens and naturalized citizens (Warren and Passel, 1987). The components of change affecting the size of the legally resident foreign-born population for 1980–88 are: admissions of lawful permanent residents, refugees, emigrants, deaths, and additions of temporary resident aliens under IRCA. The calculations are shown in table 2.1.

LEGAL RESIDENTS IN 1980 AND MORTALITY

The estimated legally resident foreign-born population of the United States in April 1980 was 12,084,000 (Warren and Passel, 1987). Deaths since 1980 are estimated with U.S. life tables for the white and Hispanic populations. The estimated loss of 1980 residents to mortality by June 1988 was 1,636,000. Over 1 million (1,097,000) of these deaths occurred in the European-born population, most of whom immigrated to the United States before 1960.

LEGAL IMMIGRANTS, 1980–88

Figures on legal immigration, representing persons who entered the United States since 1980, are derived from INS and Office of Refugee Resettlement (ORR) data. Figures for major groups of refugee arrivals,

Table 2.1 CONSTRUCTION OF ESTIMATED LEGALLY RESIDENT FOREIGN-BORN POPULATION, BY AREA OR COUNTRY OF BIRTH: JUNE 1988

(Populations in thousands; all numbers rounded independently)

Area or Country of Birth	Legal Foreign-Born Residents: April 1980			Deaths to 1980 Pop., 1980–88	Legal Immig. 1980–88	Deaths to 1980–88 Immig.	Applicants for Legal Status (I-687s)	Emig. 1980–88	Estimate, June 1988	
	Total (1) = (2) + (3)	Alien (2)	Citizen (3)	(4)	(5)	(6)	(7)	(8)	All Periods (1) + (5) + (7) − (4) − (6) − (8)	Entered since 1960[a]
All countries	12,084	5,965	6,119	1,636	4,911	76	1,745	1,097	15,929	12,473
North America	3,666	2,433	1,233	358	1,665	22	1,521	414	6,058	5,472
Mexico	1,400	1,195	205	108	587	6	1,219	107	2,985	2,985
Other North America	2,266	1,238	1,028	250	1,078	16	303	307	3,073	2,487
South America	466	335	131	23	322	4	74	73	762	711
Europe	5,283	1,450	3,833	1,097	528	10	33	267	4,470	1,959
Asia	2,460	1,629	831	144	2,229	39	82	272	4,316	4,048
Africa and Oceania	209	119	90	15	166	2	36	71	323	277

Note: Data on I-687 applications for legal status were provided by Michael Hoefer, Statistics Office, U.S. Immigration and Naturalization Service, and are based on applications filed and processed as of May 9, 1989.

a. Components of population estimate not shown separately; includes Mexicans who entered before 1960.

as obtained from the ORR, are included in the estimate at date of entry. Between 1980 and June 1988 146,000 Cubans and Haitians, 576,000 Indochinese, and 49,000 persons from Europe and the Soviet Union legally entered the United States. INS figures on immigrants admitted for permanent residence for a given year include numerous persons who entered the U.S. legally in an earlier year and are "adjusting their status." To prevent double counting, those refugees adjusting status to permanent resident alien from the groups added separately are not counted as immigrants.[5]

The component of change for legal immigration during 1980–88 amounts to 4,911,000 persons. These legal immigrants are primarily from North America (1,665,000) and Asia (2,229,000). Mexico sent the largest number of legal immigrants, about 587,000. China and Korea together accounted for 624,000 immigrants during this period.

EMIGRATION FROM THE UNITED STATES

Emigration of foreign-born (and native-born) persons from the United States is not tracked by any administrative records system. However, demographic research has shown that emigration of legal immigrants during the 1960s and 1970s was significant, averaging over 100,000 persons per year (Warren and Kraly, 1985; Warren and Peck, 1980). Consistent with this research, the Census Bureau currently incorporates an allowance of 133,000 foreign-born emigrants and 27,000 native-born emigrants annually in postcensal population estimates (U.S. Bureau of the Census, 1986). For the 1980s, the only direct measures of emigration come from the Census Bureau's innovative application of multiplicity sampling surveys in the July 1987 CPS. Initial analyses of these data corroborate the assumption that 160,000 persons emigrate from the United States annually (Woodrow and Passel, 1989).

The estimates of the legally resident foreign-born population, derived in table 2.1, incorporate an assumption of 133,000 emigrants annually since April 1980. This level of emigration amounts to 1,097,000 persons for the 1980–88 period.[6] These emigrants are distributed to country or region of birth and periods of entry based on the historical pattern of levels and rates of emigration described in the research literature (Warren and Kraly, 1985).

APPLICANTS FOR LEGALIZATION UNDER IRCA

Aliens with continuous residence in the United States in an unlawful status since January 1, 1982, were eligible for temporary resident status under the main legalization program. During the application period, which ran from May 5, 1987, to May 4, 1988, a total of 1,745,000 aliens applied for legalization under this "general amnesty" provision of IRCA. We designate this group of aliens as "I-687 applicants."

The figures for I-687 applications represent a maximum of those who will ultimately become lawful permanent residents of the United States. Of those applying for legalization, a small proportion, perhaps 5 percent, may not receive approval. To qualify for permanent resident status, those receiving temporary resident status must apply within a specified time period and meet some other criteria. Some may fail to do so; others may leave the United States or die. Nonetheless, in these estimates, we used the 1.75 million I-687 applicants as an initial estimate of the number added by IRCA to the legally resident foreign-born population in June 1988.

Over 1.2 million, or 70 percent, of the I-687 applicants are from Mexico. The second largest group, those from El Salvador, accounts for 144,000 applicants, or 8 percent of the total. Guatemala and Colombia supplied another 53,000 and 27,000 of the applicants, respectively. No other country accounted for as many as 20,000 applicants. Males account for 57 percent of the total. The vast majority of the I-687 applicants are young adults, with ages 15–44 representing 81 percent of the applicants. The characteristics of this population (e.g., country of birth, period of entry) are described more fully in Hoefer (1989) and U.S. Immigration and Naturalization Service (INS) (1989a).

Another group of aliens, called special agricultural workers (SAWs), received legal status as temporary residents under IRCA. Aliens who had worked at least 90 days in U.S. agriculture were eligible to apply as SAWs under the legislation, and approximately 1.3 million aliens did so. Little is known regarding the residency status of the SAWs and their dates of entry into the U.S. The SAWs are not necessarily residents of the U.S. in fact or under census and CPS residency rules. The number of SAWs counted as part of the U.S. population is not known. Some of our analyses suggested that only a very few SAWs appear in the CPS data. Consequently, we did not include them in the estimate of the legally resident foreign-born population. The effect of SAWs on the estimated undocumented population is discussed in a separate section of this chapter.

ESTIMATED LEGALLY RESIDENT FOREIGN-BORN POPULATION

The estimate of legal foreign-born residents of the United States for June 1988 was obtained by adding to the estimate of 12.1 million for April 1980 a total of 4.9 million legal immigrants during the 1980–88 period and 1.7 million I-687 applicants under IRCA, and by subtracting 1.7 million deaths and 1.1 million emigrants. As stated, the resulting estimate of 15,929,000 legal foreign-born residents for June 1988 does not, at this point, include an allowance for SAWs (see table 2.1).

Overall, the estimated legally resident foreign-born population increased by 32 percent, from 12.1 million in April 1980 to 15.9 million in June 1988. The number of legal residents increased for every region of birth except Europe. The number of European-born legal residents declined from 5.3 million in 1980 to 4.5 million in 1988. The legally resident population born in Mexico is the largest single group. It more than doubled, from 1.4 million to 3.0 million over the same interval; most of the increase was accounted for by the 1.2 million I-687 applicants under IRCA.

Our analysis focuses primarily on immigrants who entered the United States after 1960, because previous research found evidence of undocumented immigrants who entered before 1960 only for Mexico (Warren and Passel, 1987).[7] The number of legal foreign-born residents who entered since 1960[8] is 12,473,000. Over 5 million (5,472,000) were from North American countries. Over 4 million (4,048,000) were from Asian countries. The number of European-born legal residents who entered since 1960 is 1,959,000—considerably smaller than the 2,510,000 who entered before 1960.

CHARACTERISTICS OF THE FOREIGN-BORN POPULATION INCLUDED IN THE JUNE 1988 CPS

This section, including tables 2.2 and 2.3, describes the characteristics of the foreign-born population included in the June 1988 CPS without regard to legal status. These descriptions are not based on the derived estimates of legal foreign-born residents, but, rather, on the data as collected in the CPS. Data are shown both without (table 2.2) and with (table 2.3) adjustment for misreporting of nativity by the Mexican-born population.

Country of Birth and Period of Entry

The foreign-born population in June 1988, as measured by the CPS, was 16,967,000. Mexico is the largest single country of birth,

Table 2.2 FOREIGN-BORN POPULATION BY AREA OR COUNTRY OF BIRTH AND PERIOD OF IMMIGATION: JUNE 1988 CURRENT POPULATION SURVEY

(Populations in thousands; all numbers rounded independently)

Area or Country of Birth	All Periods	1986–88	1982–85	1980–81	1975–79	1970–74	1960–69	Before 1960
All countries	16,967	1,565	2,461	2,050	2,850	2,150	2,748	3,143
North America	7,408	551	1,184	1,014	1,358	1,063	1,382	856
Mexico	3,867	295	629	545	956	604	502	337
Other North America	3,542	257	556	469	403	459	880	519
South America	799	130	96	147	111	95	176	44
Europe	3,974	263	262	126	265	313	737	2,007
Asia	4,505	553	850	749	1,058	639	434	223
Africa and Oceania	280	66	69	15	58	41	19	12

Source: June 1988 Current Population Survey (CPS). See text for details.
Note: Unknowns are allocated. Data do not include adjustment for misreporting of nativity by Mexican-born aliens.

Table 2.3 FOREIGN-BORN POPULATION BY AREA OR COUNTRY OF BIRTH AND PERIOD OF IMMIGRATION: JUNE 1988, JUNE 1986, AND NOVEMBER 1979 CURRENT POPULATION SURVEYS AND 1980 CENSUS

(Populations in thousands; all numbers rounded independently)

Area or Country of Birth	All Periods of Entry				Entered since 1960[a]			
	June 1988 CPS	June 1986 CPS	November 1979 CPS	1980 Census	June 1988 CPS	June 1986 CPS	November 1979 CPS	1980 Census
All countries	17,185	16,237	13,198	14,139	14,379	13,069	8,760	9,230
North America	7,626	7,118	5,203	5,150	7,108	6,502	4,494	4,344
Mexico[a]	4,085	3,852	2,824	2,531	4,085	3,852	2,824	2,531
Other North America	3,542	3,265	2,379	2,619	3,023	2,650	1,670	1,813
South America	799	710	556	596	755	668	469	531
Europe	3,974	4,139	4,732	5,423	1,966	1,949	1,500	1,790
Asia	4,505	4,023	2,509	2,672	4,283	3,721	2,135	2,328
Africa and Oceania	280	248	197	297	268	229	161	238

Sources: Unpublished tabulations from June 1988 CPS, June 1986 and November 1979 CPS data based on analysis by Passel and Woodrow (1987).

Note: All data include adjustment for misreporting of nativity by Mexican-born aliens. See text for details.

a. Foreign-born population entered since 1960 includes Mexican-born population entering before 1960.

accounting at that time for 3,867,000 persons, or 23 percent of the foreign-born population. The Mexican-born population represented a little more than one-half of the population born in North American countries, as 3,542,000 persons came from other countries of North America. Europe was the birthplace of an estimated 3,974,000 persons, fewer than the number born in Asia—4,505,000. Over 1 million persons (1,079,000) were born in South America and Africa/Oceania combined.

Europe dominates as the place of birth among pre-1960 entrants, accounting for almost two-thirds of the 3.1 million pre-1960 entrants in the June 1988 CPS. Following the elimination of the national origin quota system in 1965, legal immigration from Asian and North American countries increased and the European nations' importance as source countries of immigrants diminished. The June 1988 CPS data reflect these changing origins and increased levels of immigration.[9] According to the June 1988 CPS, the number of foreign-born persons who entered during 1970–79 exceeded the number who entered during the 1960s. This pattern of higher net immigration (as of June 1988) in the 1970s holds for North America, Mexico separately, Europe, and Asia. Even though the 1980s were not yet complete, the June 1988 CPS showed that immigration from Other North America, South America, and Asia for the decade already exceeded the levels of the 1970s. In addition, for the remaining areas of the world (that is, Mexico, Europe, and Africa/Oceania), the 1980s achieved levels comparable to those for the entire 1970s.

Changes over Time

The foreign-born population increased from a total of 13,198,000 in November 1979 to 17,185,000 in June 1988, an increase of 3,987,000, or 30 percent.[10] The population born in Asia increased dramatically—almost doubling, from 2.5 million to 4.5 million—over the eight and one-half year period. At the same time, the population born in Europe declined by about 758,000, or 16 percent, reflecting mortality and emigration of this generally "old" immigrant cohort. Almost 9 million persons (8,760,000) entered the United States between 1960 and 1979, according to the November 1979 CPS.[11] The June 1988 CPS showed only 8,086,000 persons who entered during that period. This cohort should continue to decrease in size as emigration and mortality take their toll, since, by definition, it cannot be replenished.

Between June 1986 and June 1988, the total foreign-born population increased by almost 1 million. For the population born in Mexico, the June 1988 figure of 4,085,000 does not differ significantly from the June 1986 figure of 3,852,000. For Asia, the two-year increase was over 500,000. The changes shown in table 2.3 for populations born in South America, Europe, and Africa/Oceania, although consistent with INS data on admissions, are not statistically significant.

ESTIMATES OF THE UNDOCUMENTED IMMIGRANT POPULATION AND THE IMPACT OF IRCA

The impact of IRCA in the context of the current research involves three phases of the law: (1) the legalization program for aliens continuously resident in an unlawful status since January 1, 1982; (2) increased border enforcement to prevent entries without inspection; and (3) employer sanctions to force undocumented aliens in the United States to leave. All three phases were intended to act in concert to reduce, and eventually eliminate, the undocumented immigrant population. Although others have tried to disentangle the separate effects of these three phases of the law (White, Bean, and Espenshade, forthcoming) we make no such attempt in this discussion.

The simplest evaluation of IRCA's impact on undocumented immigration to the United States is to measure whether the undocumented population in June 1988 is larger or smaller than it was before the legislation was enacted. However, since the legislation itself enabled many undocumented residents to legalize their status, a smaller undocumented population in 1988 would not necessarily indicate lower levels of *net* undocumented immigration since passage of the legislation in late 1986 and implementation of the legalization programs and employer sanctions in 1987–88. Thus, in addition to measuring the size of the undocumented population, it is necessary to assess whether population change due to undocumented immigration is smaller after IRCA than before.

Assessing the impact of IRCA would ideally rely on decomposition of the undocumented population to three periods of immigration to the United States: before 1982, 1982–86, and 1987–88. The legislation called for legalization for persons continuously resident in an undocumented status since 1981, so their numbers should be dramatically reduced by 1988. Undocumented persons who entered after 1981 or were not otherwise eligible for legalization under IRCA's employer sanctions should have experienced difficulties in the U.S. labor market as the sanctions took effect. Thus, this population should have at least decreased, if not substantially, since 1986. Finally, the increased border enforcement provisions of IRCA were intended to curtail entries without inspection after 1986, so that the number of undocumented entrants in 1987–88 should be reduced.

The residual methodology can supply estimates for each of these time periods. However, the precision of the estimates is limited by the sampling variability of the CPS-based estimates. Furthermore, the accuracy of the residual estimates depends on accurate reporting of dates of entry by CPS respondents and consistency between these responses and the dates of entry shown in the administrative records used to construct the estimate of legal foreign-born residents. For the most part, the residual estimates of undocumented immigrants by period of entry are meaningful and interpretable. However, minor reporting/estimation problems for European immigrants and more serious ones for Asian immigrants preclude definitive estimates for these areas and for total undocumented immigration. Our approach to assessing IRCA with the June 1988 CPS involves three sets of estimates: (1) an estimate of the size of the undocumented population included in the June 1988 CPS, broken down by period of entry; (2) comparison of the June 1988 estimate with estimates for earlier dates; and (3) comparison of 1987–88 entrants from the CPS and from INS records.

Undocumented Immigrants in the June 1988 CPS and June 1986 CPS

PRINCIPAL RESULTS FOR JUNE 1988

The estimate of undocumented immigrants included in the June 1988 CPS is the difference between the June 1988 CPS foreign-born population (as shown in table 2.3) and the estimated legally resident foreign-born population (as shown in table 2.1). This difference is shown in table 2.4, broken down by period of entry (pre-82 and 1982 or later) and by country or region of birth. Comparable figures for the June 1986 CPS are also shown.

The residual estimate for June 1988 shows 1,906,000 undocumented immigrants included in the CPS. Of these, 1,100,000, or 58 percent, are from Mexico. The rest of North America (which includes Caribbean countries) accounts for another 536,000 undocumented immigrants in the June 1988 CPS, or 28 percent of the estimated

Table 2.4 FOREIGN-BORN POPULATION IN THE CURRENT POPULATION SURVEY, ESTIMATED LEGAL FOREIGN-BORN RESIDENTS, AND ESTIMATED UNDOCUMENTED POPULATION IN THE CPS, BY AREA OR COUNTRY OF BIRTH AND PERIOD OF IMMIGRATION: JUNE 1986 AND JUNE 1988

(Populations in thousands; all numbers rounded independently)

Area or Country of Birth	Date of Survey	Entered 1960[a] or Later			Entered after 1981			Entered 1960[a]–81			
		Foreign-Born (CPS)	Legal Residents (Est.)	Undocumented (Diff.)[b]	Foreign-Born (CPS)	Legal Residents (Est.)	Undocumented (Diff.)	Foreign-Born (CPS)	Legal Residents (Est.)	I-687 Applicants	Undocumented (Diff.)
All countries	June '88	14,379	12,473	1,906	4,051	3,359	692	10,328	7,369	1,745	1,214
	June '86	13,069	9,911	3,158	2,917	2,316	601	10,152	7,595	(X)	2,557
North America	June '88	7,108	5,471	1,636	1,761	1,053	708	5,347	2,897	1,521	928
	June '86	6,502	3,658	2,845	1,203	682	521	5,299	2,976	(X)	2,323
Mexico	June '88	4,085	2,985	1,100	948	389	559	3,137	1,378	1,219	541
	June '86	3,852	1,657	2,195	704	260	443	3,148	1,397	(X)	1,751
Other North America	June '88	3,023	2,486	536	813	664	149	2,210	1,520	303	388
	June '86	2,650	2,000	650	499	421	78	2,151	1,579	(X)	572
South America	June '88	755	712	43	226	233	-7	528	405	74	50
	June '86	668	575	93	136	157	-22	532	418	(X)	114
Europe	June '88	1,966	1,959	7	526	376	149	1,441	1,550	33	-142
	June '86	1,949	1,894	55	366	285	81	1,583	1,609	(X)	-27
Asia	June '88	4,283	4,049	233	1,403	1,584	-181	2,879	2,384	82	414
	June '86	3,721	3,563	158	1,115	1,116	-1	2,606	2,447	(X)	159
Africa and Oceania	June '88	268	283	-15	135	113	22	133	134	36	-37
	June '86	229	221	8	96	77	20	133	145	(X)	-12

Note: Estimates of legal foreign-born residents and of the undocumented population in the June 1986 CPS are consistent with Woodrow et al. (1987).

a. Includes Mexicans who entered before 1960.

b. Diff. = difference.

total. The estimates shown for other regions in table 2.4 are not statistically significant. Table 2A.1 is the source of standard errors used to test comparisons in this chapter for statistical significance. (The estimate of 233,000 for Asia is not significant at a 90 percent confidence level, but would be if it were about 276,000.)

About 692,000 undocumented immigrants entered during the 1982–88 period. Most of these were from Mexico (559,000). The only other significant estimates for the 1982–88 period are for Asia and Europe. However, because of estimation problems associated with reporting of date of entry, neither of these estimates is particularly meaningful. For Asia, the estimate for legal residents exceeded the estimate of the foreign-born population entered after 1981, resulting in a negative estimate for the undocumented population of − 181,000. This estimate is more than offset by the large positive estimate for the 1960–81 period. For Europe, the estimate for the 1982–88 period is significant and positive (149,000), but is counterbalanced by an equally large negative value for the earlier period.

Among undocumented immigrants in 1988, 1,214,000 had entered in 1960–81. The estimates for North America, Mexico, and Other North America for this period—of 928,000, 541,000, and 388,000, respectively—are statistically significant. The estimates for Europe and Asia are also significant, − 142,000 and 414,000, respectively. However, as discussed in the preceding paragraph, these results for Europe and Asia are not meaningful because of problems associated with reporting of dates of entry.

According to the estimates in table 2.4, the June 1988 CPS showed a greater number of undocumented immigrants who had entered in 1960–81 than after 1981.[12] The earlier period accounted for 1,214,000 undocumented immigrants, or 64 percent of the total. However, the large and partially offsetting estimates by period for Asia and Europe point to problems with measurement error. If Asian countries are excluded, the estimates of undocumented immigrants in the June 1988 CPS for the 1960–81 and post-1981 periods do not differ significantly.

PRINCIPAL RESULTS FOR JUNE 1986

The estimated number of undocumented immigrants included in the June 1986 CPS is 3,158,000. (The results shown in table 2.4 are from Woodrow et al., 1987.) Of these, 2,195,000, or 70 percent, are from Mexico. About 650,000, or 21 percent, are from other North American countries. As with the estimates for June 1988, the estimates for other regions are not statistically significant.

As of June 1986, about 601,000 undocumented immigrants, or 19 percent, had entered during 1982–86. Most of these were from Mexico (443,000). The remaining 2,557,000 undocumented immigrants in June 1986 (or 81 percent) had entered before 1982. Significant numbers had entered before 1982 from North America (2,323,000), Mexico (1,751,000), and Other North America (572,000).

In the June 1986 estimates, a greater number of undocumented immigrants had entered in 1960–81 (2,557,000) than after 1981 (601,000). For Mexico, the estimate of 1,751,000 pre-1982 entrants greatly exceeded the estimate of 443,000 for 1982–86 entrants. For countries of Other North America, the pre-1982 immigrants (572,000) exceeded the nonsignificant estimate of 78,000 for undocumented immigrants who entered after 1981. The estimates by period of entry from the June 1986 CPS do not seem to be affected by reporting and measurement problems to the same degree as the June 1988 estimates. None of the period-specific or overall estimates for Europe or Asia is statistically significant, although the period estimates for each area have opposite signs.

Change in the Undocumented Population

Comparison of the June 1988 and June 1986 estimates shows that there are significantly fewer undocumented immigrants in the June 1988 CPS than in the June 1986 CPS. This pattern holds true for all countries, North America, and Mexico specifically. For the post-1981 period, the overall estimates for the undocumented population do not differ significantly in 1988 and 1986 (692,000 and 601,000, respectively), even though the 1988 figure covers more than eight years and the 1986 figure covers only a little more than six years.

The decrease in the undocumented population between 1988 and 1986 is concentrated among the pre-1982 entrants. The number of undocumented immigrants who had entered before 1982 dropped by over 50 percent, from 2,557,000 in 1986 to 1,214,000 in 1988. For Mexico, the number of undocumented immigrants who entered before 1982 declined by an even greater percentage, almost 70 percent, from 1,751,000 in 1986 to 541,000 in 1988.

EFFECT OF I-687 LEGALIZATIONS

Direct comparison of the undocumented population in 1986 and 1988 fails to separate the effects attributable to two very different processes: first, formerly undocumented aliens becoming legal residents under the provisions of IRCA (i.e., the newly legal I-687 applicants); and second, actual population change due to undocumented immigration, either net inflow from new undocumented immigration or net outflow due to IRCA. To measure the actual impact of undocumented immigration over the 1986–88 period, we had to include the I-687 applicants in the 1986 estimate of the legally resident foreign-born population, even though they were not legal residents at the time. This procedure was equivalent to subtracting the I-687 applicants from the June 1986 CPS estimates of undocumented immigrants. The result of this calculation was an estimate of undocumented immigrants in June 1986 who were "not expected to legalize."[13]

The June 1986 CPS contained 1,413,000 undocumented immigrants who were "not expected to legalize" (see table 2.5). Of these, 976,000, or 70 percent, were from Mexico. Another 347,000 were from Other North American countries. The June 1986 estimates for all countries in both periods of entry (1960–81 and after 1981), Mexico in both periods, and Other North America in the 1960–81 period are statistically significant. None of the other entries in table 2.5 for either period is significant.

Allowing for the presence of the 1.745 million legalizing aliens in the June 1986 CPS, how does the undocumented population in 1988 compare with the undocumented, "not expected to legalize" population in 1986? Overall, the figures in table 2.5 show an increase of 493,000 in the number of undocumented immigrants between the June 1986 CPS and the June 1988 CPS, but this difference is *not statistically significant* at a 90 percent confidence level.[14] However, even though the difference is not significant, it is consistent with the increase one would expect given past trends (Woodrow et al., 1987). Thus, the entire decrease in the undocumented population from 3.1 million in 1986 to 1.9 million in 1988 is attributable to the newly legal I-687 applicants (i.e., to formerly undocumented immigrants changing their status to legal residents under the provisions of IRCA).

POPULATION CHANGE FROM UNDOCUMENTED IMMIGRATION SINCE 1980

Population change from undocumented immigration can be represented by the difference between the residual estimates of the undocumented population for the various dates. Table 2.6 compares the CPS-based estimates of June 1988, June 1986, and November 1979 and the 1980 Census-based estimate. To control for the effect of IRCA through the I-687 applicants, estimates of the undocumented population for dates before 1988 are compared with the combined undocumented and legalizing populations in June 1988. The

Table 2.5 ESTIMATES OF UNDOCUMENTED IMMIGRANTS INCLUDED IN THE JUNE 1988 CURRENT POPULATION SURVEY AND UNDOCUMENTED IMMIGRANTS "NOT EXPECTED TO LEGALIZE" IN THE JUNE 1986 CURRENT POPULATION SURVEY, BY AREA OR COUNTRY OF BIRTH AND PERIOD OF IMMIGRATION

(Populations in thousands; all numbers rounded independently)

Area or Country of Birth	Total			Entered after 1981			Entered 1960[a]–81		
	June 1988 CPS	June 1986 CPS	Diff.[b]	June 1988 CPS	June 1986 CPS	Diff.	June 1988 CPS	June 1986 CPS	Diff.
All countries	1,906	1,413	493	692	601	91	1,214	812	401
Non-Asian countries	1,673	1,337	336	873	601	271	800	735	65
North America	1,636	1,323	313	708	521	187	928	802	126
Mexico	1,100	976	124	559	443	116	541	533	8
Other North America	536	347	189	149	78	71	388	269	119
South America	43	19	24	−7	−22	15	50	41	9
Europe	7	22	−15	149	81	68	−142	−60	−83
Asia	233	77	157	−181	−1	−180	414	77	337
Africa and Oceania	−15	−28	13	22	20	2	−37	−48	11

Source: Table 2.4.
a. Includes Mexicans who entered before 1960.
b. Diff. = difference.

Table 2.6 ESTIMATED ANNUAL CHANGE IN UNDOCUMENTED IMMIGRANT POPULATION BASED ON COMPARISON OF JUNE 1988 CURRENT POPULATION SURVEY, EARLIER CURRENT POPULATION SURVEYS, AND THE 1980 CENSUS, BY AREA OR COUNTRY OF BIRTH: 1986–88, 1979–88, AND 1980–88

(Populations in thousands; all numbers rounded independently)

Area or Country of Birth	June 1988 CPS Foreign-Born Population[a] (All Ages)	Estimated Undocumented Immigrant Population				Combined Undocu-mented and Legalizing Population June 1988	Estimated Gross Change					Estimated Annual Change				
		CPS 1988	CPS 1986	1979	1980 Census		1986 to 1988	1979 to 1988	1980 Census to 1988	1979 to 1986	1980 Census to 1986	1986 to 1988	1979 to 1988	1980 Census to 1988	1979 to 1986	1980 Census to 1986
All countries	14,379	1,906	3,158	1,724	2,057	3,651	493	1,927	1,595	1,434	1,102	246	224	193	218	176
Mexico	4,065	1,100	2,196	1,436	1,131	2,319	122	882	1,188	760	1,065	61	103	144	115	170
Other Latin America	3,453	572	736	339	452	941	205	602	489	397	285	102	70	59	60	46
Europe and Canada	2,291	16	60	−150	175	56	−4	206	−119	210	−115	−2	24	−14	32	−18
Asia, Africa, and Oceania	4,551	218	166	99	299	335	170	237	36	67	−133	85	28	4	10	−21

Sources: Warren and Passel (1987); Woodrow, Passel, and Warren (1987); Passel and Woodrow (1987).
Note: See text for limitations and methodology.
a. Foreign-born population entered since 1960 plus Mexican-born persons entering before 1960.

estimate of total change for each period is shown; the differences are also converted to average annual change.

None of the measures of total change between 1986 and 1988 is significant, as was noted before. However, the four measures of total change between either 1979 or 1980 and either 1986 or 1988 are statistically significant. Likewise, the estimated change for Mexico in each of the same four periods is significant. For Other Latin America, the changes between the 1979 CPS or the 1980 Census and the 1988 CPS are significant. Finally, for Europe and Canada combined, each of the changes between 1979 and 1986 or 1988 is significant. None of the changes for Asia/Africa/Oceania is statistically significant.

Overall, there is a high degree of similarity in the estimates of average annual change from undocumented immigration for the various periods. All of the estimates fall roughly in the range of 175,000 to 250,000 per year. Mexico and Other Latin America[15] predominate as countries of origin of the undocumented immigrants and, very roughly, to approximately the same degree. (The results in table 2.6 are also discussed later in this paper.)

Pre-IRCA Undocumented Immigrants Who Did Not Legalize

Based on the estimates of undocumented immigrants in tables 2.4 and 2.5 for June 1986 and 1988, an undocumented population of substantial size persists after IRCA. Apparently, there are over 1 million undocumented aliens remaining, according to the various CPS-based estimates. This population presumably includes both persons eligible for legalization who chose not to apply and others who were ineligible, either because they entered the U.S. after the January 1, 1982, cutoff date or they failed to meet other eligibility criteria. Our analysis can only focus on the date-of-entry criterion, however.

There is one major anomaly in the tables that complicates the analysis of the period-of-entry data. Although the overall estimates of undocumented immigrants from Asia for 1986 and 1988 are consistent with one another (158,000 and 233,000, respectively), the estimates by period of entry for June 1988 show a negative estimate for post-1981 entrants and a positive estimate for 1960–81, despite nonsignificant estimates for both periods in the 1986 estimates. This pattern could result from changes in reporting of date of entry by Asian immigrants; errors in constructing the estimated legally resident population; coverage of recent Asian immigrants, refugees, and other nonimmigrants adjusting their immigration status; or other errors. Because of this estimation problem, the analysis of the period-of-entry data focuses on non-Asian undocumented immigrants, rather than all immigrants.

The estimates of undocumented immigrants in 1988 and the "not expected to legalize" population in 1986 are similar for the total and for each of the individual areas. For non-Asian countries, there were 1,673,000 undocumented immigrants in 1988 and 1,337,000 in 1986; the difference of 336,000 is not statistically significant (see table 2.5). The June 1988 CPS includes an estimated 800,000 undocumented immigrants from non-Asian countries who entered the U.S. before the IRCA cutoff date of January 1, 1982. This figure does not differ significantly from the 1986 estimate of 735,000 non-Asian undocumented immigrants who are "not expected to legalize." One possible interpretation of the persistence of a pre-cutoff population of undocumented immigrants into 1988 is that INS enforcement activities and the employer sanctions provisions of IRCA may not have resulted in emigration of long-term undocumented residents, especially in light of IRCA's "grandfather" clause regarding employer sanctions.

The data from table 2.5 can also be used to gauge the effectiveness of the I-687 legalization program. The entire group of pre-1982 undocumented immigrants can be compared directly with the I-687 legalization applicants, since they share one key criterion—entry into the U.S. before 1982.[16] For all non-Asians, the group that did not legalize is almost half (44 percent) as large as the group that applied for legalization, according to the June 1986 CPS.[17] In other words, about two-thirds of the pre-1982 undocumented immigrants (non-Asians) who were in the country in June 1988 completed I-687 applications. For Mexicans, the 533,000 that did not legalize is 45 percent as large as the 1,219,000 that did, implying that nearly one of every three Mexican undocumented immigrants living in the U.S. since before January 1, 1982 did not apply for legalization.

Both the June 1988 and June 1986 CPS show a significant number of undocumented immigrants who entered the United States after the IRCA cutoff date and were, thus, not eligible for legalization under IRCA's general amnesty. For countries outside Asia, the June 1988 CPS includes an estimated 873,000 undocumented immigrants. Mexico accounts for 559,000, or about 64 percent, of non-Asian undocumented immigrants who entered after 1981. The June 1986 CPS includes 601,000 non-Asian undocumented immigrants who entered after the January 1, 1982 cutoff date (statistically not different from the 873,000 in 1988). Mexico accounts for 443,000, or 74 percent, of the non-Asians.

Post-IRCA Undocumented Immigration

It is apparent from the figures in tables 2.4, 2.5, and 2.6 that the June 1988 CPS did not identify a "huge influx" of post-IRCA immigrants (i.e., persons who entered the United States in 1987 or 1988 after the passage of IRCA). Because of the relatively small numbers of immigrants during the 18 months from 1987 through June 1988, CPS data on this group are limited in terms of definitive conclusions. However, the data do provide some indications relating to the flow of undocumented immigrants in the post-IRCA period.

COMPARISON OF JUNE 1988 AND JUNE 1986 CPS ESTIMATES

The overall population change due to undocumented immigration between 1988 and 1986 of 493,000, while substantively large, was not statistically significant for all countries. Nor were the changes for any of the specific countries or regions statistically significant (tables 2.5 and 2.6). For the overall amount of change due to undocumented immigration for all countries between 1986 and 1988 to be significant at a 90 percent confidence level, the estimate would have to be at least 10 percent greater.

The importance of this issue, that is, whether there was net undocumented immigration between 1986 and 1988, requires closer scrutiny as to possible sources of estimation and measurement error associated with the estimate of undocumented aliens in the June 1988 CPS. Since the INS had not completed the processing of I-687 applications, we incorporated the total number of applicants in the computation of the legally resident foreign-born population. The number of actual approvals will be less than the 1,745,000 figure used in our calculations, probably by over 65,000.[18] If the estimate of the legally resident foreign-born population incorporated an estimate of the ultimate number of I-687 approvals, then the estimated undocumented population would be higher by the number of denials. If these denied individuals were not included in the 1986 estimates, then the net change due to undocumented immigration would approach or exceed a statistically significant amount. Thus, when both sampling variability and possible nonsampling estimation errors are taken into account, population change due to undocumented immigration between the June 1986 and June 1988 CPS should be considered significant and consistent with continued net undocumented immigration into the United States.

The estimated annual change of 246,000[19] due to undocumented immigration for the 1986-88 period does not differ in a statistically significant way from estimates for 1979–88 (224,000) and 1980–88 (193,000). Nor is this amount of change different from the levels for periods prior to IRCA (i.e., 1979–86 [218,000] and 1980-86 [176,000]). Although the differences in estimates of annual change by country across the various periods are not generally statistically significant, an interesting hypothesis is suggested by table 2.6. Although Latin America is still by far the predominant source of undocumented immigration, the relative importance of Mexico as the source of undocumented immigration appears to have lessened somewhat for 1986–88. At the same time, Other Latin American countries and Asia appear to have increased in importance as sources of undocumented immigration in the post-IRCA period, according to this analysis of differences between the June 1986 and June 1988 Current Population Surveys.

1987–88 ENTRANTS

An even more direct assessment of recent undocumented immigration can be attempted with the June 1988 CPS. From the CPS, foreign-born persons who reported entering the United States in 1987 or 1988 are tabulated. The number of legal entrants in the same period is then obtained from INS and ORR data. The difference provides a measure of "new" undocumented immigrants since the passage of IRCA. It should be stressed again that this particular estimate is very sensitive to reporting problems for date of entry and that the sampling variability of the resulting estimates is large relative to the quantities of undocumented immigration being estimated. Thus, the entire analysis can be expected to lead to only tentative conclusions, at best.

The difference between 1987–88 entrants according to the CPS and the number legally admitted in the interval does not provide significant evidence of new undocumented immigration for all countries combined. Specifically, the overall estimate of 70,000 undocumented entrants for 1987–88 is a statistically nonsignificant amount (table 2.7). However, for two areas of origin, Mexico and Europe, the CPS figures are significantly higher than the legal admissions. This pattern may indicate new undocumented immigrants who entered during 1987–88 or nonimmigrant visa overstayers who appeared in the CPS.

For Asia, the CPS figure is significantly less than the legal admissions, and the negative figure for Other North America is nearly significant. This pattern strongly suggests problems with measuring date of entry consistently in the various administrative record sys-

Table 2.7   FOREIGN-BORN POPULATION FROM THE JUNE 1988 AND JUNE 1986 CURRENT POPULATION SURVEYS AND ESTIMATED LEGAL FOREIGN-BORN ENTRANTS: JANUARY 1987–JUNE 1988 AND JANUARY 1985–JUNE 1986

(Populations in thousands; all numbers rounded independently)

Area or Country of Birth	January 1987–June 1988			January 1985–June 1986		
	Foreign-Born Population (CPS)	Estimated Legal Entrants	Difference	Foreign-Born Population (CPS)	Estimated Legal Entrants	Difference
All countries	948	878	**70**	1,010	867	**144**
North America	360	304	**56**	395	261	**134**
Mexico	216	103	**113**	257	96	**161**
Other North America	144	201	**−57**	138	165	**−27**
South America	76	63	**13**	52	62	**−9**
Europe	199	94	**105**	162	106	**56**
Asia	287	385	**−98**	359	407	**−48**
Africa and Oceania	26	32	**−6**	43	32	**11**

Note: Estimates of legal entrants are based on admissions of lawful permanent residents, Indochinese refugees, and European refugees. CPS data are not adjusted for misreporting of nativity by Mexican-born aliens.

tems and the CPS, in addition to problems related to sampling variability. Most of the discrepancy for Asia appears to be related to adjustment of status during 1987–88 by nonimmigrants other than Indochinese refugees who had actually entered the United States before 1987.

Table 2.7 also includes comparisons of the foreign-born populations entering in 1985–86 from the June 1986 CPS and legal entrants during this time period. These comparisons offer another opportunity to assess the applicability of the technique in a situation similar to 1987–88. For the 1985–86 period, the differences shown, which represent "new" undocumented immigrants over an 18-month period, are significant for North America, Mexico, and Europe. The reporting problems that led to significant negative differences for the 1987–88 comparisons appear to have been less in this earlier period, as the negative differences for the 1985–86 period are not statistically significant.

For these two short time intervals of 1.5 years each, the foreign-born populations by birthplace from the 1986 and 1988 surveys do not differ significantly. In addition, comparison of the "estimates" of undocumented immigrants in these analyses of 1987–88 and 1985–86 entrants suggests that there were no significant changes between 1988 and 1986 in short-term undocumented immigration. However, it is apparent that Mexico continues as an important source of undocumented immigrants for both the 1987–88 period and the 1985–86 period.

These analyses of tables 2.6 and 2.7 do not present a strong, definitive picture of post-IRCA undocumented immigration. Both sets of estimates point to a continued flow of new undocumented immigrants from Mexico. The evidence from table 2.6 of continued (and even slightly increased) undocumented immigration from Asia and the rest of Latin America is not supported by the data in table 2.7. On the other hand, the evidence from table 2.7 for Europe as a source of new undocumented immigration is contradicted by table 2.6.

Effect of SAWs on the Estimates of Undocumented Immigrants

Up to this point, this discussion has not included the persons who will legalize as special agricultural workers (SAWs) under IRCA. These individuals have not been included in the estimate of the legally resident foreign-born population for two major reasons. First, it is not known how many of them are (or will be) residents of the

United States. Second, they are not thought to be covered in the CPS. If the CPS does, in fact, include SAWs, then the estimate of 1.9 million undocumented immigrants also includes SAWs and overstates the size of the undocumented population by the number of SAWs included in the CPS. This section of the chapter describes the SAW population, with a particular emphasis on residence in the U.S., and then develops estimates of undocumented immigrants in the CPS based on alternative scenarios regarding the SAW population.

ARE SAWs INCLUDED IN THE CPS?

In one of the big surprises during IRCA implementation, over 1.3 million persons applied for legalization under the SAW program (INS, 1989b).[20] In California, for example, the applicants for legalization as SAWs exceeded the total number of people (not just seasonal workers) thought to be in the entire agricultural labor force of the state (Martin and Taylor, 1988). The SAW applicants included even a higher proportion of Mexican-born persons than had the I-687 applicants. Over 80 percent of the SAW applicants, or more than 1.06 million persons, were born in Mexico. Only two other countries had more than 20,000 applicants: Haiti with 45,000 and El Salvador with 25,000. The SAW applicants were also disproportionately male, about 82 percent, to a much greater extent than the I-687 applicants. In addition, the SAWs were younger than the I-687 applicants (median age of 28 years versus 31 years, respectively) and had a greater concentration in the 15–44 age group (91 percent versus 81 percent, respectively).

The requirements for achieving SAW status under IRCA were minimal. Applicants only to show proof of having worked in U.S. seasonal agricultural services for 90 days during the year May 1, 1985, through May 1, 1986, and the 90 days did not have to be continuous. Even with these minimal requirements, there is suspicion in many circles of substantial fraud in the SAW program. In California, for example, the number of SAW applicants is thought to be three or four times the total number of eligible farmworkers, legal or illegal (Martin and Taylor, 1988).

The principal issue regarding SAWs and the estimates of undocumented immigrants included in the CPS is whether the SAWs are interviewed and counted in the CPS as residents of (or workers in) the United States. Unfortunately, very little is known about the residence history of SAWs or the number who reside in the U.S. on a permanent basis. Individuals working in agriculture could be interviewed if contacted while working. However, if the person only lives in the U.S. while working in seasonal agriculture, he or she would not be considered a U.S. resident by census residence rules.

The available evidence supports the notion that virtually none of the SAWs are included in the CPS as *agricultural workers*. The latest CPS-based estimate is that there were 138,000 Hispanic farmworkers in the U.S. in 1988 (U.S. Bureau of the Census, 1989). This figure is dwarfed by the more than 1 million Hispanic applicants for SAW status.

ALTERNATIVE SCENARIOS

The estimates of the undocumented population in the CPS are based on the assumption that SAWs are not included in the CPS. In light of the evidence just cited, this simplistic assumption seems to be a plausible starting point. However, given that significant numbers of fraudulent applications are likely to be approved, it is necessary to investigate the effect on our estimates of various numbers of permanent residents among the SAW applicants. Definitive information about the permanence of the SAW population will not become available until SAWs adjust to permanent residence. Until then, assumptions about the residence of SAWs must suffice.[21]

Even with the consensus that not all of the SAW applicants and eventual SAWs are persons who actually worked in agriculture, there is no agreement as to how many SAWs or truly seasonal agricultural workers there are. Perhaps 600,000 applicants may actually be persons with work experience in seasonal agricultural services (Martin, 1989). The remainder, which we designate as "pseudo-SAWs," include a diverse selection among three major groups of undocumented immigrants:

1. Persons who resided in the United States since before January 1, 1982, but could not, or chose not to, assemble proof for an I-687 application;
2. Persons who entered the United States after January 1, 1982, and reside permanently in the U.S.;
3. Persons who commute between the United States and another country, usually Mexico, and live in the other country.

Refining the estimate of legal foreign-born residents in June 1988 would involve partitioning the SAW applicants among these three groups and true agricultural workers. Obviously, this would be an extremely imprecise or impossible undertaking. We can, however,

model the impact of including SAWs by relying on known characteristics of SAW applicants and making assumptions about their
residence histories.

The first step in developing age-sex and country-of-origin distri-
butions can be based on the applicant data from the INS (1989b).
Two different totals for approvals are assumed, 1.0 and 1.2 million.[22]
About 85 percent of the approvals are assumed to be from Mexico,
slightly more than 80 percent are male, and over 90 percent are 15–
44 years of age, with none under age 15. And, finally, we used some
information on the two different groups of SAW applicants: Group
I applicants (100,000) who provided evidence that they had worked
at least 90 days in seasonal agriculture in each of the three years
1983–84, 1984–85, and 1985–86; and Group II applicants (1,200,000)
who provided evidence of working at least 90 days in seasonal agriculture only in 1985–86.[23]

Four specific assumptions were developed to illustrate a range of
effects of including SAWs in the estimates of the legally resident
foreign-born population for June 1988. The assumptions vary the
average amount of time that the SAWs spend in the United States
and, thus, affect the number of person-years included in the estimates
of legal foreign-born residents. The greater the number of SAWs
included as part of the legally resident population in the CPS, the
smaller the estimate of undocumented immigrants in the June 1988
CPS. The resulting estimates, by country of birth and sex, are shown
in table 2.8. The four illustrative scenarios are:

A) Each SAW resided in the United States, on average, for three
   months. This assumption implies that 250,000 or 300,000 SAWs
   would be included in the survey estimates.
B) Each SAW resided in the United States, on average, for six months.
   This assumption implies that 500,000 or 600,000 SAWs would
   be included in the survey estimates.
C) Each SAW resided in the United States permanently. This assumption implies that 1,000,000 or 1,200,000 SAWs would be
   included in the survey estimates.
D) 100,000 applicants reside continuously in the United States (Group
   I, defined in the preceding paragraph); of the remaining applicants, 450,000 or 500,000 SAWs resided permanently in the United
   States and 450,000 or 500,000 SAWs resided in the United States
   for six months, on average (Group II). This assumption implies
   that 775,000 or 850,000 SAWs would be included in the survey
   estimates.

Table 2.8 ESTIMATES OF THE UNDOCUMENTED POPULATION INCLUDED IN THE JUNE 1988 CURRENT POPULATION SURVEY BASED ON ALTERNATIVE ASSUMPTIONS ABOUT INCLUSION OF SPECIAL AGRICULTURAL WORKERS (SAWs)

(Populations in thousands; all numbers rounded independently)

Area or Country of Birth and Sex	Zero SAWs (0)	1,000,000 SAW Approvals Specific Assumption				1,200,000 SAW Approvals Specific Assumption			
		(A)	(B)	(C)	(D)	(A)	(B)	(C)	(D)
All countries	1,906	1,656	1,406	906	1,131	1,606	1,306	706	981
Mexico	1,100	888	675	250	442	845	590	80	314
All other	806	768	731	656	689	761	716	626	667
Males	784	584	384	−16	164	544	304	−176	44
Mexico	580	410	240	−100	53	376	172	−236	−49
All other	203	173	143	83	110	167	131	59	92
Females	1,123	1,073	1,023	923	968	1,063	1,003	883	938
Mexico	520	478	435	350	388	469	418	316	363
All other	603	596	588	573	580	594	585	567	575

Notes: General assumptions are that the number of SAW approvals will range between 1,000,000 and 1,200,000; the percentage of SAWs who are from Mexico equals 85; and percentage of SAWs who are male equals 80.

Specific assumptions regarding inclusion of SAWS are: (0), No SAWs included in June 1988 CPS. (A), Average SAW resided in United States for three months. (B), Average SAW resided in United States for six months. (C), All SAWs resided in United States permanently. (D), Mixed assumption—Group I applicants permanently resident: 100,000; Group II applicants: 450,000–550,000 permanently resident; 450,000–550,000 residend in United States for six months.

Based on this broad range of assumptions, the undocumented population in June 1988 could range from 706,000 to 1,906,000. However, because the SAW applicants include such a high percentage of Mexican males, the lowest estimates of undocumented immigrants under assumptions C and D produce results with an unacceptable demographic structure. Specifically, these assumptions result in negative or very small estimates of undocumented Mexican males in the June 1988 CPS. If these variants are excluded as implausible, the various assumptions yield estimates of the undocumented immigrant population included in the June 1988 CPS in the range of 1.1–1.9 million.

Additional calculations could be prepared under alternative assumptions, but all would be merely hypothetical and illustrative. The calculations shown in table 2.8 are sufficient to make certain conclusions. First, *an undocumented population of substantial size continues to exist in the United States*. Second, to the extent that the CPS includes persons who will be approved as SAWs, *the undocumented population could have a higher percentage of females than the pre-IRCA undocumented population*, perhaps exceeding 50 percent female. Also, undocumented Mexican immigrants comprise a smaller proportion of the undocumented population than before the enactment of IRCA. In fact, Mexicans may no longer constitute a majority of the undocumented population.

The inclusion of SAWs in the estimated undocumented population included in the CPS probably has less of an effect on the measures of average annual change due to undocumented immigration than on the estimated number of undocumented immigrants. Population change due to undocumented immigration is measured in table 2.6 by comparing estimates of the undocumented population prior to IRCA with estimates of the combined undocumented plus the legalizing population after IRCA. The combined size of this latter group is not affected by the SAW assumptions, so that there would be no change in the measure of annual change. On the other hand, the estimate of average annual change due to undocumented immigration would be affected by the inclusion of SAWs in the June 1988 CPS, but not earlier Current Population Surveys. To the extent that this phenomenon occurs, the estimates in table 2.6 would overstate the measure of average annual change for periods ending in 1988.

Measurement of average annual change due to undocumented immigration depends upon comparability of census and survey coverage of the foreign-born, legally resident, and undocumented populations. Because census and CPS data are not comparable, as noted earlier, associated change measures should be cautiously regarded and estimates based on CPS to CPS comparisons should be preferred. It should be noted, however, that if the passage of IRCA has influenced CPS coverage of legally resident and undocumented immigrants by encouraging or discouraging participation in the CPS, measurement of change using the 1988 CPS will be consequently affected. Unfortunately, only an awareness of these potential biases, and not an assessment of their magnitude, is possible with the existing data.

DISCUSSION AND CONCLUSION

Has IRCA worked? The research reported here says "yes," "no," and "we're not sure." First, IRCA has clearly reduced the number of undocumented immigrants in the country by the nearly 1.7 million persons who will be granted legal status under the general amnesty and by some unknown fraction of the more than 1.3 million SAW applicants. However, IRCA clearly has not entirely eliminated all undocumented immigrants from the population living in the United States. *As stated, significant numbers of undocumented immigrants remain in the United States.*

It has been conjectured that "an estimated 1.7 to 2.9 million persons resided illegally in the United States at the beginning of 1989" (INS, 1989a: 30). The research reported here is entirely consistent with this conjecture. We found 1.9 million undocumented immigrants included in the June 1988 CPS. Two factors can modify this estimate. First, the CPS-based estimate obviously makes no allowance for persons not included in the CPS. Although there is no direct estimate of how many undocumented immigrants are not counted in the CPS, some evidence from the studies of undocumented immigrants in the 1980 Census suggests reasonable limits. Analysis of the 1980 Census results suggested that 20 percent to 40 percent of the undocumented immigrants residing permanently in the country were not included in the census (Passel, 1985). A similar range may by reasonable for the CPS as well. On the other hand, the estimate of the legally resident foreign-born population in 1988 does not specifically include any of the SAW applicants. Accordingly, the estimate of undocumented immigrants included in the CPS would be overstated exactly to the extent that SAW applicants are counted in the CPS. Offsetting this overstatement is any underestimation of the undocumented population caused by the assumption that the CPS includes either all of the foreign-born population or all of the population estimated as legally resident in the country.

The CPS results show that there could be more than 1 million undocumented immigrants who have resided in the United States for seven or more years (i.e., since before the IRCA cutoff date of January 1, 1982). These individuals may have been unable to gather the necessary proof to apply for amnesty or may be planning to reside in the United States for only a short while more. Nonetheless, these results suggest that as many as two-thirds of the current undocumented population are persons who met the entry date requirement to be eligible for amnesty under IRCA. Put another way, *about two-thirds of those who appear to have been eligible for the general amnesty (based on their dates of entry) actually applied.*

The undocumented population in the United States decreased between the June 1986 CPS and the June 1988 CPS, because 1.7 million formerly undocumented immigrants became legal residents through the general amnesty program. However, after this group is taken into account, our research suggests that the remaining undocumented population may actually have increased between June 1986 and June 1988, although the results are not definitive. Thus, *IRCA has not cut off the flow of new undocumented immigrants to the United States. But, we are not able to make a determination from the available evidence of whether IRCA has reduced the flow of undocumented immigrants to below the pre-IRCA estimates.* We found no significant difference in the average annual population change attributable to undocumented immigration for the 1986–88 period as compared to the 1979–86 or 1980–86 periods. Nor were there significant differences when the 1987–88 undocumented entrants were compared with the 1985–86 undocumented entrants.

There are some suggestions in the analyses that there have been changes in the composition of the undocumented population and shifts in the composition of the inflow of undocumented immigrants. Tabulations of the undocumented population classified by sex show that *females constitute a majority of the non-Mexican undocumented population.* If the June 1988 CPS included even a moderate number of SAWs, *the post-IRCA undocumented population from Mexico may also be majority female.* Both of these populations would, thus, have undergone major changes from their pre-IRCA compositions.

Analyses of 1986–88 changes (table 2.6) and 1987–88 entrants (table 2.7) suggest that *Mexicans may represent a smaller proportion of the net flow of undocumented immigrants than before the enact-*

ment of IRCA. Although the differences are not statistically significant, both analyses suggest the shift from Mexico, but they provide contradictory indications as to whether the larger flows are from Other Latin American countries, Asia, or Europe. Alternative scenarios regarding inclusion of SAWs in the CPS also support the notion of a shift in composition. Finally, the SAW scenarios suggest strongly that *Mexicans may no longer represent a majority of the remaining resident population of undocumented immigrants.*

Methodological Issues and Future Research

The residual methodology has been extremely valuable in measuring the size of the undocumented population and change over time due to undocumented immigration. However, assessing change for a two-year period requires a degree of sensitivity and refinement of the residual methodology that may be difficult to achieve. In particular, variations in survey coverage of the foreign-born population or undocumented population could limit comparability of data over time. Intersurvey differences in reporting period of immigration and varying levels of nonresponse and misresponse also complicate analysis. Ultimately, the accuracy of the analysis of period-of-entry data requires consistency of reporting over time as well as between the CPS and the administrative systems of the INS and the ORR. Future research will reevaluate the November 1979, April 1983, June 1986, and June 1988 CPS datasets in terms of data quality, consistency, and potential errors of data modifications.

The independent population estimates by age, sex, race, and Hispanic origin used to inflate survey results to provide national-level estimates are based on a methodology that allows for net change due to undocumented immigration of 200,000 per year. Complete assessment of the impact of IRCA would iterate the estimation reported here after reweighting the survey results to independent population controls with different estimated net change due to undocumented immigration. However, this modeling is unlikely to affect our major findings, as the survey controls are not specific by nativity. Nevertheless, this investigation and 1990 Census research to estimate the undocumented population are essential in corroborating the results of CPS research studies on undocumented immigration during the 1980s.

Measurement of the size of the resident undocumented population and recent and future changes in this population are crucial for adequately evaluating past legislation and for considering new immigration reform. Proposed legislation is designed to place a cap on annual legal immigration as well as to revise the categories of admission as lawful permanent residents. The impacts of legal immigration reform on undocumented immigration are unknown; changes could possibly lead to undocumented entries or prolonged stays in the United States by persons joining immediate or close relatives and violating the terms of their nonimmigrant visas.

Notes

This chapter is a revised version of a paper presented at the Urban Institute conference on "Illegal Immigration Before and After IRCA," on July 21, 1989, in Washington, D.C. The paper reports the general results of research undertaken while both authors were employed by the U.S. Bureau of the Census. The views expressed are attributable to the authors and do not necessarily reflect those of the Bureau of the Census or The Urban Institute. The June 1988 Current Population Survey was partially funded by the Immigration and Naturalization Service.

1. The estimates for the undocumented population for previous dates theoretically include the group of aliens who legalized under IRCA's general amnesty. Thus, in estimating population change due to undocumented immigration for pre-IRCA and post-IRCA periods, one must take into account the legalizing aliens and make assumptions about their dates of entry and inclusion in previous CPS supplements.

2. The Current Population Survey is a monthly survey funded by the U.S. Bureau of Labor Statistics and conducted by the Bureau of the Census. The sample is a national probability sample of approximately 58,000 households located in 729 sample areas representing 1,973 counties, independent cities, and minor civil divisions of the United States (see U.S. Bureau of the Census, 1978). The survey results are weighted to agree with independent population estimates of the civilian noninstitutional population by age and sex for race groups and for Hispanic/non-Hispanic categories. The independent population estimates are based on 1980 census counts updated with components of change for births, deaths, legal immigration, undocumented immigration, and emigration (U.S. Bureau of the Census, 1986, 1987; Passel, 1986).

3. Reasonable alternative approaches include: allocating according to the survivors of those who misreported in 1980, with the remainder going to post-1980 periods; allocating entirely to the 1982–86 period; or allocating pro rata within age-sex groups. Although there was no significant misreporting among the Mexican origin population in June 1988, the number reporting as native-born in the Central and South American and "Other Hispanic" categories was 16 percent higher in June 1988 than in June 1986. This difference may represent an actual increase, misreporting, or correction of previous misreporting.

4. The estimates of Warren and Passel (1987) correct for some misreporting by persons born abroad of American parents, but only for specific countries of birth.

5. The figures for legal immigration derived in this manner differ slightly from those used by the Bureau of the Census (1986, 1987) in official population estimates.

6. Previous work on measuring the undocumented immigrant population has incor-

porated a range of emigration estimates (Woodrow et al., 1987). We have chosen a single figure in this study for ease of presentation, based on the July 1987 CPS results. Different levels of emigration would affect the resulting estimates of undocumented immigration on a one-for-one basis, with higher emigration implying lower undocumented immigration and vice versa.

7. The final column of table 2.1 shows the estimated legally resident foreign-born population that had entered after 1960 plus Mexicans who entered before 1960. The presence of non-Mexican undocumented aliens who entered before 1960 is unlikely. In fact, all undocumented aliens continuously resident since January 1, 1972, are eligible to apply for permanent resident status under IRCA.

8. Throughout this chapter, we use the phrase "entered since 1960" to include all persons who entered the U.S. since 1960 plus the Mexican-born population that entered the U.S. before 1960 (but only the Mexican-born population).

9. Data from a census or survey (such as those shown in table 2.2) cannot strictly be interpreted as trends in immigration. Rather, the distribution by period of entry reflects the net effect of immigration during the period less the cumulative effects of emigration and mortality over the varied intervals from immigration to the date of the survey. Within the limitations of the data, the data in table 2.2 represent the composition of the foreign-born population at the survey date, and they approximate trends in immigration.

10. We focus our attention on comparisons of the June 1988 CPS and the November 1979 CPS as providing the best measure of change since 1980. The CPS, in general, appears to cover the foreign-born population less well than the 1980 Census and has greater sampling variability, but yields a more complete estimate for the population born abroad of American parents. Consequently, comparisons of June 1988 CPS estimates of the foreign-born population with the 1980 Census would tend to understate the amount of growth, particularly for some regions of birth. Comparisons among CPS data sources provide more accurate assessments of change in the foreign-born population. See also "Comparability of 1980 Census Data and CPS Data," in the section on "June 1988 Current Population Survey" in this chapter.

11. Recall that this group includes persons born in Mexico who entered the U.S. before 1960.

12. The difference between the 1,214,000 immigrants who entered in 1960–81 and the 692,000 who entered in 1982 or later tests as significant at an 89 percent confidence level.

13. An alternative approach involves comparing the 1986 estimated undocumented population (3,158,000) with the 1988 estimate of undocumented immigrants plus the legalized aliens (3,522,000). This approach yields results that are equivalent, in terms of population change from undocumented immigration, to the results obtained using the method presented in the text.

14. In fact, of the differences between the 1988 estimated undocumented populations and the 1986 "not expected to legalize" populations shown in table 2.5 for all periods and for the 1960–81 and post-1981 periods of entry, only the difference of 337,000 for Asia for 1960–81 is statistically significant. This difference is nearly offset by the negative (and nonsignificant) difference of −181,000 for the post-1981 period. As discussed earlier, these large and offsetting differences appear to be the result of measurement/estimation problems surrounding the reporting of dates of entry. Consequently, in subsequent analyses of table 2.5, the focus will be of the non-Asian countries.

15. In this context, Other Latin American includes all countries in the Caribbean, Central America, or South America.

16. The group that did not apply may not have been eligible for legalization because

they failed to meet other of IRCA's criteria. Thus, this analysis speaks only to the date-of-entry criterion.

17. The June 1986 CPS is used for this calculation because it more closely represents the population in the country when IRCA was passed in October 1986. However, because of the similarity of the estimated undocumented population in June 1988 to the "not expected to legalize" population in June 1986, it hardly matters which group is used for comparison. For example, using the June 1988 CPS would give a figure of 46 percent for the non-Asian comparison cited in the text.

18. Through November 2, 1989, the INS had approved 95.1 percent of 1,651,000 I-687 applicants processed (INS, 1989b). This approval rate applied to all applicants would yield 65,000 fewer legal residents than the figure used in the calculations.

19. Use of the higher figure for 1986–88 of 275,000, which incorporates I-687 denials, does not alter the statements in this paragraph.

20. The statistical information on SAW characteristics in this section comes from the INS (1989b).

21. A related problem that will continue to affect analytic work on the CPS and population estimates in the 1990s, even after the SAWs have adjusted their status, is the residence status of replenishment agricultural workers (RAWs). These persons will be able to work legally in the U.S. and may or may not reside in the U.S. They must work at least 90 days per year in seasonal agricultural services for three consecutive years.

22. By November 1989, only about 525,000 SAW applications had been processed with an approval rate of 93.4 percent (INS, 1989b). Because of certain judicial rulings, INS is finding it difficult to deny SAW applications for fraud (Martin, 1989). As a result, it appears that the higher assumption will be closer to the actual number of approvals.

23. All of these years run from May 1 through May 1.

References

Creighton, Kathleen and Robert Wilkinson. 1984. "Redesign of the Sample for the Current Population Survey." *Employment and Earnings* 31 (May): 7–10.

Hoefer, Michael D. 1989. "Characteristics of Aliens Legalizing under IRCA." Paper presented at the annual meeting of the Population Association of America, Baltimore, Mar. 28–30.

INS. *See* U.S. Immigration and Naturalization Service.

Martin, Philip L. 1989. "SAWs, RAWs, and Farmworkers in California." Nov. 10. University of California at Davis. Photocopy.

Martin, Philip L., and J. Edward Taylor. 1988. "Harvest of Confusion: SAWs, RAWs, and Farmworkers." Working Paper PRIP-UI-4. Washington, D.C.: Urban Institute, December.

Passel, Jeffrey S. 1985. "Undocumented Immigrants: How Many?" In *Proceedings of the Social Statistics Section of the American Statistical*

Association, 1985 65–71. Washington, D.C.: American Statistical Association.

_____. 1986. "Changes in the Estimation Procedure in the Current Population Survey Beginning in January 1986." *Employment and Earnings* 33 (Feb.): 7–10.

Passel Jeffrey S., and Karen A. Woodrow. 1987. "Change in the Undocumented Alien Population in the United States, 1979–1983." *International Migration Review* 21 (4): 1304–34.

U.S. Bureau of the Census. 1978. *The Current Population Survey: Design and Methodology.* Technical Paper no. 40. Washington, D.C.: U.S. Government Printing Office.

_____. 1986. "Estimates of the Population of the United States by Age, Sex, and Race: 1980 to 1985." *Current Population Reports*, series P-25, no. 985. Washington, D.C.: U.S. Government Printing Office.

_____. 1987. "Estimates of the Population of the United States by Age, Sex, and Race: 1980 to 1986." *Current Population Reports*, series P-25, no. 1000. Washington, D.C.: U.S. Government Printing Office.

_____. 1989. "Rural and Rural Farm Population: 1988." *Current Population Reports*, series P-20, no. 439. Washington, D.C.: U.S. Government Printing Office.

U.S. Immigration and Naturalization Service. 1980 to 1988. *Statistical Yearbook of the Immigration and Naturalization Service.* Washington, D.C.: U.S. Government Printing Office.

_____. 1989a. "International Migration to the United States." *The President's Comprehensive Triennial Report on Immigration, 1989*, 1–31. Washington, D.C.: U.S. Government Printing Office.

_____. 1989b. "Provisional Legalization Application Statistics: November 2, 1989." Statistics Division, Office of Plans and Analysis, U.S. Immigration and Naturalization Service. Washington, D.C.: U.S. Government Printing Office.

Warren, Robert, and Ellen Percy Kraly. 1985. *The Elusive Exodus: Emigration from the United States.* Population Trends and Public Policy Occasional Paper no. 8. Washington, D.C.: Population Reference Bureau.

Warren, Robert and Jeffrey S. Passel. 1987. "A Count of the Uncountable: Estimates of Undocumented Aliens Counted in the 1980 United States Census." *Demography* 24 (3, Aug.): 375–93 and unpublished technical appendix.

Warren, Robert, and Jennifer Marks Peck. 1980. "Foreign-born Emigration from the United States." *Demography* 17 (1, Feb.): 71–84.

White, Michael J., Frank D. Bean, and Thomas J. Espenshade. Forthcoming. "The U.S. 1986 Immigration Reform and Control Act and Undocumented Immigration to the United States." *Population Research and Policy Review.*

Woodrow, Karen A., and Jeffrey S. Passel. 1989. "Estimates of Emigration

Based on Sample Survey Data from Resident Relatives." Report prepared for the Office of Information and Regulatory Affairs, Office of Management and Budget. Washington, D.C.: U.S. Bureau of the Census, April.

Woodrow, Karen A., Jeffrey S. Passel, and Robert Warren. 1987. "Preliminary Estimates of Undocumented Immigration to the United States, 1980–86: Analysis of the June 1986 Current Population Survey." In *Proceedings of the Social Statistics Section of the American Statistical Association, 1987*. Washington, D.C.: American Statistical Association.

APPENDIX

Table 2A.1 APPROXIMATE STANDARD ERRORS AND CONFIDENCE
INTERVALS FOR FOREIGN-BORN POPULATIONS: JUNE 1988
CURRENT POPULATION SURVEY

(Populations rounded to hundreds)

Population and Size of Estimate	Standard Error	90% Confidence Interval	
		Lower Bound	Higher Bound
Total: Born in Mexico, Other North America, or South America			
10,000,000	244,700	9,608,500	10,391,500
9,000,000	250,700	8,598,900	9,401,100
8,000,000	252,700	7,595,700	8,404,300
7,000,000	250,700	6,598,900	7,401,100
6,000,000	244,700	5,608,500	6,391,500
5,000,000	234,300	4,625,100	5,374,900
4,000,000	218,900	3,649,800	4,350,200
3,000,000	197,300	2,684,300	3,315,700
2,000,000	167,200	1,732,500	2,267,500
1,000,000	122,400	804,200	1,195,800
900,000	116,500	713,600	1,086,400
800,000	110,200	623,700	976,300
700,000	103,400	534,600	865,400
600,000	96,000	446,400	753,600
500,000	87,900	359,400	640,600
400,000	78,900	273,800	526,200
300,000	68,600	190,200	409,800
200,000	56,200	110,100	289,900
100,000	39,800	36,300	163,700
Born in Europe			
4,000,000	127,800	3,795,500	4,204,500
2,000,000	97,600	1,843,800	2,156,200
Born in Asia, Africa, or Oceania			
4,000,000	168,600	3,730,200	4,269,800
2,000,000	128,800	1,793,900	2,206,100

Source: Statistical Methods Division, U.S. Bureau of the Census, Washington, D.C.

ANNUAL ESTIMATES OF NONIMMIGRANT OVERSTAYS IN THE UNITED STATES: 1985 TO 1988

Robert Warren

This chapter presents annual estimates of the number of persons admitted temporarily to the United States who were still in the country more than nine months after the end of their period of admission. The estimates were developed by the U.S. Immigration and Naturalization Service (INS) to measure the level of unauthorized migration to the United States and to evaluate the impact of the Immigration Reform and Control Act of 1986 (IRCA) on this part of the illegally resident population.[1] Estimates of nonimmigrant overstays are shown for the two years before and two years after the passage of IRCA. These estimates were derived from statistics collected in the INS Nonimmigrant Information System (NIIS), an automated database designed to record the arrival and departure of the millions of non-U.S. citizens admitted temporarily each year.

The tables in this chapter contain estimates of nonimmigrant overstays by country of citizenship for 1985 to 1988, state of destination for 1986 to 1988, and age for 1987 and 1988. The estimates were made separately for each mode of arrival (air, sea, land) and for broad classes of admission. Although, as will be described, the estimates have limitations, they provide an empirical basis for evaluating the effects of IRCA on the flow of illegal migration from most of the countries of the world. A significant decline after 1986 in the number of temporary migrants who fail to depart, or an increase in the level of departure of illegal residents, would indicate that IRCA has made it more difficult for unauthorized aliens to obtain employment in the United States.

The statistics presented here show that for many countries of origin there was a drop in the number of overstays in 1987, the first year after IRCA's passage, followed by an increase in 1988 to about the 1986 (pre-IRCA) level. The number of overstays from some countries declined steadily from 1985 to 1988, whereas for other countries the number increased rapidly throughout the period. In contrast to the number of overstays, the annual rate of overstay declined to 1.9

percent in both 1987 and 1988, compared to 2.4 percent in each of the two years prior to passage of the act.

The top six states of destination—New York, California, Florida, New Jersey, Illinois, and Texas—each had lower rates of overstay in 1988 than in 1986. However, many states had higher numbers in 1988 than in 1986. One exception was Illinois, which showed steady declines in both numbers and rates of overstay. The other leading states of destination had significant drops in 1987, followed by increases in 1988 to the 1986 levels.

DEFINITIONS

The following terms are used in this chapter to describe the procedure for estimating the number of temporary migrants who failed to depart within their authorized period of admission.

Nonimmigrant—A non-U.S. citizen admitted to the United States for a temporary, specified period. Examples include tourists, temporary visitors for business, diplomats, students, and temporary workers. A list of the nonimmigrant categories is presented in table 3A.1.

Overstay—A nonimmigrant who failed to depart within the authorized period of admission. The data on "apparent overstays" used to make these estimates were compiled at least nine months after admission and include only those nonimmigrants who were expected to depart. Nonimmigrants with longer periods of admission and those who overstayed briefly but departed are not included in these estimates.

Nonimmigrant Information System (NIIS)—An automated data collection system used by the INS to record the arrival and departure of nonimmigrants. Arriving nonimmigrants present an arrival/departure form (I-94) to an INS inspector, who collects the arrival part of the form. The matching departure forms are collected by representatives of transportation companies and by INS personnel at land ports upon departure. A list of the variables in NIIS is shown in table 3A.1.

Expected departure—A nonimmigrant whose period of admission ended before the creation of the data tapes used to make these estimates. Expected departures are total arrivals, minus nonimmigrants who adjust to permanent resident status, minus those with valid nonimmigrant visas at the time the estimates are made. Examples of the latter category include students, exchange visitors, and other relatively long-term nonimmigrants.

Apparent overstay—A term used by the INS to refer to a nonimmigrant arrival form without a matching departure form. The majority of apparent overstays are the result of the incomplete collection of departure forms. Actual overstays are also included in this category.

System error—A term used to classify a nonimmigrant who departed or obtained an extension of stay as an apparent overstay. In addition to the incomplete collection of departure forms, system error also includes the failure to enter all extensions of stay in the system and other relatively smaller sources of error, such as keying errors and lost departure forms.

ESTIMATION PROCEDURE

Most of the millions of nonimmigrant arrival forms collected each year by INS inspectors are later matched to corresponding departure forms; those that are not matched are termed *apparent overstays*. The approach used in this chapter involved estimating how many of these apparent overstays were the result of system error (incomplete collection of departure forms, etc.) and how many were the result of nonimmigrants failing to depart. The estimation procedure was carried out within different categories of admission to take account of possible variations in rates of system error due to mode of travel (air, sea, land) and class of admission (tourists, visitors for business, others). In each category of nonimmigrant admission, a single rate of system error was estimated. The rate of system error was subtracted from the rate of apparent overstay for each country; the remainder is the estimated rate of overstay.

Estimates of System Error

System error was estimated by first identifying a group of countries that have very few actual overstays; that is, countries for which all of the apparent overstays can be assumed to be the result of system error. Twelve countries were selected on the basis of five criteria: (1) low backlogs for immigrant visas; (2) low numbers of applicants for legalization; (3) low numbers of alien apprehensions by the INS; (4) low estimates of undocumented aliens counted in the 1980 U.S. Census; and (5) low rates of apparent overstay. The 12 countries, which were exceptionally low on each of these indicators, are: Belgium, Finland, Norway, Sweden, Switzerland, Singapore, Saudi Arabia, Kuwait, Australia, New Zealand, Netherland Antilles, and Suriname. These countries were used in the estimation of system error in each category of admission. Also, to maintain consistency over time, the same 12 countries were used in deriving the estimates shown here for 1985–88.

Table 3.1 illustrates the procedure used to estimate the rate of system error for temporary visitors for pleasure who arrived during the October 1986–March 1987 period. After rates of apparent overstay were computed for each country, the mean and standard deviation of the 12 rates were calculated. Finally, the estimated rate of system error was set at one standard deviation above the mean of the 12 rates.[2]

Estimates of Overstays

Rates of system error were computed for each mode of arrival and broad class of admission; the error rates were used to estimate the number of overstays by country of citizenship, state of destination and five-year age group. The estimation of nonimmigrant overstays by country of citizenship is illustrated in table 3A.2. A rate of apparent overstay was calculated for each country using statistics from the Nonimmigrant Information System. Then, for each country, the

Table 3.1 COMPUTATION OF SYSTEM ERROR FOR NONIMMIGRANTS
ARRIVING OCTOBER 1986 TO MARCH 1987

(Temporary visitors for pleasure arriving by air)

Country of Citizenship	Expected Departures	Apparent Overstays	Percentage Apparent Overstay
Belgium	19,777	2,020	10.21
Netherlands Antilles	5,627	540	9.60
Norway	21,687	1,965	9.06
Sweden	50,410	4,439	8.81
Kuwait	1,203	104	8.65
Saudi Arabia	4,894	409	8.36
Switzerland	51,311	4,176	8.14
Australia	68,356	5,533	8.09
New Zealand	28,333	2,243	7.92
Suriname	4,233	335	7.91
Singapore	8,306	481	5.79
Finland	17,201	983	5.71

Mean apparent overstay: 8.19%
Standard deviation: 1.33%
Estimated system error: 9.52%

Source: The Nonimmigrant Information System (NIIS) of the U.S. Immigration and Naturalization Service (INS).

estimate of system error was subtracted from the rate of apparent overstay. The remainder was multiplied by the number of expected departures to estimate the number of overstays.

The procedure for deriving estimates of overstays by state of destination and age required one additional step to make the results consistent with the figures for country of citizenship. The total numbers estimated for countries were accepted as the control totals for the estimates by state and age. Within each category of admission, an initial set of calculations was done for each state using the procedures already described. The resulting estimates of overstays differed from the totals estimated for countries. To make the totals consistent, the rate of system error was adjusted so that the total numbers of overstays by state of destination agreed with those for countries. The same procedure was followed to derive estimates within age groups consistent with those for country and state of destination.

Assumptions and Limitations

Two important assumptions are implicit in the estimation procedure. First, the rates of apparent overstay for the 12 selected countries are assumed to represent system error and to include very few actual overstays. This is probably a sound assumption, because the data available indicate that those countries have very few unauthorized migrants in the United States. On the other hand, how well these countries represent the level of error that occurs throughout the system cannot be determined. It could be the case, for example, that these countries have generally lower than average rates of error, thus inflating the estimates of overstays. It is doubtful, however, that the opposite is true, because the 12 countries used to estimate system error have consistently low rates of apparent overstay relative to all other countries. In general, the estimation procedure is more likely to overestimate than underestimate the number of overstays.

The second broad assumption of the estimation procedure is that a single point estimate of system error applies to every country of origin within a particular category of admission. Even though the 12 countries used to estimate system error are geographically diverse, it is possible that some areas of the world have different rates of system error. For example, some airlines might do a better job of emphasizing the collection of I-94 departure forms. On the other hand, the high volume of departures through a relatively small number of airports in the United States probably has the effect of "homogenizing" this aspect of system error.

Even though the validity of the underlying assumptions cannot be tested with the resources available, it should be noted that in general the results correspond closely to other information available about the countries of origin and states of destination of unauthorized migrants in the United States. Also, it is possible that the data are relatively more comparable across time than within years, because the same assumptions and procedures were used to derive the estimates for each year.

These estimates cover only a part of the population migrating illegally to the United States. They include only persons arriving through authorized ports of entry with nonimmigrant visas. They exclude persons entering surreptitiously across land borders. Also, nonimmigrant students who overstay their visas are not included in these estimates. Students are excluded because their period of admission is relatively long, and the current estimates were made about 9 to 15 months after admission.

The estimates of nonimmigrant overstays presented here do not represent net growth of the illegal population. Statistics on the departure of nonimmigrants who overstayed in previous years would be needed to estimate net change in the population of overstays. Statistics on departures by period of entry are available from the Nonimmigrant Information System. These sets of data are being tabulated and analyzed; preliminary results indicate that they will be useful for estimating the net flow of nonimmigrant overstays.

RESULTS

The volume of nonimmigrant arrivals increased from about 9.4 million in 1985 to about 14.3 million in 1988, an increase of just over 50 percent. During the 1985 to 1988 period the annual number of overstays fluctuated in the 217,000 to 255,000 range (tables 3.2 and 3.3). The total number of overstays increased by 12 percent in 1986, dropped by 7 percent in 1987 (the year following passage of IRCA), then increased by about 13 percent in 1988. The overall rate of nonimmigrant overstay dropped from 2.4 percent in both 1985 and 1986 to 1.9 percent in the two years after the passage of IRCA. The total level of system error dropped steadily, from 10.3 percent in 1985 to 8.1 percent in 1988. As table 3.2 shows, the rate of system error was highest for nonimmigrants arriving by land (about 26 percent) and considerably lower for those traveling by air.

Table 3.2 SELECTED NONIMMIGRANT STATISTICS: 1985–88

(Numbers in thousands)

Type of Estimate	Fiscal Year of Entry			
	1985	1986	1987	1988
Total arrivals	9,414	10,343	12,153	14,273
Expected departures	9,083	10,039	11,707	13,748
Estimated overstays	217	243	226	255
Percentage overstay	2.4	2.4	1.9	1.9
Percentage of system error	10.3	9.5	8.8	8.1
Air	9.2	8.4	8.0	7.2
Sea	21.4	19.9	15.7	13.6
Land	26.6	25.6	24.6	26.2

Source: Table 3.3 and statistics from the Nonimmigrant Information System (NIIS) of the U.S. Immigration and Naturalization Service (INS).

Continent of Origin

North America was the leading area of origin of nonimmigrant overstays and also had the largest increases in overstays between 1985 and 1988, principally because the estimates for Mexico more than doubled during the period (table 3.4). The estimated number of overstays from Central America also increased during the period, although the figure for 1987 was lower than for 1986. Estimated overstays from Europe declined by more than 25 percent between 1985 and 1988. Asia, the second leading continent of origin, was estimated to have just over 50,000 overstays each year. The estimated number of overstays from Africa increased from 10,000 in 1985 to 14,000 in 1988. Table 3.5 shows estimated numbers and rates of overstays by continent of origin and class of admission for 1985–88.

Country of Origin

Mexico was the leading country of origin in 1988, with an estimated 55,800 overstays, or 21.9 percent of the total (table 3.6). Haiti, the Philippines, and Poland each accounted for approximately 14,000 overstays; no other country had as many as 10,000. The top 10 countries, shown in table 3.6, accounted for more than half of all overstays. The estimated percentage overstay for these 10 countries combined was 7.6 percent, compared to an average of 1.0 percent for all other countries. The top 5 countries—Mexico, Haiti, the Philippines, Poland and India—were among the leading countries of application for legal residence under IRCA, although such comparisons can be misleading because of differences in the time periods involved. Table 3.7 shows annual estimates of the number and percentage overstay for 75 countries for 1985–88.

Trends in Overstays by Country

For many of the 75 countries shown in table 3.7, the estimated number of overstays was roughly the same throughout the four-year period. This was not the case for the countries listed in table 3.8. Two of the leading countries of overstays, Mexico and Poland, showed clear trends in the level of overstays—and the changes were in the opposite directions. The estimated number for Mexico more than doubled, reaching 55,800 in 1988, while estimated overstays from Poland dropped by nearly 30 percent during the period. Information about the reasons for these changing levels of overstay would be

Table 3.3 ESTIMATED NONIMMIGRANT OVERSTAYS, EXPECTED
DEPARTURES, AND PERCENTAGE OF SYSTEM ERROR: FISCAL
YEARS 1985–88

(Numbers in thousands; rounded independently)

Class and Mode of Arrival	Fiscal Year of Entry							
	Estimated Overstays				Percentage Overstay			
	1985	1986	1987	1988	1985	1986	1987	1988
TOTAL	217	243	226	255	2.4	2.4	1.9	1.9
Air	200	224	197	222	2.4	2.4	1.8	1.7
Sea	2	2	1	2	1.1	0.8	0.6	0.6
Land	15	17	28	32	3.3	3.7	5.9	6.1
B1	29	29	30	33	1.6	1.5	1.4	1.4
Air B1[a]	24	24	26	28	1.4	1.3	1.3	1.3
Sea B1	—[b]	—	—	—	2.5	3.5	1.6	2.5
Land B1	4	5	4	5	6.8	7.7	5.7	7.1
B2	168	183	167	205	2.6	2.5	1.9	1.9
Air B2[c]	159	173	148	182	2.6	2.6	1.8	1.8
Sea B2	1	1	1	2	0.8	0.4	0.4	0.6
Land B2	9	10	18	21	2.4	2.6	4.7	4.9
Other	20	30	29	17	2.8	3.6	3.5	2.0
Air transit	5	6	2	1	2.0	2.5	1.0	0.3
Air workers	2	4	4	5	3.9	6.0	5.0	5.4
Air other	11	16	16	6	2.6	3.4	3.4	1.3
Sea other	—	1	—	—	4.4	5.1	4.0	3.1
Land other	2	3	7	5	7.8	8.1	17.9	24.2

(Continued)

Table 3.3 ESTIMATED NONIMMIGRANT OVERSTAYS, EXPECTED
DEPARTURES, AND PERCENTAGE OF SYSTEM ERROR: FISCAL
YEARS 1985–88 *(Continued)*

(Numbers in thousands; rounded independently)

Class and Mode of Arrival	Fiscal Year of Entry							
	Expected Departures				Percentage System Error			
	1985	1986	1987	1988	1985	1986	1987	1988
TOTAL	9,083	10,039	11,707	13,748	10.3	9.5	8.8	8.1
Air	8,490	9,373	10,992	12,935	9.2	8.4	8.0	7.2
Sea	137	199	229	293	21.4	19.9	15.7	13.6
Land	457	468	486	521	26.6	25.6	24.6	26.2
B1	1,785	1,929	2,120	2,330	9.0	8.7	8.6	7.8
Air B1	1,717	1,860	2,049	2,255	8.6	8.3	8.2	7.3
Sea B1	7	7	9	9	22.4	21.6	18.2	14.0
Land B1	61	62	62	66	19.1	19.3	20.5	21.7
B2	6,566	7,265	8,740	10,583	10.7	9.4	8.6	8.1
Air B2	6,080	6,717	8,144	9,871	9.3	8.2	7.7	7.1
Sea B2	120	178	210	280	22.3	20.0	15.3	13.6
Land B2	366	370	386	432	28.6	26.7	25.8	27.6
Other	733	845	848	834	10.1	11.5	11.1	8.5
Air transit	232	240	259	287	12.4	12.9	13.2	11.4
Air workers	58	70	76	85	13.6	18.0	16.8	10.6
Air other	403	486	464	436	7.7	8.8	8.1	5.9
Sea other	10	13	10	4	9.8	16.7	22.0	7.4
Land other	30	36	38	23	16.9	24.1	18.9	14.3

Source: Statistics from NIIS.
a. B1 = Temporary visitors for business.
b. Dash (—) = rounds to zero.
c. B2 = Temporary visitors for pleasure, see table 3A.1 for other classes of admission.

useful for understanding the impact of IRCA on the flow of illegal migration to the United States.

State of Destination

Not surprisingly, the leading states of destination of nonimmigrant overstays are the states where most of the foreign-born population reside (legally and illegally). The rates of overstay for each of the top six states were lower in 1988 than in 1986, with Illinois having the largest drop, from 9 percent in 1986 to 5 percent in 1988 (table 3.9). The estimated numbers of overstays going to most of these states dropped in 1987 compared to 1986, then increased in 1988 to about the same

Table 3.4 ESTIMATED OVERSTAYS BY AREA OF ORIGIN: 1985–88

(Numbers in thousands; rounded independently)

Area of Origin	Fiscal Year of Entry			
	1985	1986	1987	1988
TOTAL	217	243	226	255
North America	79	95	99	118
Mexico	25	33	41	56
Central America	11	15	12	16
Other North America	44	47	45	46
Asia	55	58	50	54
Europe	45	49	38	33
South America	15	18	14	19
Africa	10	13	14	14
Oceania	2	2	2	2
Stateless and unknown	11	8	10	15

Source: Tables 3.5 and 3.7.

level estimated for 1986. The exceptions are Illinois, which declined in both 1987 and 1988, and Texas, which was unchanged. The estimated number for New York, the leading state of destination, was about 10 percent higher in 1988 than in 1986. Table 3.10 shows annual estimates of overstays for each state and outlying area of destination.

Age

Estimates of nonimmigrant overstays by age and class of admission for 1987 and 1988 are shown in table 3.11 and 3.12. As would be expected, most of the estimated overstays are in the 15- to 44-year age range. For temporary visitors for business, about 90 percent were 15 to 44 years of age; in the "All Other" category, about 80 percent were 15 to 44. Note that children usually have the same class of admission as their parents; thus the 1,600 estimated "business" overstays under age 15 in 1988 shown in table 3.11. It is somewhat surprising that such a high proportion of tourists (temporary visitors for pleasure) are estimated to overstay in the under-15 and 45-and-over age groups. Two possible explanations for this are that (1) the estimates are overstated in these age groups, and (2) relatively more persons who overstay in these age groups later depart, producing the higher concentration in the 15-to-44 age group usually observed for longer-term residents.

Table 3.5 ESTIMATED NONIMMIGRANT OVERSTAYS, BY CONTINENT OF
ORIGIN AND CLASS OF ADMISSION: FISCAL YEARS 1985–88

(Numbers in thousands; rounded independently)

Continent and Class	Estimated Overstays				Percentage Overstay			
	1985	1986	1987	1988	1985	1986	1987	1988
TOTAL	217	243	226	255	2.4	2.4	1.9	1.9
B1	29	29	30	33	1.6	1.5	1.4	1.4
B2	168	183	167	205	2.6	2.5	1.9	1.9
Other	20	30	29	17	2.8	3.6	3.5	2.0
Europe	45	49	38	33	1.4	1.2	0.8	0.6
B1	2	1	1	1	0.2	0.1	0.2	0.1
B2	40	44	34	31	1.8	1.6	1.0	0.7
Other	3	4	2	1	1.2	1.2	0.7	0.3
Asia	55	58	50	54	2.2	2.2	1.6	1.4
B1	7	7	7	7	1.8	1.6	1.4	1.2
B2	40	39	34	43	2.1	2.0	1.4	1.4
Other	8	12	9	5	3.8	5.0	3.6	2.1
Africa	10	13	14	14	6.8	7.5	9.3	9.0
B1	1	2	3	3	4.0	4.0	7.3	6.8
B2	8	10	10	11	8.5	9.7	11.3	11.5
Other	1	1	1	1	4.4	4.7	4.6	2.4
Oceania	2	2	2	2	0.5	0.6	0.6	0.4
B1		—[b]	—	—	0.3	0.2	0.2	0.1
B2	1	2	2	2	0.5	0.6	0.7	0.5
Other		—	—	—	1.0	1.0	1.2	0.2
North America	79	95	99	118	4.1	5.1	4.7	5.1
B1	14	16	16	19	4.7	4.9	4.4	4.9
B2	59	69	67	89	3.9	5.0	4.3	5.1
Other	6	11	15	9	4.8	7.1	9.6	7.0
South America	15	18	14	19	1.9	1.9	1.4	1.9
B1	2	3	2	2	1.7	1.8	1.5	1.3
B2	12	14	10	16	2.0	2.0	1.4	2.1
Other	1	1	1	—	1.6	1.8	1.6	0.4
Other[a]	11	8	10	15	8.0	6.3	9.2	10.9

Source: Statistics from NIIS.
a. Stateless and unknown.
b. Dash (—) = rounds to zero.

ADDITIONAL ANALYSIS

These estimates of nonimmigrant overstays will be useful for monitoring the general level of unauthorized migration from most countries of the world. However, considerably more work needs to be

Table 3.6 TOP 10 COUNTRIES OF OVERSTAYS: FISCAL YEAR 1988

Country of Citizenship	Estimated Overstays	Percentage of Total	Expected Departures	Percentage Overstay
TOTAL	254,900	100.00	13,748,100	1.9
Mexico	55,800	21.9	947,600	5.9
Haiti	14,300	5.6	89,700	16.0
Philippines	14,000	5.5	130,900	10.7
Poland	13,900	5.5	49,200	28.3
India	8,400	3.3	120,600	6.9
Trinidad and Tobago	7,500	2.9	89,400	8.4
Canada	6,300	2.5	35,500	17.7
Ireland	5,400	2.1	135,800	4.0
Colombia	5,100	2.0	155,500	3.3
Pakistan	4,600	1.8	36,200	12.7
All other	119,600	46.9	11,957,700	1.0
Top ten	135,300	53.1	1,790,400	7.6

Source: Table 3.7 and statistics from NIIS.

done to improve the estimates and to develop net, in addition to gross, estimates of overstay. The section following describes other types of analysis that would improve the utility of the estimates.

Departure Statistics

One objective of the employer sanctions provisions of IRCA is to reduce the inflow of unauthorized immigrants by limiting access to employment in this country. The type of estimates described so far will be used to evaluate that aspect of the açt. In addition to reducing the inflow, the law is also based on the assumption that illegal residents would be forced to depart if employment is restricted to only legal residents. Statistics collected in the Nonimmigrant Information System can be used to determine whether departures of illegal residents have increased as a result of the new law.

Statistics on nonimmigrant departures are collected by date of entry, date of expected departure, and date of actual departure, along with the other variables in the system (table 3A.3). To illustrate the usefulness of this information, statistics were compiled for all nonimmigrants in the *apparent overstay* category who departed during fiscal year 1988. The figures were tabulated by country of citizenship and six-month periods of entry. Estimates

Table 3.7 ESTIMATED NONIMMIGRANT OVERSTAYS, BY AREA AND
SELECTED COUNTRY OF CITIZENSHIP: 1985–88

(Numbers rounded independently)

Area or Country	Estimated Overstays				Percentage Overstay			
	1985	1986	1987	1988	1985	1986	1987	1988
TOTAL	217,300	242,700	226,500	254,900	2.4	2.4	1.9	1.9
Europe	44,600	48,900	37,600	33,300	1.4	1.2	0.8	0.6
Denmark	800	700	1,700	300	1.3	1.0	1.8	0.3
Greece	2,000	1,700	1,500	700	4.2	3.2	2.6	1.2
Hungary	500	600	500	800	3.9	3.7	3.0	4.3
Ireland	4,400	6,500	6,400	5,400	5.4	6.0	5.5	4.0
Italy	6,100	4,900	2,500	4,300	2.4	1.7	0.7	1.1
Poland	19,700	21,900	16,000	13,900	42.2	40.3	31.6	28.3
Portugal	4,400	4,700	3,500	3,600	12.9	12.9	9.1	8.0
Romania	500	700	800	700	8.9	12.0	13.1	9.2
Spain	600	1,000	1,000	500	0.6	0.8	0.7	0.2
Sweden	300	100	200	—[a]	0.2	0.1	0.1	0.0
United Kingdom	200	2,500	1,200	—	0.0	0.2	0.1	0.0
Yugoslavia	2,700	1,700	1,800	1,700	11.4	6.2	5.7	5.1
Other Europe	2,400	1,900	700	1,300	0.2	0.1	0.0	0.0
Asia	55,400	58,100	49,800	54,500	2.2	2.2	1.6	1.4
Afghanistan	300	300	400	200	27.0	25.4	27.9	17.7
Bangladesh	400	1,000	1,200	1,400	12.4	20.9	24.0	24.5
China	4,900	4,900	3,500	2,900	4.2	4.4	3.3	2.4
Hong Kong	300	200	500	1,300	0.5	0.3	0.7	1.6
India	5,200	6,800	6,700	8,400	5.4	6.4	5.9	6.9
Iran	8,100	6,200	5,200	3,400	17.7	16.2	19.5	16.5
Israel	4,800	5,100	3,100	3,600	4.3	3.8	2.2	2.3
Japan	700	1,200	100	800	0.0	0.1	0.0	0.0
Jordan	600	600	800	1,000	4.1	3.9	4.4	4.9
Korea	3,000	3,100	1,700	900	3.2	3.1	1.5	0.8
Lebanon	2,300	2,200	2,600	3,700	9.7	10.0	12.0	14.5
Malaysia	400	1,500	800	3,300	1.4	5.3	2.7	8.2
Pakistan	3,600	4,300	4,200	4,600	11.8	13.1	12.4	12.7
Philippines	15,800	15,800	14,300	14,000	14.5	13.8	12.0	10.7
Sri Lanka	500	600	700	600	8.3	9.0	11.1	9.7
Syria	500	600	500	1,400	6.1	7.6	8.3	14.1
Other Asia	3,800	3,800	3,500	2,900	1.9	1.8	1.4	1.1
Africa	10,200	12,600	14,000	14,100	6.8	7.5	9.3	9.0
Cape Verde	300	300	300	600	26.7	27.3	20.8	33.1
Egypt	2,500	2,300	1,800	1,900	9.5	9.7	7.6	7.6
Ethiopa	700	900	900	1,000	20.9	22.0	21.1	21.1
Ghana	700	600	1,400	1,200	17.1	14.8	26.2	23.1
Liberia	1,300	1,400	1,500	900	29.1	32.0	32.2	22.4
Nigeria	1,300	2,200	2,800	2,400	3.7	4.9	11.1	10.0

(Continued)

Table 3.7 ESTIMATED NONIMMIGRANT OVERSTAYS, BY AREA AND
       SELECTED COUNTRY OF CITIZENSHIP: 1985–88 *(Continued)*

(Numbers rounded independently)

Area or Country	Estimated Overstays				Percentage Overstay			
	1985	1986	1987	1988	1985	1986	1987	1988
Senegal	200	500	900	500	8.1	11.2	16.4	9.6
Sierra Leone	700	700	500	500	33.5	34.1	29.9	27.4
South Africa	500	1,200	1,000	800	1.6	3.2	3.0	2.4
Sudan	100	200	300	300	5.0	7.5	11.8	13.4
Uganda	100	100	100	200	7.0	11.5	11.5	12.4
Other Africa	2,000	2,200	2,500	3,800	5.6	5.5	6.0	8.4
Oceania	1,700	2,000	2,400	2,000	0.5	0.6	0.6	0.4
Australia	—	—	—	200	—	—	—	0.1
Fiji	400	300	500	600	8.5	5.5	9.9	11.7
New Zealand	—	—	100	100	—	—	0.1	0.0
Tonga	500	800	600	700	27.2	31.8	26.9	26.0
Trust Territory of the Pacific Islands	100	400	400	100	4.2	5.4	13.0	23.0
Western Samoa	600	500	700	300	30.2	21.1	22.7	13.3
Other Oceania	100	—	—	—	2.8	2.0	1.5	1.4
North America	79,300	94,900	98,600	117,700	4.1	5.1	4.7	5.1
Canada	9,400	6,800	6,400	6,300	18.8	15.4	15.2	17.7
Mexico	24,700	32,900	41,200	55,800	2.8	4.3	4.7	5.9
The Bahamas	5,200	7,100	5,400	2,300	2.6	3.2	2.1	0.8
Barbados	700	600	1,200	1,000	3.3	2.8	4.1	3.0
Bermuda	300	400	500	500	17.7	23.4	21.7	29.4
Cuba	1,600	1,000	700	300	13.1	25.7	17.8	11.5
Dominica	600	1,600	2,200	3,000	6.3	4.8	3.4	3.9
Dominican Republic	2,900	2,900	1,700	3,000	3.8	4.2	3.2	4.8
Grenada	300	400	600	500	11.7	11.6	13.9	11.4
Haiti	12,800	14,300	11,800	14,300	15.0	16.6	13.8	16.0
Jamaica	5,800	5,900	4,500	3,600	4.6	4.0	2.6	1.8
Trinidad and Tobago	1,100	2,500	5,500	7,500	1.3	3.5	6.8	8.4
Total, Central America	10,600	15,200	12,500	16,100	3.6	4.9	3.7	4.4
Belize	800	900	700	900	8.2	8.8	6.1	7.3
Costa Rica	100	300	200	100	0.3	0.5	0.3	0.1
El Salvador	2,100	3,000	2,200	2,300	4.1	5.7	3.9	4.1
Guatemala	2,900	4,400	3,400	4,000	4.4	6.4	4.1	4.1
Honduras	1,800	2,800	2,000	2,100	3.6	5.1	3.3	3.2
Nicaragua	2,500	2,700	2,900	4,500	12.2	14.2	14.0	18.3
Panama	300	1,100	1,200	2,300	0.6	2.3	2.4	4.3
Other North America	3,200	3,300	4,600	3,500	4.8	4.3	4.9	3.5
South America	15,300	18,100	13,800	18,800	1.9	1.9	1.4	1.9
Argentina	100	—	—	100	0.1	0.0	0.0	0.1

(Continued)

Table 3.7 ESTIMATED NONIMMIGRANT OVERSTAYS, BY AREA AND
SELECTED COUNTRY OF CITIZENSHIP: 1985–88 *(Continued)*

(Numbers rounded independently)

Area or Country	Estimated Overstays				Percentage Overstay			
	1985	1986	1987	1988	1985	1986	1987	1988
South America *(continued)*								
Bolivia	500	1,000	1,100	1,500	2.7	5.8	6.0	7.5
Brazil	1,100	1,400	100	2,800	0.6	0.6	0.0	1.0
Chile	100	600	600	700	0.3	1.2	1.1	1.1
Colombia	4,200	5,500	3,800	5,100	2.6	3.5	2.5	3.3
Equador	4,600	4,100	3,200	4,500	9.3	7.1	5.1	8.3
Guyana	2,400	2,800	2,500	1,300	17.9	15.9	14.0	8.2
Paraguay	—	—	100	100	0.9	0.6	1.9	1.6
Peru	1,800	2,400	2,100	2,400	3.1	3.8	2.8	3.1
Uruguay	200	200	100	100	1.7	1.3	0.3	0.5
Venezuela	200	100	100	100	0.1	0.1	0.1	0.1
Other S.A.	—	—	—	—	0.3	0.1	0.0	0.0
Stateless	900	1,000	1,100	1,200	10.3	9.8	11.9	14.2
Unknown	10,000	7,000	9,300	13,400	7.9	6.0	9.0	10.7

Source: Statistics from NIIS.
Note: Base of percentages is in table 3A.2.
a. Dash (—) = rounds to zero.

of nonimmigrants who overstayed in previous years and departed during fiscal year 1988 are shown in table 3.13. The departures shown there are limited to those departing nonimmigrants whose length of stay was consistent with the definition of *overstay* used in this chapter, that is, those who departed after overstaying for nine months or more. The statistics on departure were used along with the estimated overstays during 1988 to make provisional estimates of net change for the year.

The results are striking for some areas and countries. Europe, Asia, and South America had large numbers of departures relative to newly arriving overstays. For Poland the estimated number of departures, 12,400, was almost as large as the number of overstays during the year. Other countries with large numbers of departures relative to new overstays were China, Israel, Korea, and Brazil.

The total net addition of overstays from all countries was estimated to be about 174,000, as shown in table 3.13. This should be considered an upper-limit figure for net overstays, for three reasons. First, as previously discussed, the estimates of overstays tend to be maximum figures. Second, conservative assumptions were used in de-

Table 3.8 COUNTRIES WITH LARGE CHANGES IN OVERSTAYS: 1985–88

Country of Citizenship	Fiscal Year of Entry				Change, 1985–88
	1985	1986	1987	1988	
Decreases					
Poland	19,700	21,900	16,000	13,900	− 5,800
Iran	8,100	6,200	5,200	3,400	− 4,700
Canada	9,400	6,800	6,400	6,300	− 3,100
The Bahamas	5,200	7,100	5,400	2,300	− 2,900
Jamaica	5,800	5,900	4,500	3,600	− 2,200
Korea	3,000	3,100	1,700	900	− 2,100
China	4,900	4,900	3,500	2,900	− 2,000
Increases					
Mexico	24,700	32,900	41,200	55,800	+ 31,100
Trinidad and Tobago	1,100	2,500	5,500	7,500	+ 6,400
India	5,200	6,800	6,700	8,400	+ 3,200
Nicaragua	2,500	2,700	2,900	4,500	+ 2,000
Panama	300	1,100	1,200	2,300	+ 2,000
Lebanon	2,300	2,200	2,600	3,700	+ 1,400
Hong Kong	300	200	500	1,300	+ 1,000

Source: Table 3.7.

Table 3.9 TOP SIX STATES OF DESTINATION OF OVERSTAYS: FISCAL YEARS 1986–88

(Numbers in thousands; rounded independently)

State of Destination	Estimated Overstays			Percentage Overstay		
	1986	1987	1988	1986	1987	1988
TOTAL	243	227	255	2.4	1.9	1.9
New York	59	50	65	3.6	2.7	3.1
California	48	40	47	3.2	2.2	2.2
Florida	30	22	30	1.8	1.1	1.2
New Jersey	13	12	15	5.9	5.0	5.7
Illinois	21	17	14	9.0	6.8	5.0
Texas	13	13	13	2.9	3.0	2.7
All other	60	73	72	1.4	1.4	1.2
Top six	183	154	184	3.3	2.4	2.4

Source: Table 3.10.
Note: States ranked using 1988 estimates.

Table 3.10 ESTIMATED NONIMMIGRANT OVERSTAYS, BY STATE OR AREA OF
DESTINATION: FISCAL YEARS 1986–88

(Numbers rounded independently)

State or Area of Destination	Estimated Overstays			Percentage Overstay		
	1986	1987	1988	1986	1987	1988
TOTAL	242,700	226,500	254,900	2.4	1.9	1.9
Alabama	400	400	400	2.4	2.0	1.9
Alaska	100	—a	300	0.5	0.2	1.3
Arizona	4,700	6,100	4,600	8.3	9.3	6.5
Arkansas	300	400	400	6.7	6.8	5.9
California	48,000	39,500	46,500	3.2	2.2	2.2
Colorado	2,400	3,000	3,300	3.5	4.1	3.7
Connecticut	2,800	2,900	3,100	3.1	3.0	3.0
Delaware	100	100	200	1.4	1.2	1.5
District of Columbia	1,600	1,100	1,400	1.1	0.7	0.8
Florida	29,700	22,100	29,700	1.8	1.1	1.2
Georgia	1,200	800	1,400	1.4	0.8	1.3
Hawaii	600	900	400	0.1	0.1	0.0
Idaho	200	700	800	4.0	12.3	12.3
Iowa	300	700	500	2.7	5.7	3.1
Illinois	20,500	16,900	14,300	9.0	6.8	5.0
Indiana	900	1,900	1,400	3.3	5.1	4.0
Kansas	1,100	1,300	1,300	8.4	9.0	8.5
Kentucky	600	800	600	5.1	5.7	3.4
Louisiana	3,600	2,200	2,300	5.1	2.8	2.7
Maine	100	300	400	0.6	1.7	2.2
Maryland	2,800	3,800	3,600	3.1	3.9	3.5
Massachusetts	7,000	8,700	9,800	3.5	3.9	3.8
Michigan	3,800	5,000	5,200	3.7	4.4	4.3
Minnesota	700	1,700	1,100	1.6	3.5	1.9
Mississippi	300	300	500	5.8	4.7	7.4
Missouri	1,400	2,000	1,500	5.3	7.0	4.9
Montana	100	400	200	3.6	7.5	4.4
North Carolina	1,000	1,300	1,100	2.3	3.0	2.1
North Dakota	100	100	300	1.7	2.9	5.1
Nebraska	400	300	500	6.4	4.8	6.7
Nevada	200	400	300	0.4	0.6	0.4
New Hampshire	100	400	300	0.8	2.1	1.6
New Jersey	12,900	12,100	15,000	5.9	5.0	5.7
New Mexico	800	1,000	1,000	7.2	7.9	6.2
New York	58,700	50,000	64,700	3.6	2.7	3.1
Ohio	3,100	3,700	2,700	4.1	4.3	2.9
Oklahoma	1,600	1,400	1,400	9.1	8.0	7.3
Oregon	600	1,000	700	2.1	3.2	1.8
Pennsylvania	2,900	3,500	3,400	2.5	2.7	2.3
Rhode Island	1,000	1,100	1,300	6.3	7.0	7.3

(Continued)

Table 3.10 ESTIMATED NONIMMIGRANT OVERSTAYS, BY STATE OR AREA OF
DESTINATION: FISCAL YEARS 1986–88 *(Continued)*

(Numbers rounded independently)

State or Area of Destination	Estimated Overstays			Percentage Overstay		
	1986	1987	1988	1986	1987	1988
South Carolina	400	300	300	1.8	1.6	1.2
South Dakota	100	100	100	2.4	3.4	4.2
Tennessee	1,100	1,500	1,100	4.7	5.5	3.4
Texas	12,800	13,400	13,400	2.9	3.0	2.7
Utah	1,400	1,600	1,600	8.6	8.1	7.3
Vermont	400	900	800	3.0	5.3	4.9
Virginia	2,900	3,500	3,700	3.4	3.7	3.6
Washington	1,400	1,100	1,200	1.4	1.0	1.0
Wisconsin	600	900	400	1.7	2.4	1.0
West Virginia	400	200	200	8.2	3.8	3.6
Wyoming	200	200	100	6.5	7.6	4.1
Guam	500	300	400	0.1	0.1	0.1
Puerto Rico	300	700	2,400	0.3	0.6	1.8
Virgin Islands	1,300	1,500	1,100	8.0	9.6	7.1

Source: Statistics from NIIS.
Note: Year refers to fiscal year of entry.
a. Dash (—) = rounds to zero.

ciding which of the departures tabulated from the NIIS should be
included as nonimmigrant overstays from previous years. Third, a
significant component of net change in the number of overstays is
not included in table 3.13: the number of overstays who adjusted to
legal permanent residence. Including these adjustments would further reduce the net addition of overstays during the year.

More work is needed to refine the estimates of departures, and
tabulations should be made for the other years for which departure
data are available. Based on these preliminary estimates, however,
it appears that the statistics on departures from the Nonimmigrant
Information System will be valuable for estimating net overstays
and for determining whether the level of departure of nonimmigrant overstays increased after the passage of IRCA.

Other Analyses

ESTIMATES BY SEX

Separate statistics for males and females were not collected in the
Nonimmigrant Information System until January 1986. Estimates of

Table 3.11 ESTIMATED NONIMMIGRANT OVERSTAYS, BY AGE AND CLASS
OF ADMISSION: FISCAL YEARS 1987 AND 1988

(Numbers rounded independently)

Age and Class	Estimated Overstays		Percentage Overstay		Percentage of Total	
	1987	1988	1987	1988	1987	1988
ALL CLASSES						
All ages	226,500	254,900	1.9	1.9	100.0	100.0
Under 15 years	36,600	40,900	3.7	3.3	16.2	16.0
15 to 19 years	27,000	31,700	4.3	3.8	11.9	12.4
20 to 24 years	33,500	41,500	2.5	2.4	14.8	16.3
25 to 29 years	35,000	40,300	2.3	2.3	15.5	15.8
30 to 34 years	31,700	32,600	2.4	2.2	14.0	12.8
35 to 39 years	16,500	16,100	1.3	1.1	7.3	6.3
40 to 44 years	10,100	9,500	0.9	0.7	4.5	3.7
45 to 49 years	6,400	6,200	0.7	0.6	2.8	2.4
50 to 54 years	5,300	5,500	0.7	0.6	2.3	2.2
55 to 64 years	9,300	11,200	0.8	0.9	4.1	4.4
65 to 74 years	8,700	9,700	1.9	2.0	3.9	3.8
75 + years	6,400	9,700	4.1	4.7	2.8	3.8
15 to 44 years	153,700	171,700	2.1	2.0	67.9	67.3
B1 TEMPORARY VISITORS FOR BUSINESS						
All ages	30,200	33,300	1.4	1.4	100.0	100.0
Under 15 years	1,700	1,600	5.8	5.3	5.8	4.9
15 to 19 years	2,700	3,400	9.2	9.1	9.0	10.3
20 to 24 years	7,800	9,400	7.3	6.4	25.9	28.2
25 to 29 years	8,900	9,400	3.7	3.2	29.5	28.2
30 to 34 years	5,800	5,800	1.8	1.6	19.1	17.5
35 to 39 years	1,600	1,600	0.4	0.4	5.4	4.8
40 to 44 years	300	400	0.1	0.1	0.9	1.1
45 to 49 years	200	200	0.1	0.1	0.5	0.7
50 to 54 years	100	200	0.1	0.1	0.4	0.6
55 to 64 years	200	300	0.1	0.2	0.8	0.9
65 to 74 years	400	500	1.5	1.9	1.5	1.5
75 + years	300	500	3.4	3.2	1.1	1.4
15 to 44 years	27,100	30,000	1.9	1.8	89.9	90.1
B2 TEMPORARY VISITORS FOR PLEASURE						
All ages	166,900	205,000	1.9	1.9	100.0	100.0
Under 15 years	30,500	36,700	3.4	3.2	18.3	17.9
15 to 19 years	22,400	26,700	4.0	3.6	13.4	13.0
20 to 24 years	19,900	28,400	1.8	2.0	12.0	13.9
25 to 29 years	19,100	27,300	1.7	2.1	11.4	13.3
30 to 34 years	20,500	24,100	2.4	2.4	12.3	11.8
35 to 39 years	12,700	13,500	1.6	1.4	7.6	6.6

(Continued)

Table 3.11 ESTIMATED NONIMMIGRANT OVERSTAYS, BY AGE AND CLASS
OF ADMISSION: FISCAL YEARS 1987 AND 1988 (Continued)

(Numbers rounded independently)

Age and Class	Estimated Overstays		Percentage Overstay		Percentage of Total	
	1987	1988	1987	1988	1987	1988
40 to 44 years	8,600	8,500	1.2	1.0	5.2	4.2
45 to 49 years	5,600	5,600	0.9	0.7	3.3	2.8
50 to 54 years	4,800	5,100	0.9	0.8	2.9	2.5
55 to 64 years	8,900	10,700	1.0	1.1	5.3	5.2
65 to 74 years	8,000	9,200	1.9	2.1	4.8	4.5
75+ years	5,800	9,000	4.1	4.9	3.5	4.4
15 to 44 years	103,200	128,500	2.0	2.0	61.8	62.7
ALL OTHER CLASSES						
All ages	29,400	16,700	3.5	2.0	100.0	100.0
Under 15 years	4,300	2,500	6.8	4.3	14.7	15.2
15 to 19 years	1,900	1,600	4.3	2.9	6.5	9.6
20 to 24 years	5,700	3,700	5.7	3.5	19.3	22.1
25 to 29 years	7,100	3,600	5.4	2.7	24.0	21.7
30 to 34 years	5,400	2,600	4.3	2.2	18.5	15.8
35 to 39 years	2,100	1,000	1.8	0.9	7.2	6.0
40 to 44 years	1,200	600	1.3	0.7	4.1	3.9
45 to 49 years	700	400	0.9	0.6	2.3	2.2
50 to 54 years	300	200	0.6	0.5	1.0	1.2
55 to 64 years	200	200	0.5	0.4	0.7	1.0
65 to 74 years	300	—[a]	2.9	0.3	0.9	0.1
75+ years	300	200	5.0	2.2	0.9	1.3
15 to 44 years	23,400	13,200	3.8	2.1	79.6	79.0

Source: Statistics from NIIS.
a. Dash (—) = rounds to zero.

nonimmigrant overstays by sex would be useful for understanding the flow of unauthorized migration and for assessing the quality of the estimates of total overstays.

ALTERNATIVE ASSUMPTIONS

Additional estimates of overstays should be computed using alternative strategies in the estimation of system error to determine how sensitive the estimates are to the assumptions used. Also, estimates of system error could be made using a different set of "index" countries, selected less rigorously than the 12 countries used here, and allowing for greater geographic diversity. The drawback to these proposals is that the computation of these estimates requires a considerable amount of computer time and analysis.

Table 3.12 ESTIMATED OVERSTAYS BY AGE: FISCAL YEAR 1988

Age	Estimated Overstays	Percentage of Total	Expected Departures	Percentage Overstay
ALL AGES	254,900	100.0	13,748,100	1.9
Under 15	40,900	16.0	1,235,000	3.3
15 to 24	73,200	28.7	2,550,900	2.9
25 to 34	72,900	28.6	3,224,600	2.3
35 to 44	25,600	10.0	2,845,900	0.9
45 to 64	23,000	9.0	3,206,000	0.7
65 and over	19,400	7.6	685,600	2.8
15 to 44	171,700	67.3	8,621,400	2.0
Median age	26.2	—	29.0	—

Source: Table 3.11 and statistics from NIIS.

ANALYSIS OF NIIS DATA

Additional detailed analysis of the statistics on apparent overstays by class of admission is needed to "weed out" system error introduced each year because of changes in admission categories and data collection procedures, as well as other inevitable minor administrative problems. These tend to inflate the number of apparent overstays by increasing system error. In some cases the estimation procedure makes allowances for these factors, but in other cases the result is an overstatement of overstays. Consistency from year to year could be improved considerably if the statistics produced by NIIS were carefully evaluated and adjusted to reduce spurious levels of apparent overstays.

SUMMARY

The estimates presented here show that information from the Nonimmigrant Information System is valuable for making detailed estimates of the flow of nonimmigrant overstays and for assessing the impact of IRCA on the illegal population. Additional analysis will be required to improve the estimates and develop annual estimates of net change in the population of overstays.

The estimated level of overstays was higher in 1988 than before IRCA was enacted; however, the overall rate of overstay dropped from 2.4 percent in 1985 and 1986 to 1.9 percent in 1987 and 1988. The number of overstays from some countries dropped steadily from

Table 3.13 PROVISIONAL ESTIMATES OF NET OVERSTAYS: FISCAL YEAR
1988

Country of Citizenship	Entered 1988, Estimated Overstay	Overstayed prior to 1988, Departed during 1988	Estimated Net Change, 1988
TOTAL	254,900	81,300	173,700
Europe	33,300	21,500	11,800
Ireland	5,400	1,700	3,700
Italy	4,300	1,600	2,700
Poland	13,900	12,400	1,600
Portugal	3,600	700	3,000
Other Europe	6,100	5,100	800
Asia	54,500	25,600	28,900
China	2,900	4,000	−1,000
India	8,400	3,300	5,100
Iran	3,400	900	2,400
Israel	3,600	2,600	1,000
Korea	900	2,100	−1,100
Lebanon	3,700	800	2,900
Malaysia	3,300	700	2,600
Pakistan	4,600	800	3,800
Philippines	14,000	3,900	10,000
Other Asia	9,700	6,500	1,000
Africa	14,100	4,000	10,100
Egypt	1,900	700	1,100
Ghana	1,200	100	1,100
Nigeria	2,400	500	1,900
Other Africa	8,600	2,700	6,000
Oceania	2,000	2,200	−200
North America	117,700	17,000	100,600
Canada	6,300	1,800	4,500
Mexico	55,800	7,800	48,000
Dominica	3,000	200	2,700
Dominican Republic	3,000	300	2,700
Haiti	14,300	700	13,600
Jamaica	3,600	1,100	2,500
El Salvador	2,300	600	1,700
Guatemala	4,000	900	3,100
Honduras	2,100	500	1,600
Nicaragua	4,500	300	4,200
Panama	2,300	400	1,900
Trinidad and Tobago	7,500	700	6,800
Other North America	9,000	1,700	7,300

(Continued)

Table 3.13 PROVISIONAL ESTIMATES OF NET OVERSTAYS: FISCAL YEAR
1988 *(Continued)*

Country of Citizenship	Entered 1988, Estimated Overstay	Overstayed prior to 1988, Departed during 1988	Estimated Net Change, 1988
South America	18,800	9,300	9,500
Brazil	2,800	2,400	400
Colombia	5,100	1,700	3,400
Equador	4,500	700	3,800
Peru	2,400	800	1,700
Other South America	4,000	3,700	200
Stateless	1,200	100	1,100
Unknown	13,400	1,500	11,900

Source: Statistics from NIIS.

1985 to 1988. For other countries the numbers increased steadily during the period. Overstays from Mexico, the leading country of origin, more than doubled between 1985 and 1988. As expected, the leading states of destination of overstays were New York, California, and Florida, followed by New Jersey, Illinois, and Texas. In general, the rates of overstay for states dropped between 1986 and 1988, although the number of overstays was higher in 1988 than in 1986 for the majority of states.

It will be difficult to determine the effect of IRCA on the flow and size of the illegal population because of the inherent uncertainty accompanying all estimates of unauthorized migration. Also, the maximum impact of the law will not be felt for at least another year or two. At that time, improved estimates of overstays and departures derived from the Nonimmigrant Information System will be available, along with other information, to evaluate the impact of IRCA on the illegally resident population.

Notes

This chapter is from a paper originally prepared for presentation at the Urban Institute conference on "Illegal Immigration Before and After IRCA," on July 21, 1989, in Washington, D.C.

1. Computer support was provided by Michael D. Hoefer and John A. Bjerke of the Statistics Division of the INS. The original programming was done by Vicky Virgin.

2. A point above the mean of the rates was selected because the resulting estimates of overstays for these 12 countries should be at or near zero. That is, if the mean rate had been selected, estimates of overstays would have been produced for about half of the 12 countries.

APPENDIX

Table 3A.1 NONIMMIGRANT CLASSES OF ADMISSION AND VARIABLES
INCLUDED IN NONIMMIGRANT INFORMATION SYSTEM

Nonimmigrant Classes of Admission	Selected NIIS Variables
Foreign government officials and families	Country of citizenship
Temporary visitors	Country of last residence
For business (B1)	Visa-issuing post
For pleasure (B2)	Port of entry
Transit aliens	Class of admission
Treaty traders and investors and families	Date of admission
Students and families	Date admitted to
Representatives (and families) to international	Arrival/departure status
organizations	Date of departure
Temporary workers and trainees	Port of departure
Distinguished merit or ability	Mode of travel
Performing services unavailable in the	Occupation
United States	State of intended residence
Agricultural workers	Year of birth
Nonagricultural workers	Sex
Industrial trainees	Airline
Spouses and children of temporary workers	
and trainees	
Representatives (and families) of foreign	
information media	
Exchange visitors and families	
Fiancés(ées) of United States citizens	
Intracompany transferees and families	
NATO officials and families	
Unknown	

Note: For more detailed information and numbers of arrivals, see U.S. Immigration
and Naturalization Service. 1988. *Statistical Yearbook of the Immigration and Naturalization Service*. Washington, D.C.: U.S. Government Printing Office.

Table 3A.2 ILLUSTRATION OF PROCEDURE FOR ESTIMATING OVERSTAYS: B2 (TOURIST) ARRIVALS, BY AIR, OCTOBER 1986 TO MARCH 1987

Country of Citizenship	Expected Departures (1)	Apparent Overstays		Estimates	
		Number (2)	Percentage (3) = [(2) ÷ (1)] × 100	Overstay (4) = [(3) − 9.52 ÷ 100] × (1)	Error (5) = (2) − (4)
ALL COUNTRIES	3,165,945	295,836	N/A[a]	71,067	224,769
Europe	1,142,086	116,976	N/A	16,304	100,672
Austria	21,784	2,068	9.49	—[b]	2,068
Belgium	19,777	2,020	10.21	137	1,883
Denmark	22,574	3,061	13.56	912	2,149
Finland	17,201	983	5.71	—	983
France	116,088	10,597	9.13	—	10,597
Federal Republic of Germany	198,686	15,833	7.97	—	15,833
Greece	16,220	1,680	10.36	136	1,544
Ireland	29,942	6,078	20.30	3,228	2,850
Italy	90,275	9,681	10.72	1,087	8,594
Netherlands	42,401	3,961	9.34	—	3,961
Norway	21,687	1,965	9.06	—	1,965
Poland	17,971	10,192	56.71	8,481	1,711
Portugal	9,276	1,998	21.54	1,115	883
Spain	34,222	3,134	9.16	—	3,134
Sweden	50,410	4,439	8.81	—	4,439
Switzerland	51,311	4,176	8.14	—	4,176
United Kingdom	345,787	31,772	9.19	—	31,772
Other Europe	36,474	3,338	[c]	1,209[c]	2,129
Asia	997,297	46,708	N/A	16,156	30,552
Bangladesh	1,141	550	48.20	441	109
China	15,978	2,030	12.70	509	1,521
Hong Kong	16,043	1,303	8.12	—	1,303

Asia (continued)					
India	19,541	3,746	19.17	1,886	1,860
Indonesia	5,182	626	12.08	133	493
Iran	9,592	3,078	32.09	2,165	913
Israel	32,600	4,971	15.25	1,867	3,104
Japan	784,311	11,018	1.40	—	11,018
Korea	17,038	2,297	13.48	675	1,622
Kuwait	1,203	104	8.65	—	104
Lebanon	5,079	1,359	26.76	875	484
Malaysia	8,509	972	11.42	162	810
Pakistan	7,903	2,310	29.23	1,558	752
Philippines	22,027	5,836	26.49	3,739	2,097
Saudi Arabia	4,894	409	8.36	—	409
Singapore	8,306	481	5.79	—	481
Taiwan	16,355	1,451	8.87	—	1,451
Other Asia	21,595	4,167	c	2,146[c]	2,021
Africa	30,947	7,511	N/A	4,568	2,943
Egypt	4,550	1,080	23.74	647	433
Ethiopia	931	372	39.96	283	89
Ghana	1,059	483	45.61	382	101
Liberia	1,529	884	57.82	738	146
Morocco	1,494	246	16.47	104	142
Nigeria	5,223	1,501	28.74	1,004	497
South Africa	8,997	1,254	13.94	397	857
Other Africa	7,164	1,691	c	1,012[c]	679
Oceania	101,911	9,119	N/A	870	8,249
Australia	68,356	5,533	8.09	—	5,533
New Zealand	28,333	2,243	7.92	—	2,243
Other Oceania	5,222	1,343	c	870[c]	473

(Continued)

Table 3A.2 ILLUSTRATION OF PROCEDURE FOR ESTIMATING OVERSTAYS: B2 (TOURIST) ARRIVALS, BY AIR, OCTOBER 1986 TO MARCH 1987 (Continued)

Country of Citizenship	Expected Departures (1)	Apparent Overstays		Estimates	
		Number (2)	Percentage (3) = [(2) ÷ (1)] × 100	Overstay (4) = [(3) − 9.52 ÷ 100] × (1)	Error (5) = (2) − (4)
North America	564,067	78,896	N/A	25,433	53,463
Canada	1,772	693	39.11	524	169
Mexico	214,857	29,132	13.56	8,678	20,454
The Bahamas	97,877	11,649	11.90	2,331	9,318
Barbados	4,937	658	13.33	188	470
Cayman Islands	5,028	317	6.30	—	317
Dominica	14,753	1,883	12.76	479	1,404
Dominican Republic	13,449	1,603	11.92	323	1,280
Haiti	20,595	5,569	27.04	3,608	1,961
Jamaica	36,530	5,094	13.94	1,616	3,478
Netherlands Antilles	5,627	540	9.60	4	536
Trinidad and Tobago	19,730	3,370	17.08	1,492	1,878
Costa Rica	22,487	2,068	9.20	—	2,068
El Salvador	17,212	2,506	14.56	867	1,639
Guatemala	28,180	4,075	14.46	1,392	2,683
Honduras	17,956	2,178	12.13	469	1,709
Nicaragua	8,107	2,209	27.25	1,437	772

	(1)	(2)			
Panama	20,916	2,404	11.49	413	1,991
Other North America	14,054	2,948	c	1,612[c]	1,336
South America	297,830	30,599	N/A	4,736	25,863
Argentina	60,957	4,589	7.53	—	4,589
Bolivia	5,096	903	17.72	418	485
Brazil	81,061	7,273	8.97	—	7,273
Chile	13,243	1,499	11.32	238	1,261
Colombia	42,149	5,453	12.94	1,440	4,013
Ecuador	19,526	2,959	15.15	1,100	1,859
Guyana	3,630	1,005	27.69	659	346
Paraguay	2,140	254	11.87	50	204
Peru	25,056	3,203	12.78	818	2,385
Suriname	4,233	335	7.91	—	335
Uruguay	4,028	396	9.83	13	383
Venezuela	36,704	2,730	7.44	—	2,730
Other South America	7	0	c	0	0
Stateless	1,536	321	20.90	175	146
Unknown	30,271	5,706	18.85	2,824	2,882

Notes: Data from columns (1) and (2) are from the NIIS. Error rate = 9.52% (see table 3.1).

a. N/A = Not applicable.

b. Dash (—) = Countries with rates of apparent overstay rates below 9.52, which were assumed to have no overstays.

c. The estimates were done separately for each country. The number for "other" in column 4 is the sum of the estimated overstays for the countries not shown separately in this table.

Table 3A.3 EXPECTED DEPARTURES BY COUNTRY OF CITIZENSHIP: FISCAL
YEARS 1985–88

(Numbers rounded independently)

Country of Citizenship	Fiscal Year of Entry			
	1985	1986	1987	1988
TOTAL	9,083,200	10,039,500	11,717,400	13,748,100
Europe	3,272,300	3,937,800	4,866,600	5,922,100
Denmark	60,700	74,800	94,800	106,000
Greece	48,700	52,900	55,400	56,500
Hungary	13,100	15,000	16,000	18,000
Ireland	81,700	108,500	117,400	135,800
Italy	251,700	287,000	349,400	389,200
Poland	46,600	54,400	50,600	49,200
Portugal	34,200	36,300	38,400	45,400
Romania	5,300	5,700	6,400	8,100
Spain	109,800	123,500	144,600	181,800
Sweden	123,600	144,600	182,100	229,700
United Kingdom	1,017,700	1,240,400	1,467,300	1,894,000
Yugoslavia	23,700	27,200	31,300	33,500
Other Europe	1,455,600	1,767,400	2,312,800	2,774,900
Asia	2,491,900	2,664,100	3,139,600	3,774,400
Afghanistan	1,300	1,200	1,400	1,300
Bangladesh	3,400	4,600	5,100	5,800
China	116,500	110,600	107,200	121,100
Hong Kong	59,000	69,400	72,100	81,200
India	95,800	106,900	112,900	120,600
Iran	45,900	38,000	26,800	20,400
Israel	111,500	133,800	142,700	156,600
Japan	1,539,100	1,657,700	2,086,000	2,606,100
Jordan	15,700	15,700	17,600	19,400
Korea	92,700	101,700	112,000	123,600
Lebanon	23,700	22,100	21,800	25,700
Malaysia	28,700	27,400	29,100	40,200
Pakistan	30,700	32,900	33,900	36,200
Philippines	108,600	113,900	119,100	130,900
Sri Lanka	6,500	6,700	6,400	6,600
Syria	8,200	7,600	6,200	9,800
Other Asia	204,600	214,000	239,300	269,000
Africa	150,200	169,000	151,000	155,900
Cape Verde	1,100	1,200	1,600	1,800
Egypt	26,000	23,900	23,300	24,500
Ethiopia	3,200	3,900	4,300	4,700
Ghana	3,800	4,000	5,200	5,200
Liberia	4,400	4,500	4,600	4,000
Nigeria	34,600	44,100	25,200	24,300

(Continued)

Table 3A.3 EXPECTED DEPARTURES BY COUNTRY OF CITIZENSHIP: FISCAL
YEARS 1985–88 *(Continued)*

(Numbers rounded independently)

Country of Citizenship	Fiscal Year of Entry			
	1985	1986	1987	1988
Africa *(continued)*				
Senegal	2,500	4,400	5,600	5,100
Sierra Leone	2,000	2,100	1,700	1,700
South Africa	34,000	38,200	35,000	35,500
Sudan	2,200	2,300	2,300	2,400
Uganda	900	1,000	1,100	1,300
Other Africa	35,600	39,400	41,100	45,500
Oceania	326,500	357,600	390,300	469,500
Australia	229,600	234,500	251,800	304,900
Fiji	4,800	5,100	4,800	5,000
New Zealand	83,900	104,300	121,600	150,900
Trust Territory of the Pacific Islands	2,300	6,700	3,000	500
Tonga	1,700	2,500	2,400	2,500
Western Samoa	2,100	2,300	3,300	2,500
Other Oceania	2,100	2,200	3,300	3,200
North America	1,922,900	1,856,300	2,103,400	2,290,500
Canada	49,900	43,800	42,100	35,500
Mexico	887,100	763,100	875,800	947,600
The Bahamas	200,900	224,900	257,500	285,100
Barbados	21,700	22,800	28,700	33,700
Bermuda	1,900	1,900	2,300	1,600
Cuba	11,900	3,800	3,700	3,000
Dominica	9,400	34,000	64,100	75,300
Dominican Republic	78,200	68,300	54,800	63,000
Grenada	3,000	3,500	4,000	4,700
Haiti	85,700	86,100	85,700	89,700
Jamaica	125,800	145,500	173,300	195,200
Trinidad and Tobago	85,200	71,500	80,300	89,400
Total, Central America	294,400	309,600	338,200	366,400
Costa Rica	51,100	55,200	57,100	57,100
El Salvador	51,400	52,600	55,000	56,900
Guatemala	66,200	67,700	83,200	98,800
Honduras	50,300	55,800	60,400	64,600
Nicaragua	20,300	19,100	20,400	24,400
Panama	45,400	48,900	50,900	52,000
Belize	9,800	10,300	11,200	12,500
Other North America	67,800	77,600	92,800	100,200
South America	783,600	928,600	954,200	1,001,800
Argentina	90,700	177,100	166,000	127,400

(Continued)

Table 3A.3 EXPECTED DEPARTURES BY COUNTRY OF CITIZENSHIP: FISCAL
YEARS 1985–88 *(Continued)*

(Numbers rounded independently)

Country of Citizenship	Fiscal Year of Entry			
	1985	1986	1987	1988
South America *(continued)*				
Bolivia	16,900	17,900	18,500	19,700
Brazil	181,900	234,200	235,600	275,500
Chile	43,200	46,500	50,800	62,400
Colombia	160,300	157,300	152,900	155,500
Equador	49,800	58,100	62,900	54,700
Guyana	13,700	17,400	17,700	16,100
Paraguay	4,800	5,500	6,700	7,100
Peru	58,500	62,800	76,300	80,100
Uruguay	12,200	14,500	16,500	17,900
Venezuela	145,400	128,600	136,400	167,200
Other South America	6,300	8,700	13,900	18,200
Stateless	8,800	10,000	9,200	8,800
Unknown	127,000	116,000	103,300	125,200

Source: NIIS.
Note: Denominators for rates are shown in table 3.7.

Chapter Four

POST-IRCA CHANGES IN THE VOLUME AND COMPOSITION OF UNDOCUMENTED MIGRATION TO THE UNITED STATES: AN ASSESSMENT BASED ON APPREHENSIONS DATA

Frank D. Bean, Thomas J. Espenshade, Michael J. White, and Robert F. Dymowski

The Immigration Reform and Control Act (IRCA) of 1986 is a complex piece of legislation intended to achieve a number of different objectives, chief among them being to reduce the number of illegal migrants coming to and residing in the United States (Bean, Vernez, and Keely, 1989). The major provision adopted to accomplish this objective followed a recommendation in the final report of the Select Commission on Immigration and Refugee Policy (1981) and involves the imposition of sanctions on employers for hiring undocumented workers. Other features of the legislation that have implications for illegal immigration include provisions authorizing enhanced resources for the U.S. Border Patrol, passed in an attempt to increase the likelihood of apprehension of illegal crossers at the southern land border of the country, and provisions establishing two legalization programs, the principal one of which was targeted at the population of illegal aliens who had been residing in the country for several years.[1]

These provisions were designed to reduce the stock and flow of undocumented migrants in several ways. First, the employer sanctions provisions of IRCA establish penalties for employers who knowingly hire undocumented workers. All employers are subject to these sanctions, the intent of which is to eliminate employment opportunities for illegal aliens in the United States and thereby remove a major motivation for workers to enter the country without proper documentation.[2] Employers are required to verify each new employee's eligibility to work in the country by inspecting appropriate documents (for example, various combinations of the following are acceptable: a passport, resident alien card, birth certificate, Social Security card, and driver's license). Those who knowingly hire undocumented workers are subject to civil fines ranging from $250 to $2,000 for each undocumented migrant in the case of a first offense and to criminal penalties of up to six months in prison for a "pattern and practice" of employing illegal workers.

Second, IRCA provided for increased enforcement capabilities within the U.S. Immigration and Naturalization Service (INS). For example, INS funding for enforcement activities jumped from $361 million in fiscal year (FY) 1986 to $391 million in FY 1987, to $480 million in FY 1988, and to $541 million in FY 1989. The number of Border Patrol personnel was also substantially increased, from 3,687 in FY 1986 to 4,919 in FY 1989 (Bean et al., 1989).

Third, two legalization programs extended temporary resident alien status to groups of undocumented immigrants. The general legalization program involved those who could prove they were residing in the United States continuously since January 1, 1982. Such persons may later adjust to permanent resident alien status, provided they can demonstrate a minimal understanding of English and a basic knowledge of U.S. civics and history. In addition, special agricultural workers (SAWs) were initially granted temporary resident alien status and then permanent resident alien status at the end of one year if they were able to show that they had worked at least 90 days in U.S. perishable agriculture in each of the years 1984, 1985, and 1986. Other agricultural workers qualify for permanent resident alien status at the end of two years if they are able to show they had worked at least 90 days in the 12 months preceding May 1, 1986. By the time the application periods for these programs had ended, 1.77 million applications for temporary resident alien status had been filed through the general legalization program and an additional 1.3 million through the SAW program (U.S. Immigration and Naturalization Service, 1989).[3]

PURPOSE AND RATIONALE

This chapter seeks to assess the extent to which these provisions had the effects of (1) reducing the size of the undocumented population in the country, (2) changing the volume of illegal flows of migrants coming into the country, and (3) changing the composition of illegal flows coming into the country. Ascertaining the first is easier than ascertaining the second and third. The enrollment of over 3 million persons in IRCA's two legalization programs has substantially reduced the size of the illegal population residing in the United States, simply by reclassifying as legal temporary resident aliens some persons who were formerly present as illegal aliens. But ascertaining the degree to which the volume and composition of the flow coming into the country has changed as a result of IRCA is not so readily apparent. Even a straightforward examination of seemingly relevant statistics must be undertaken with caution, because the values of such statistics may fluctuate over time as a result of both IRCA-related and non-IRCA-related factors.

As discussed in the introduction to this volume, the question of the extent to which IRCA has changed illegal stocks and flows is most completely addressed by examining several different kinds of data, each of which provides information about different parts of the stock or different segments of the flow. This chapter focuses primarily on the Mexican segment of the flow. The data examined are U.S. Immigration and Naturalization Service apprehensions data, which are counts of the number of times persons entering the country illegally were apprehended by the Border Patrol or other INS enforcement personnel within a given period of time.[4] Our primary research strategy is to develop and estimate the parameters of a statistical model that incorporates both IRCA and non-IRCA variables that might be thought to influence either apprehensions or the flow of illegals coming to the country.[5] We then use the model to estimate the extent to which changes since the passage of the legislation can be attributed to IRCA and non-IRCA-related factors.

Analyses of apprehensions data using such models are a worthwhile exercise for two reasons. First, a relationship appears to exist between the number of apprehensions and the number of attempts to cross the border illegally. Some observers have suggested that such data are not particularly useful because some persons are apprehended more than once and because, it is alleged, the data have sometimes been manipulated to serve the purposes of the Immigration and Naturalization Service; others have often seemed to imply that such data, when multiplied by a factor to take into account the number of crossers going unapprehended, indicate the number of illegal aliens residing in the country who entered at the border (McDonnell, 1989). We do not agree with either view. Rather, we argue that apprehensions data provide a reflection, although only a partial one, of the volume of illegal crossings, and are particularly useful for indicating periodic changes in the number of such crossings, especially to the extent that it can be assumed over time that there is a fairly constant relationship between crossers and apprehensions (North and Wagner, 1981; Hill, 1985; and Bean et al., 1989).

Second, figures on gross changes in apprehensions (that is, figures that do not break the changes down into constituent parts) have been widely cited in the press, both as indicating changes in illegal immigration before IRCA and as indicating decreases since IRCA (Suro, 1989; Mathews, 1988). For example, the volume of total INS apprehensions declined from 1,767,400 in FY 1986 to 1,190,488 in FY 1987—a drop of 33 percent in one year. Data for FY 1988 show a further decrease to 1,009,145 apprehensions, and the figure for FY 1989 was 954,119 (U.S. Immigration and Naturalization Service, 1989b; Hoefer, 1989). This latter figure gives a total decline since 1986 of 46 percent. A quantitative assessment that decomposes such changes into IRCA-related and non-IRCA-related parts is needed to tell how much, if any, of the gross changes observed are the result of the legislation in general and certain provisions of the legislation in particular.

In addition to the possibility that IRCA may have changed the magnitude of the flow, the legislation may also (or even independently) have affected the composition of undocumented migration. The flow of Mexican male migrants across the southern border has been characterized as predominantly labor migration, that is, as migration motivated primarily by the possibility of finding work in the United States (Portes and Bach, 1985; Portes, 1983). However, Mexican female migrants and their children and non-Mexican migrants (most of whom are Central American in origin) also enter the United States illegally at the southern border. This latter migration is more heterogeneous and is less likely to consist primarily of labor migrants. Hence, one might hypothesize that this segment would be less affected by the employer sanctions provisions of IRCA, which are designed to deter labor migration, than would the migration of Mexican males. Moreover, it is possible that these flows may be moving in a reverse direction from that of Mexican males. Thus, the flows of undocumented Mexican women and minors and of non-Mexicans might have increased at the same time that the flow of undocumented Mexican males might have decreased.

KINDS OF APPREHENSIONS STATISTICS

The total number of INS apprehensions occurring in a given year results from activities undertaken by both the Border Patrol, which is the main enforcement arm of the INS, and the Investigations Unit, which is responsible for interior operations. Most of the illegal aliens apprehended in the United States are arrested by the Border Patrol; most are caught near the U.S.-Mexican border; and most entered the United States without inspection by the INS. Data for FY 1987 are instructive (U.S. Immigration and Naturalization Service, 1988). First, of the 1.19 million apprehensions made in that year, 1.17 million were credited to the Border Patrol. The remaining 22,000 arose from the investigations unit.[6] Second, the INS is divided for administrative purposes into four regions and 33 districts. Five of these districts touch the 1,900-mile southern border with Mexico (El Paso, Harlingen, and San Antonio in the state of Texas; Phoenix in Arizona; and San Diego in California). Together, these five districts accounted in 1987 for more than 97 percent of all aliens deported or required to depart. Third, 98 percent of all apprehensions in 1987 comprised aliens who entered the country without inspection. The small remaining fraction of apprehensions consisted of persons who entered with fraudulent documentation, or who entered legally but subsequently violated the terms of their visa by, for example, accepting unauthorized employment or overstaying the length of their visa (Levine et al., 1985).

Given that an overwhelmingly high proportion of apprehensions are made by the Border Patrol at the Mexican border, we focus here on INS Border Patrol apprehensions at the southern land border of the country. These consist of two types—linewatch and non-linewatch apprehensions. The former are apprehensions resulting from time spent guarding the border against smuggling and illegal entry of aliens. They include apprehensions by Border Patrol agents engaged in surveillance; tower watch; patrolling along the border on foot, horseback, or in some kind of vehicle; as well as other operations designed to prevent illegal entry. As implied by the nature of the activity, nearly every linewatch apprehension (roughly 98 percent) is of a person apprehended trying to enter the United States without appropriate entry documents. Non-linewatch operations involve several kinds of activities—non-linewatch patrols, farm and ranch checks, traffic checks, transportation checks, city patrols, and other activities.[7]

In this analysis of the volume of illegal crossings, we examine linewatch and non-linewatch apprehensions separately. The former may provide a somewhat better basis than the latter for assessing changes in the flow of illegal migrants for two reasons. First, linewatch apprehensions occur right at the border and do not involve the different kinds of enforcement activities that are involved in non-linewatch apprehensions. As a result, they are less likely than non-linewatch apprehensions to fluctuate over time as a result of changing enforcement strategies adopted by the Border Patrol (North, 1988; Bean et al., 1989). Farm and ranch checks have historically generated a higher "yield" than other types of activities (North and Wagner, 1981). To the extent that this kind of activity is disproportionately undertaken in a given period, it could affect the number of apprehensions in that period. However, because farm and ranch checks cannot be undertaken without a warrant since the passage of IRCA, the months since IRCA may especially be affected.

Second, a large proportion of non-linewatch apprehensions consists of persons who have been in the country four days or longer, with the numbers varying considerably depending upon the method of apprehension. As table 4.1 indicates, almost 98 percent of linewatch apprehensions occur at entry, whereas only one out of every seven non-linewatch apprehensions does. Also, one-quarter of non-linewatch apprehensions arise after an alien has been inside the

Table 4.1 TYPE OF APPREHENSION BY LENGTH OF TIME ILLEGALLY IN THE UNITED STATES: ALL SECTORS, JANUARY 1977–SEPTEMBER 1989

Type of Apprehension	Total	Length of Time Illegally in the United States			
		Apprehended at Entry	Within 72 hours	4–30 days	30 + days
Total apprehensions	12,117,073	7,944,033	2,973,805	608,926	590,309
	100.0	65.6	24.5	5.0	4.9
Linewatch	7,446,006	7,281,152	121,240	25,950	17,664
	100.0	97.8	1.6	0.3	0.2
Non-linewatch	4,671,067	662,881	2,852,565	582,976	572,645
	100.0	14.2	61.1	12.5	12.3
Patrols	427,024	1,415	246,640	125,203	53,766
	100.0	0.3	57.8	29.3	12.6
Farm and ranch checks	436,262	6,465	173,367	152,905	103,525
	100.0	1.5	39.7	35.0	23.7
Traffic checks	1,126,475	206,646	758,198	82,525	79,106
	100.0	18.3	67.3	7.3	7.0
Transportation checks	1,314,705	306,306	906,525	41,156	60,718
	100.0	23.3	69.0	3.1	4.6
City patrols	649,152	36,723	320,652	105,477	186,300
	100.0	5.7	49.4	16.2	28.7
Other[a]	717,449	105,326	447,183	75,710	89,230
	100.0	14.7	62.3	10.6	12.4

a. "Other" includes boat patrols, crewmen-stowaways, and deportable aliens turned over to the Border Patrol by other agencies.

United States for four or more days. This fraction tends to be even higher in the case of all categories of non-linewatch activity except traffic and transportation checks. In short, non-linewatch apprehensions consist of sizable proportions of persons who have been in the country for some time. Their change over time may reflect changes in the stock of illegal immigrants, in enforcement strategies, and in the flow of undocumented migrants. Also, they may vary because the number of non-linewatch apprehensions may depend on the number of linewatch apprehensions (i.e., the more successful the Border Patrol is in catching persons upon entry, the fewer numbers will be at risk of being apprehended as a result of non-linewatch activities).

Information on changes in the number of Border Patrol linewatch and non-linewatch apprehensions thus provides a partial basis for assessing whether the monthly number of illegal southern border crossings into the United States (or the magnitude of the "flow" of undocumented migrants) has changed since the passage of IRCA. We assess this change using time-series analyses of linewatch and non-linewatch apprehensions data from FYs 1977 through 1989. This time period includes several years of data before the 1982 economic decline in Mexico that was brought about by the global collapse in oil prices, as well as data for the three FYs since IRCA became law in November 1986. To assess the extent to which IRCA might have influenced the composition of undocumented flows, we conducted similar time-series analyses of total Border Patrol apprehensions at the southern land border. These analyses focus on changes in the apprehensions of Mexican males, of Mexican females and children, and of non-Mexicans. Unfortunately, we cannot disaggregate these data by linewatch or non-linewatch activity, because data on apprehensions by gender and country of origin are not available in this form.

As already noted, to be most useful for assessing the degree to which IRCA has affected the nature and degree of illegal border crossings into the United States, apprehensions data must be "freed" of other factors that influence their magnitude, including many that have nothing to do with IRCA. Before drawing conclusions about whether changes over time in various kinds of apprehensions might be attributed to IRCA, it is necessary to control for the non-IRCA-related factors that might account for changes in apprehensions. Our strategy here is to account for a wide range of factors that might influence the flow coming into the country by developing and estimating a statistical model for various kinds of apprehensions data.

DEVELOPING A MODEL OF THE PROCESS

This section describes the model and related variables used to analyze monthly statistics on Border Patrol apprehensions at the southern border. The model is intended to conceptualize the flow of undocumented migration to the United States, with the discussion focusing on the model's application to the analysis of linewatch apprehensions. Although data on linewatch apprehensions may provide better information on changes in flows than data on non-linewatch and total apprehensions, we use the model (with minor modifications) to analyze non-linewatch and total apprehensions as well.

The Model

The process of undocumented migration to the United States leading to apprehension *at the U.S.-Mexican border* depends upon three factors: the population at risk of migrating illegally to the United States, the propensity of this population to migrate, and the probability of being apprehended at the border.[8] The product of the first two factors is the number of border crossings in undocumented status in a specified time interval. Because some fraction of these crossings results in apprehension at the point of entry to the United States, the multiplication of all three elements corresponds to the number of linewatch apprehensions along the U.S.-Mexican border per time period. Our analytic strategy models the data on linewatch apprehensions by considering the determinants of these three components.

Because Mexican mortality declined for nearly three decades before fertility began to fall in the late 1970s, the population in the prime migrating ages has been increasing in recent years (Alba and Potter, 1986; Massey, 1988). A convincing measure of this growing population at risk is the size of the young-adult population in Mexico.[9] An additional aspect to consider, however, is the effect of the SAW legalization program in IRCA. Special agricultural workers who have been granted legal temporary resident alien status may now move back and forth between the United States and Mexico without fear of apprehension when returning to the United States. The effect of IRCA's provisions for SAW legalization, therefore, may be to reduce the size of the pool of persons at risk of being apprehended.

A second factor determining the level of apprehensions at the U.S.-Mexican border is the rate of undocumented migration from the pool of eligibles. This propensity is likely to be substantially motivated by an evaluation of comparative economic opportunities in the United States versus Mexico. To the extent that this is the case, such influences as relative unemployment rates, wage opportunities, and income levels in the two countries are likely to play important roles in this evaluation. In addition, a component of labor demand for low-wage farmworkers in California and in other parts of the American Southwest is highly seasonal, building during the spring planting months, reaching a peak during the summer harvest, and then tapering off significantly in the winter (Espenshade and Taylor, 1988). One may expect this influence to be reflected in seasonal variations in the tendency to migrate illegally to the United States. Finally, other factors associated with IRCA may also affect the outcome. Beliefs by prospective undocumented migrants that IRCA's employer sanctions provisions have substantially reduced the probability of locating employment in the United States and/or that the Border Patrol has increased its enforcement effort to such a level rendering any attempted border crossing extremely costly will reduce the incentive to migrate. IRCA may also have dampened the incentives for undocumented migrants living in the United States prior to IRCA to circulate back and forth between the United States and Mexico, out of concern that they might have a difficult time locating new employment upon their return.[10] These forces operating in the post-IRCA period may exhibit both secular and seasonal tendencies as migrants adjust their perceptions to new realities.[11]

Third, the probability that an undocumented migrant will be apprehended at the U.S.-Mexican border depends directly on the enforcement effort mounted by the Immigration and Naturalization Service. Two prominent factors affecting INS effort are the human and physical resources devoted to enforcement. These include, among other things, the number of hours Border Patrol officers are stationed along the line and the capital equipment at their disposal in the form of motor vehicles, infrared sensing devices, and the like.

The preceding discussion suggests that monthly variations in the level of apprehensions of undocumented migrants along the southern U.S. border may be conceptualized as the outcome of a process much like an economic production process in which the volume of output (in this case apprehensions) depends upon inputs of labor, capital, and resources. Labor and capital inputs correspond to INS enforcement effort and reflect the probability of being apprehended. The resources or raw materials can be represented by the number of border crossings by undocumented migrants within a specified time interval. It is clear that the level of apprehensions will be zero if either the probability of being apprehended or the number of border crossings is zero. This reasoning suggests a production function involving multiplicative terms.

In particular, we assume that

$$Y = P * m * \pi, \text{ where} \tag{4.1}$$

Y = level of monthly linewatch apprehensions along the U.S.-Mexican border,

P = population at risk of migrating in undocumented status to the United States,

m = monthly rate of undocumented migration to the United States, and

π = probability that an illegal immigrant crossing the U.S.-Mexican border is apprehended by a linewatch officer.

If we postulate that the natural logarithm of each term on the right side of equation (4.1) is linearly related to a set of underlying behavioral determinants (X_i), then we have

$$\ln Y = \beta_0 + \beta_1 X_1 + \beta_2 X_2 + ... + \beta_k X_k + u, \tag{4.2}$$

where u is a stochastic error term. With this formulation, each coefficient on an X variable represents the estimated relative or proportional change in Y corresponding to a one-unit change in X. This is the equation we will use for estimation purposes.

Variables and Data

The variables used in the regression analysis, together with the hypothesized signs of their regression coefficients, are listed and defined in table 4.2. The variables MEXPOP and SAWS affect the population at risk of migrating illegally to the United States in different ways. Because the great majority of undocumented migrants across the southern U.S. border are born in Mexico, we have used the size of the young adult population in Mexico (ages 15–34) as a rough proxy for the expanding at-risk population. At the same time, the presence of a growing number of legalized special agricultural workers who receive legal temporary resident alien status and who continue to circulate between Mexico and the United States should reduce the number of undocumented travelers to this country.

Several factors are assumed to be related to the rate of undocumented migration from Mexico to the United States. Principal among these is a comparison of relative economic opportunities in Mexico and the United States, captured by relative wage and unemployment ratios (WAGERATIO and UNEMPRATIO variables, respectively).[12] Improving conditions on the U.S. side of the border and/or worsening circumstances in Mexico (reflected in unemployment rates or in wage rates) should accelerate the rate of migration. Second, we hypothesized that seasonal variations in demand for low-wage agricultural workers in the American Southwest are related to incentives for undocumented migration. These demands are typically least during the winter months and accelerate as the planting and harvest seasons unfold. We incorporated these seasonal effects through a set of monthly dummy variables, JAN to NOV.

Third, if IRCA is successful in reducing the flow of undocumented immigrants into the United States, then there should be fewer apprehensions along the U.S.-Mexican border in the post-IRCA period than during pre-IRCA months, all other things held constant. We attributed this hypothesized negative effect, measured by the variable POSTIRCA, to the possibility that employer sanctions and stepped-up border enforcement may have altered perceptions of the likelihood of being able to enter the United States illegally and locate subsequent employment. Because perceptions and, therefore, the incentives and risks associated with undocumented migration may change as employer sanctions and other provisions of IRCA become more fully implemented, this effect of IRCA may be strengthened or weakened in the second and third years of the legislation. We included the variables YEAR2 and YEAR3 to allow for these possibilities. In addition to a secular trend, IRCA's success in affecting undocumented migration may also possess seasonal elements (SPRING and SUMMER variables), especially if there is a seasonal component to agricultural labor demand. We expected these seasonal IRCA effects to be greatest during the spring months when agricultural labor demand is building. The variables SPRING2, SPRING3, SUMMER2 and SUMMER3 were included to test whether seasonal effects in the post-IRCA period are altered in the second and third years of IRCA.

The final explanatory variables in table 4.2, LWHOURS, NLWHOURS and CAPINV, are related to the probability of being apprehended along the southern U.S. border. Increases in both the number of U.S. Border Patrol officer linewatch or non-linewatch hours and the amount of physical capital (for example, unattended electronic ground sensors, lighting, a variety of imaging devices, and transportation vehicles) employed in the enforcement effort were assumed to raise the probability of apprehension.[13] Because of the logarithmic nature of equation (4.2) and the requirement that probabilities lie between zero and one, we have used reciprocals of these

Table 4.2 VARIABLE NAMES, DEFINITIONS, SOURCES OF DATA, AND EXPECTED SIGNS OF ESTIMATED COEFFICIENTS

Variable Name	Definition	Data Source	Expected Sign of Coefficient
Dependent Variables:			
LWAPPS	Natural log of monthly linewatch apprehensions along the U.S.-Mexican border	U.S. Border Patrol reports of field operations	N/A[a]
NLWAPPS	Natural log of monthly non-linewatch apprehensions along the U.S.-Mexican border	U.S. Border Patrol reports of field operations	N/A
MMAAPPS	Natural log of monthly apprehensions of Mexican males along the U.S.-Mexican border	U.S. Border Patrol reports of field operations	N/A
MFAPPS	Natural log of monthly apprehensions of Mexican females and children along the U.S.-Mexican border	U.S. Border Patrol reports of field operations	N/A
Explanatory Variables:			
MEXPOP	Mexican population 15–34 years of age (in millions)	International Division, U.S. Bureau of the Census	+
SAWS	Cumulative number of SAW applications (in millions)	U.S. Immigration and Naturalization Service	−
UNEMPRATIO	Ratio of U.S. male unemployment rate (percent) to Mexican male unemployment rate (percent)	U.S. Bureau of Labor Statistics, Employment and Earnings; International Labor Office, Bulletin of Labor Statistics; World Bank	−

Variable	Definition	Source	Expected sign
WAGERATIO	Ratio of hourly wage rate in U.S. nonagricultural sector (in Mexican pesos) to hourly earnings in Mexican manufacturing sector (in pesos)	U.S. Bureau of Labor Statistics, Employment and Earnings; International Labor Office, Bulletin of Labor Statistics; World Bank	+
JAN–NOV	Monthly dummy variables for seasonal labor demand (December is omitted month)	Each monthly dummy = 1 for that month and = 0 elsewhere	+
POSTIRCA	Deterrent efficacy of IRCA	Dummy variable (= 1 for Nov. 1986 through Oct. 1988)	–
YEAR2	Altered IRCA effect in second year of post-IRCA period	Dummy variable (= 1 for Nov. 1987 and all subsequent months)	?
YEAR3	Altered IRCA effect in third year of post-IRCA period	Dummy variable (= 1 for Nov. 1988 through Sept. 1989)	?
SPRING	Spring effect in post-IRCA period	Dummy variable (= 1 in Mar.–June months of post-IRCA period)	–
SUMMER	Summer effect in post-IRCA period	Dummy variable (= 1 in July–Oct. months of post-IRCA period)	?
SPRING2	Altered spring effect in year 2 of post-IRCA period	SPRING*YEAR2	?
SPRING3	Altered spring effect in year 3 of post-IRCA period	SPRING*YEAR3	?
SUMMER2	Altered summer effect in year 2 of post-IRCA period	SUMMER*YEAR2	?
SUMMER3	Altered summer effect in year 3 of post-IRCA period	SUMMER*YEAR3	?
LWHOURS	Reciprocal of U.S. Border Patrol officer linewatch hours devoted to appropriate enforcement activity (hours in millions).	U.S. Border Patrol sector reports of field operations	–

(Continued)

Table 4.2 VARIABLE NAMES, DEFINITIONS, SOURCES OF DATA, AND EXPECTED SIGNS OF ESTIMATED COEFFICIENTS
(Continued)

Variable Name	Definition	Data Source	Expected Sign of Coefficient
NLWHOURS	Reciprocal of U.S. Border Patrol officer non-linewatch hours devoted to appropriate enforcement activity (hours in millions)	U.S. Border Patrol sector reports of field operations	—
CAPINV	Reciprocal of the sum of INS capital investment for enforcement purposes in months 7–18 prior to observation month (capital expenditures in millions or constant 1988 U.S. dollars)	Office of Management and Budget, *Budget of the United States Government*, appendix material for INS	—

a. N/A = not applicable.

labor and capital variables. Negative coefficients imply that the probability of being apprehended grows as labor and capital inputs increase.

Altogether the model in equation (4.2) is estimated from 153 monthly observations from January 1977 to September 1989. The estimation results are discussed in the next section.

EMPIRICAL RESULTS

This section presents information on basic trends in the various kinds of apprehensions, the results of estimating the statistical models, and, based on these results, calculations of the amount of the change in apprehensions following IRCA that is attributable to each of three factors: (1) changes in INS effort, (2) the operation of the agricultural legalization program, and (3) the remaining effects of IRCA.

Descriptive Results

Figures 4.1, 4.2, and 4.3 show the monthly levels of total, linewatch and non-linewatch apprehensions for FYs 1977–89. Two observations about these data are useful at this point. First, each of the monthly series of apprehensions exhibits a strong seasonal pattern, peaking in spring months and usually reaching a low in December. This pattern coincides with what observers on the Mexican side of the border have noted is a tendency for illegal Mexican migration to reach its height in spring months and its nadir in December (Massey, Alarcón, Durand, and González, 1987). Hence, the fact that apprehensions exhibit a similar seasonal pattern provides important evidence that they are indeed correlated with undocumented flows. Second, each of the series shows the highest monthly levels of apprehensions in 1986 and lower levels thereafter, coinciding with the passage of IRCA in October 1986. Interestingly, whatever the reason for the post-1986 declines, apprehensions since IRCA have not fallen to the levels existing before the collapse of oil prices in 1982 and the subsequent deterioration in the Mexican economy. Assessing the extent to which these declines might be attributable to IRCA or to other factors is the objective of our statistical analyses.

Before moving to the results of these analyses, it is also interesting to examine the apprehensions data on an annual basis, together with information on the annual number of hours devoted to linewatch

Figure 4.1 TOTAL APPREHENSIONS AT BORDER

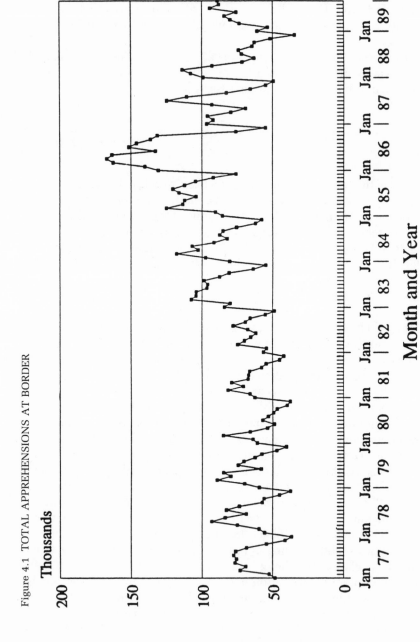

Figure 4.2 LINEWATCH APPREHENSIONS AT BORDER

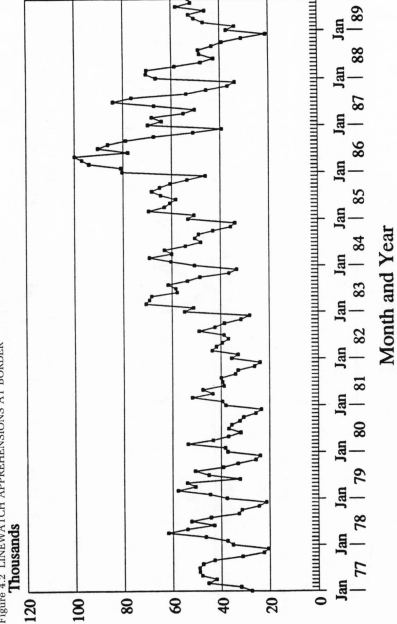

Figure 4.3 NON-LINEWATCH APPREHENSIONS AT BORDER

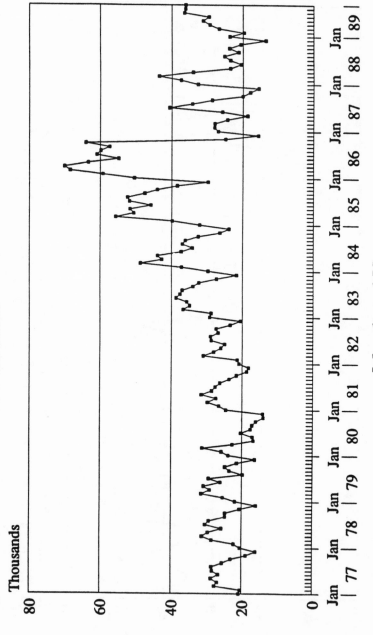

and non-linewatch activities. The latter provides an indication, as previously noted, of fluctuations in enforcement effort. These data are presented in table 4.3. In addition to yearly totals, the table shows yearly averages for three periods. The first (1977–82) consists of the years before the oil price collapse in 1982; the second (1983–86), the years after the collapse but before the passage of IRCA; and the third (1987–89), the years since the passage of the legislation. During the first period, linewatch apprehensions increased and then declined, as did linewatch hours. Linewatch apprehensions per hour also declined slightly. Non-linewatch apprehensions remained rather steady, although hours increased and apprehensions per hour declined. During the second period, both types of apprehensions increased substantially and, after an initial lag, so did hours and apprehensions per hour of effort. During the third period, linewatch apprehensions decreased substantially, although hours remained at high levels, except in 1987 when Border Patrol personnel were assigned heavy responsibilities in connection with the campaign to educate employers about the sanctions provisions of the legislation (Bean et al., 1989; Fix and Hill, 1990). Linewatch apprehensions per hour also declined substantially. Non-linewatch apprehensions fell even more precipitously (both absolutely and relative to hours), even though non-linewatch hours continued to increase, reflecting dramatically the reallocation of non-linewatch personnel into other types of activities.

What do the descriptive data reveal about changes in the composition of apprehensions? Figure 4.4 shows the monthly series for Mexican males and for Mexican females and children (monthly data for non-Mexicans are not shown because apprehensions of this group are not sufficiently numerous to yield a stable monthly series), and table 4.4 shows the annual data and period averages. The time-series for males and for females and children shown in figure 4.4 track each other rather closely, except during 1988 and 1989, when the fraction of females and children among those apprehended increased noticeably. By the end of the period the number of Mexican women and children apprehended in 1989 exceeded the level recorded in every previous year observed except the peak year of 1986. Among non-Mexicans, after falling in the year immediately after IRCA's passage, apprehensions increased dramatically thereafter, reaching a level in 1989 that exceeded all of the levels recorded before 1986.

In sum, both linewatch and non-linewatch apprehensions have fallen since the passage of IRCA, with the apprehensions of Mexican males exhibiting an especially steep decline. After an initial drop,

Table 4.3 AVERAGE ANNUAL LINEWATCH AND NON-LINEWATCH APPREHENSIONS, ENFORCEMENT HOURS, AND APPREHENSIONS PER HOUR: FISCAL YEARS 1977–89

Fiscal Year	Linewatch (LWA)			Non-linewatch (NLWA)		
	Apprehensions	Hours	LWA/Hours	Apprehensions	Hours	NLWA/Hours
1977	441,265	1,740,446	0.254	281,142	1,843,235	0.153
1978	481,612	1,762,616	0.273	300,029	1,970,476	0.152
1979	488,941	1,935,926	0.253	298,911	2,105,045	0.142
1980	428,966	1,815,797	0.236	255,237	2,030,831	0.126
1981	452,421	1,929,448	0.234	290,484	2,307,437	0.126
1982	443,437	1,871,173	0.237	295,772	2,334,868	0.127
1983	644,411	1,976,126	0.326	384,063	2,476,150	0.155
1984	623,944	1,843,179	0.339	428,090	2,432,609	0.176
1985	666,402	1,912,895	0.348	509,992	2,698,041	0.189
1986	946,341	2,401,575	0.394	656,806	3,374,131	0.195
1987	747,055	2,546,397	0.293	359,913	3,617,289	0.099
1988	612,653	2,069,498	0.296	315,171	3,800,325	0.083
1989	521,623	2,570,331	0.203	326,917	4,187,362	0.078
Period	Mean	Mean	LWA/Hours	Mean	Mean	NLWA/Hours
1977–82	456,107	1,842,568	0.248	286,929	2,098,649	0.137
1983–86	720,275	2,033,444	0.354	494,738	2,745,233	0.180
1987–89	627,110	2,395,409	0.262	334,000	3,868,325	0.086

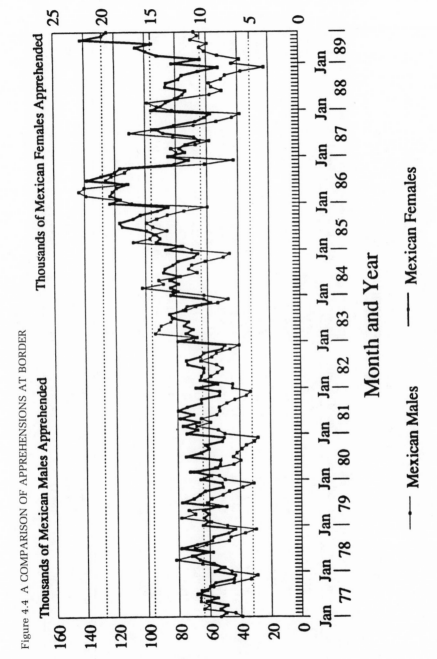

Figure 4.4 A COMPARISON OF APPREHENSIONS AT BORDER

Table 4.4 AVERAGE ANNUAL APPREHENSIONS (MEXICAN MALES, MEXICAN FEMALES AND CHILDREN, AND NON-MEXICANS), ENFORCEMENT HOURS, AND APPREHENSIONS PER HOUR: FISCAL YEARS 1977–89

Year	Mexican Males	Mexican Females and Children	Non-Mexicans	Enforcement Hours	Mexican Males per Hour	Mexican Females and Children per Hour	Non-Mexicans per Hour
1977	613,572	100,607	8,228	3,583,681	0.1712	0.0281	0.0023
1978	660,821	111,976	8,844	3,733,092	0.1770	0.0300	0.0024
1979	662,446	114,225	11,181	4,040,971	0.1639	0.0283	0.0028
1980	558,005	112,629	13,569	3,846,628	0.1451	0.0293	0.0035
1981	600,974	127,454	15,387	4,236,885	0.1418	0.0301	0.0036
1982	606,319	119,377	13,513	4,206,041	0.1442	0.0284	0.0032
1983	878,552	132,193	17,729	4,452,276	0.1973	0.0297	0.0040
1984	881,933	146,900	24,918	4,275,788	0.2063	0.0344	0.0058
1985	975,307	170,904	30,183	4,610,936	0.2115	0.0371	0.0065
1986	1,345,362	216,039	41,746	5,775,706	0.2329	0.0374	0.0072
1987	941,195	152,426	13,347	6,163,686	0.1527	0.0247	0.0022
1988	761,708	146,697	20,419	5,869,823	0.1298	0.0250	0.0035
1989	632,605	176,127	39,808	6,757,693	0.0936	0.0261	0.0059

Period	Mean	Mean	Mean	Mean	Mexican Males per Hour	Mexican Females and Children per Hour	Non-Mexicans per Hour
1977–82	617,023	114,378	11,787	3,941,216	0.1566	0.0290	0.0030
1983–86	1,020,289	166,509	28,644	4,778,677	0.2135	0.0348	0.0060
1987–89	778,503	158,417	24,525	6,263,734	0.1243	0.0253	0.0039

however, apprehensions of Mexican females and children and of non-Mexicans have increased, and substantially so in FY 1989. To ascertain the extent to which these post-IRCA changes in apprehensions might be attributed to the legislation, we estimated the time-series models, which provide a means of controlling for the influence of other variables that may affect the level of apprehensions.

Regression Estimates

Because ordinary least-squares estimates with time-series data typically exhibit serial correlation in the residuals, we estimated the models with a Yule-Walker two-step procedure (SAS Institute, 1984). A first-order autoregressive term was sufficient to capture the serial correlation; higher-order terms were not significant. The estimated regression equations for linewatch and non-linewatch apprehensions appear in table 4.5.[14] Several initial observations are worth making. First, as would be expected if linewatch apprehensions provide a somewhat better indicator of undocumented flows than non-linewatch apprehensions, the fit of the model to the data is better in the case of linewatch than non-linewatch apprehensions (R^2 = 0.941 versus 0.923, respectively). Second, the monthly dummies, which are coded to reflect differences relative to the low month of December, are strongly statistically significant and show the seasonal pattern of a spring peak and winter trough in apprehensions, which is what would be expected if apprehensions are correlated with undocumented flows. Third, this seasonal pattern is stronger and more statistically significant in the case of linewatch apprehensions, which again is what would be expected given the preceding reasoning. Fourth, even though the seasonal pattern is not so pronounced in the case of non-linewatch apprehensions, it is nonetheless quite strong, suggesting that these apprehensions are also associated with undocumented flows, even though they may be more likely to reflect other sources of variation as well.

For each of the variables listed in table 4.2 about whose coefficient there is an hypothesis, the estimated coefficients are all in the expected direction, and with the exception of the SAWs variable for linewatch apprehensions, the coefficients are all statistically significant. As already noted, the models account for a substantial amount of the variation in the dependent series, which is often the case in time-series regressions. It might be thought that this is owing mostly to the monthly dummies, but this is not the case. These variables alone account for only 39.4 and 26.3 percent of the variation in

Table 4.5 REGRESSION RESULTS FOR THE LOGARITHM OF MONTHLY
LINEWATCH AND NON-LINEWATCH APPREHENSIONS, 1977–89

Variable	Linewatch	Non-linewatch
MEXPOP	0.047**	0.061**
	(4.076)	(3.560)
SAWS	−0.397	−0.680*
	(−1.505)	(−2.140)
UNEMPRATIO	−0.118**	−0.202**
	(−3.140)	(−4.484)
WAGERATIO	0.049**	0.038*
	(2.507)	(1.681)
JAN	0.476**	0.375**
	(14.282)	(8.741)
FEB	0.541**	0.483**
	(13.994)	(10.381)
MAR	0.716**	0.641**
	(16.803)	(11.779)
APR	0.666**	0.560**
	(16.335)	(10.961)
MAY	0.630**	0.485**
	(15.233)	(9.449)
JUN	0.550**	0.459**
	(13.676)	(9.190)
JUL	0.612**	0.520**
	(15.052)	(10.433)
AUG	0.576**	0.430**
	(14.062)	(8.532)
SEP	0.430**	0.352**
	(10.626)	(7.046)
OCT	0.288**	0.307**
	(7.114)	(6.222)
NOV	0.126**	0.174**
	(3.985)	(4.572)
POSTIRCA	−0.267**	−0.764**
	(−3.499)	(−8.466)
YEAR2	0.106	0.163
	(0.901)	(1.155)
YEAR3	0.121	0.583
	(0.374)	(1.495)
SPRING	−0.228**	−0.232**
	(−2.793)	(−2.350)
SUMMER	0.001	0.097
	(0.013)	(0.833)
SPRING2	0.112	0.257
	(0.875)	(1.671)

(Continued)

Table 4.5 REGRESSION RESULTS FOR THE LOGARITHM OF MONTHLY
LINEWATCH AND NON-LINEWATCH APPREHENSIONS, 1977–89
(Continued)

Variable	Linewatch	Non-linewatch
SUMMER2	0.006	0.043
	(0.036)	(0.213)
SPRING3	0.133	0.356**
	(1.117)	(2.646)
SUMMER3	0.061	0.230
	(0.453)	(1.492)
LWHOURS	−0.134**	—
	(−5.183)	
NLWHOURS	—	−0.119**
		(−3.574)
CAPINV	−0.888*	−1.034*
	(−2.108)	(−2.054)
INTERCEPT	10.031**	9.315**
	(34.496)	(19.254)
RHO(1)	−0.358**	−.360**
	(−4.292)	(−4.317)
R^2	0.941	0.923
N	153	153

Note: T-statistics are in parentheses.
 * $p \leq .05$, one-tail test.
** $p \leq .01$.

linewatch and non-linewatch apprehensions, respectively. Tests of
the equivalence of the models between the first and second halves
of the series were conducted and these indicated that the coefficients
on the regressors are statistically equivalent in the 1977–83 period
and the 1983–89 period. Because the results for linewatch and non-
linewatch apprehensions are similar, they are discussed here primarily in terms of the findings for the former.

The two groups that are hypothesized to affect the population at
risk of migrating illegally to the United States are seen to have the
expected impact on the pattern of apprehensions. First, the Mexican
population 15–34 years old totaled roughly 23 million persons in
1980 and was growing at about 90,000 persons per month in 1986.
An increase of 1 million Mexicans aged 15–34 translates to nearly
a 5 percent increase in monthly linewatch apprehensions. Thus, the
effect of Mexican population growth in the mid- 1980s was to raise
the number of linewatch apprehensions by about 4,200 over the same
month in the previous year. Because the time trend in population is

smoothly monotonic, its inclusion may also capture other similarly shaped trends, such as the growth of social networks, as described by Massey and España (1987) and the spread of information.

Second, the legalization program for special agricultural workers may have removed from the at-risk population a group of seasonal farmworkers having a disproportionately high tendency to circulate back and forth between Mexico and the United States. Prior to IRCA these individuals would return to the United States in undocumented status; now with the legalization program, they may come and go lawfully. Hence, the model includes the cumulative number of SAWs who have filed for legalization by the end of each month. As expected, the SAWs variable's coefficient is negative and implies nearly a 40 percent reduction in linewatch apprehensions for every million SAW applications (and a 68 percent reduction for non-linewatch apprehensions). Stated another way, the results are consistent with the notion that the number of linewatch apprehensions per month declined by one for every 48 persons who had applied for the SAW program. Because this measure is correlated with others in the model, it is difficult to separate effects in the post-IRCA period.

Economic conditions in the United States and Mexico have an important influence on the border apprehension series. For each one-unit increase in the ratio between U.S. and Mexican hourly wages (WAGERATIO), for example, monthly linewatch apprehensions are predicted to increase by 4.9 percent. In the late 1970s this wage ratio varied between 2.5 and 3.5, but following the economic crisis in 1982, Mexican wages deteriorated substantially. By the time of IRCA's passage in November 1986 the U.S. wage stood at roughly eight times the Mexican wage, a change since the late 1970s large enough to bring about a 20 percent increase in apprehensions net of other factors. Since mid-1987, relative conditions in Mexico have improved, bringing the ratio down to just under five by the end of the series in September 1989. The coefficient for the ratio of the unemployment rates in the United States and Mexico (UNEMPRATIO) also takes on the expected negative sign, indicating that a rise in the ratio of one unit is associated with a 12 percent decline in linewatch apprehensions.[15]

As noted, the seasonal pattern observed in figures 4.1, 4.2, and 4.3 is clearly reflected in the set of monthly coefficients. Each coefficient represents the average percentage increase in apprehensions in that month in relation to December. For example, the volume of linewatch apprehensions in March is typically 72 percent above the December level. Apprehensions are usually lowest between October and December. In addition to implying that apprehensions are correlated with flows, this pattern is consistent with the hypothesis that seasonal factors, including the seasonal nature of agricultural farmwork and the desire among many nonagricultural workers to spend the winter in Mexico, provide much of the motivation to cross the border at certain times. This basic monthly pattern persists in the post-IRCA period, although it is modified in a way we discuss next.

We now turn to the measures of resources and enforcement effort by the Immigration and Naturalization Service. As expected, an increase in the number of Border Patrol officer linewatch hours (LWHOURS) leads to greater numbers of apprehensions, an effect that statistically is highly significant. To see the effect more concretely, consider an increase of linewatch hours from 200,000 (approximately the monthly average during FY 1986) to 210,000. This 5 percent increase would lead to a 3.2 percent increase in apprehensions, or almost 2,600 per month, over the levels of effort being realized in FY 1986. Except for the monthly dummy variables, linewatch hours provides the largest single t-statistic among variables in the linewatch equation. The effect of capital budget expenditures (CAPINV) is statistically significant and of the expected sign. Using budget and apprehensions values for FY 1986, we estimate that each additional million dollars of capital expenditures (1988 dollars) predicts an increase in monthly apprehensions of about 0.6 percent, or a decline of about 500 apprehensions per month from the time of IRCA's passage.

In addition to the impacts of its SAWs legalization program and the intensified INS effort, IRCA doubtless also had the effect of balkanizing circulatory flows of undocumented workers. Because of employer sanctions and other widely advertised features of the new legislation, prospective undocumented workers in Mexico might have been less willing to come north. At the same time, illegal immigrants with jobs in the United States might have been less willing to give them up in exchange for a return trip home. The construction of a set of dummy variables to capture this effect of IRCA enabled us to observe how this pattern might have changed over time. The underlying effect, which we have labeled POSTIRCA in table 4.2, indicates that, in the post-IRCA period, monthly apprehensions have been 27 percent less than in the pre-IRCA period, everything else held constant. This basic post-IRCA effect is, of course, susceptible to modification. The coefficients on YEAR2 and YEAR3 indicate that, in the second and third years following IRCA's passage, the net effect weakened slightly to 16 percent and 15 percent reductions, respectively, in apprehensions, but this apparent relaxation in IRCA's influence is not statistically significant. In the case of non-linewatch apprehensions, however, the post-IRCA reduction observed in the first year was cut substantially by the third year. But even the YEAR3 effect is not statistically significant in the non-linewatch equation.

We find a strong negative "spring effect" in the post-IRCA period. For the months between (and including) March and June, apprehensions have been down an additional 23 percent net of all the other variables in the model (for both linewatch and non-linewatch apprehensions). When the POSTIRCA and SPRING effects were combined, we found that linewatch apprehensions in the period from March 1987 to June 1987 were substantially below comparable levels in the pre-IRCA period, and non-linewatch apprehensions even more so.[16] Because the coefficients on SPRING2 and SPRING3 are positive, there is a suggestion of weaker "spring effects" in 1988 and in 1989 (an effect that is statistically significant for non-linewatch apprehensions in 1989). Thus, in those months during which the volume of apprehensions is usually the greatest (due, one suspects, to the influx of agricultural and other seasonal workers), the falloff in apprehensions is pronounced, although not so large that it completely offsets the seasonal pattern observed in figures 4.1, 4.2, and 4.3. Summer effects are generally negligible.

Table 4.6 presents the time-series regression coefficients for the apprehensions of Mexican males and of Mexican females and children. These analyses, respectively, include the number of male and female SAWs as independent variables rather than the total number of SAWs. We do not present the results for non-Mexicans, because the model did not fit the data very well in their case (R^2 = 0.332), which is not surprising given the small (and temporarily unstable) number of apprehensions, as well as the fact that much of the non-Mexican flow is Central American in origin and not motivated primarily by economic reasons. In the cases of Mexican males and of females and children, however, the models fit the data well (R^2 = 0.947 and 0.943, respectively), and the patterns of the coefficients parallel for the most part the results for linewatch and non-linewatch apprehensions.

There are some interesting differences, however. One that is consistent with the hypothesis that the migration of females and children as compared to that of males is more motivated by noneconomic reasons is the statistical insignificance of the WAGERATIO variable in the female equation. Another is that the seasonal pattern is less pronounced for females and peaks in July and August, rather than in the spring. Also, the SAWs variable does not exert a statistically significant effect in the case of females and children, as would be expected given the relatively light female participation in the program. Finally, by the third year after IRCA, apprehensions of females and children showed a statistically significant increase from the declines observed in the first year. This is revealed in the coefficients for SUMMER3 and SPRING3, which are large enough, when combined with the other post-IRCA coefficients, to indicate an increase in apprehensions by the third year net of the influence of other factors.

Components of Change in Apprehensions

As a step towards assessing IRCA's impact on undocumented immigration to the United States, we first calculated the influence of the new legislation on recent levels of linewatch and non-linewatch apprehensions of illegal migrants. These estimates depend on how many apprehensions one might reasonably expect to have observed in the post-IRCA period had the 1986 reforms not passed. IRCA's combined effects on apprehensions could then be gauged by subtracting the monthly number of linewatch apprehensions that were observed from the number anticipated in the absence of IRCA. In addition, it is of considerable policy interest to know the relative contributions of each of IRCA's several dimensions to this aggregate difference.

To maintain internal consistency, we used the estimated regression equations reported in table 4.5 to calculate the amount of the monthly change in apprehensions in the post-IRCA period attributable to each of three sources: (1) changes in INS effort, (2) the SAWs legalization program, and (3) the remaining effects of IRCA. We made four separate calculations. First, to estimate the monthly number of linewatch apprehensions in the absence of IRCA, we set the SAWs variable and all nine IRCA-related variables (POSTIRCA, SPRING, SPRING2, SPRING3, SUMMER, SUMMER2, SUMMER3, YEAR2, and YEAR3) equal to zero and assumed that the two INS effort variables (capital investment and hours) stayed constant at their FY 1986 average values. The remaining variables in the equations in table 4.5 were assumed to take on their actual values. Then, beginning with November 1986, the expected number of linewatch apprehensions was calculated month by month to September 1989. Second, to isolate the effect of changes in INS effort under IRCA, the first calculation was repeated by substituting the actual values of hours (HOURS) and

Table 4.6 REGRESSION RESULTS FOR THE LOGARITHM OF MONTHLY
APPREHENSIONS OF MEXICAN MALES AND FEMALES AND
CHILDREN, 1977–89

Variable	Males	Females and Children
MEXPOP	0.032**	0.057**
	(2.580)	(6.231)
SAWS	−0.883**	−0.716
	(−2.695)	(−0.637)
UNEMPRATIO	−0.160**	−0.122**
	(−4.487)	(−4.696)
WAGERATIO	0.054**	0.001
	(2.833)	(−0.001)
JAN	0.434**	0.287**
	(12.031)	(10.572)
FEB	0.560**	0.215**
	(14.486)	(7.449)
MAR	0.720**	0.232**
	(15.610)	(6.784)
APR	0.680**	0.204**
	(16.197)	(6.546)
MAY	0.614**	0.222**
	(14.342)	(7.001)
JUN	0.559**	0.206**
	(13.744)	(6.805)
JUL	0.591**	0.391**
	(14.267)	(12.701)
AUG	0.543**	0.313**
	(12.949)	(10.049)
SEP	0.418**	0.216**
	(10.055)	(7.003)
OCT	0.302**	0.158**
	(7.187)	(5.028)
NOV	0.160**	0.036**
	(4.931)	(1.471)
POSTIRCA	−0.460**	−0.350**
	(−6.180)	(−6.359)
YEAR2	0.142	−0.006
	(1.221)	(−0.070)
YEAR3	0.386	−0.084
	(1.161)	(−0.336)
SPRING	−0.214**	−0.178**
	(−2.639)	(−2.969)
SUMMER	0.072	−0.110
	(0.759)	(−1.563)
SPRING2	0.178	0.111
	(1.398)	(1.166)

(Continued)

Table 4.6 REGRESSION RESULTS FOR THE LOGARITHM OF MONTHLY
APPREHENSIONS OF MEXICAN MALES AND FEMALES AND
CHILDREN, 1977–89 *(Continued)*

Variable	Males	Females and Children
SUMMER2	0.053	0.039
	0.313	(0.305)
SPRING3	0.280**	0.354**
	(2.504)	(4.274)
SUMMER3	0.186	0.443**
	(1.471)	(4.750)
LWHOURS	−0.348**	—
	(−5.562)	
NLWHOURS	—	−0.280**
		(−6.081)
CAPINV	−1.114**	0.101
	(−2.764)	(0.343)
INTERCEPT	10.935**	8.689**
	(27.993)	(30.349)
RHO(1)	−0.312**	−0.288**
	(−3.671)	(−3.362)
R^2	0.947	0.943
N	153	153

Note: T-statistics are in parentheses.
** $p \le .01$.

capital budget expenditures (CAPINV) during the post-IRCA period. The difference between the predicted values of apprehensions in steps 1 and 2 is the partial effect of IRCA due to changes in INS effort.

Third, to separate the effect of the SAW legalization program, the calculation in step 2 was repeated by substituting the observed values of the SAWs variable for zeroes. The difference between the predicted number of apprehensions in steps 2 and 3 was attributable to IRCA's SAW program. Fourth, the calculation in step 3 was repeated by giving all nine IRCA-related variables their actual values. Given the good fit of the models to the data, the predicted values from step 4 of apprehensions come close to those for observed apprehensions in each month. The difference between steps 3 and 4 in the predicted apprehensions values is a measure of the non-SAW-related and non-INS-effort-related effects of IRCA.[17] Finally, the difference between the first and fourth sets of estimates of apprehensions provides an indication of the amount of change in apprehensions (that is, the "total" IRCA effect) occurring in each month of the post-IRCA period. This total IRCA effect and its three separate components are displayed month by month in tables 4.7 and 4.8.[18]

The numbers in these tables that are in parentheses represent negative values and imply that the associated component lifted the level of apprehensions in that month above the level that would have been expected in the absence of IRCA. This outcome occurs only in the case of IRCA's influence on changes in INS effort. Border Patrol linewatch hours increased through the latter part of 1986 and into early 1987, and then declined through the remainder of 1987 and 1988, before increasing again in 1989. Non-linewatch hours increased throughout the post-IRCA years. However, our measure of applicable capital expenditures devoted to enforcement decreased for the most part until April 1987, after which it substantially increased. Because values of the two INS effort variables sometimes moved in opposite directions in the post-IRCA period, they tended to have somewhat offsetting effects. Their combined net effect raised linewatch and non-linewatch apprehensions in many of the months following IRCA's passage above the level anticipated without IRCA. In November 1986, for example, the 8 percent increase in linewatch hours over the FY 1986 average combined with a 27 percent decline in capital expenditures to produce a rise of 1,378 linewatch apprehensions.

In the second year, however, IRCA had the apparent effect of lowering linewatch apprehensions. In June 1988, for example, the number of linewatch hours logged by Border Patrol agents was 20 percent below FY 1986 levels, so that, despite a near doubling of relevant capital budget inputs, there was a net reduction in apprehensions of over 10,000. These results suggest that trends in Border Patrol linewatch hours are more influential predictors of variations in apprehensions than trends in the capital budget measure, a conclusion consistent with the relative magnitudes of their coefficients' respective t-statistics in table 4.5.

Both the SAWs effect and the remaining IRCA effects consistently worked to lower linewatch and non-linewatch apprehensions, either by reducing the size of the population at risk of migrating illegally or by slowing the migration rate. The SAWs effect in tables 4.7 and 4.8 was zero prior to June 1987 when applications for the legalization program began to be received. Then as the SAW program got underway, its monthly impact on linewatch apprehensions also grew. IRCA's remaining effects reduced apprehensions from the outset; the largest impacts tend to be registered in the spring months between March and June.

By September 1989 the cumulative total reduction in linewatch apprehensions due to IRCA amounted to nearly 1,132,000, and the reduction in non-linewatch apprehensions amounted to about 1,173,000. Taken together, these quantities represent a drop to approximately 2.6 million from the 4.9 million linewatch and non-linewatch apprehensions we estimate would have materialized between November 1986 and September 1989 in IRCA's absence. The net shift in INS resources and effort had the effect of masking some of this decline. That is, were it not for the increases in INS resources and effort, the drop would have been even greater (specifically, about 104,000 apprehensions greater).[19] Of the estimated change in apprehensions *not due to changes* in INS resources or effort (1,132,000 − 35,000 + 686,000 + 626,000 = 2,409,000), the agricultural legalization program (the SAW program) accounted for 52.1 percent ({[568,000 + 686,000] ÷ 2,409,000} x 100), and the remaining effects of IRCA for 47.9 percent ([{529,000 + 626,000] ÷ 2,409,000} x 100).[20]

We also carried out this type of analysis for the apprehensions of Mexican males and of Mexican females and children using the coefficients in table 4.6. The results are summarized in table 4.9. Again, had it not been for increases in INS effort and resources, apprehensions would have declined even more than they did (279,000 and 30,000 for males and for females and children, respectively). Of the change *not due to* changes in INS effort and resources, the SAW program accounted for 62.4 percent of the decline that occurred in the case of males and for 21.5 percent of the decline in the case of females and children. The remaining effects of IRCA accounted for 37.6 and 78.5 percent of the decline among these two groups, respectively.

DISCUSSION

The preceding results considerably refine our understanding of the reasons for the post-IRCA decline in linewatch and non-linewatch apprehensions. In particular, they suggest that IRCA has not exerted a simple or uniform influence on apprehensions, but, rather, has resulted in several effects sometimes working in offsetting directions.

Table 4.7 REDUCTION IN LINEWATCH APPREHENSIONS DUE TO IRCA'S PROVISIONS, INCLUDING CHANGES IN INS ENFORCEMENT, SAWS LEGALIZATION, AND REMAINING IRCA EFFECTS

Month (1)	INS Enforcement		SAWs		Remaining IRCA Effect		Total	
	Monthly (2)	Cumulative (3)	Monthly (4)	Cumulative (5)	Monthly (6)	Cumulative (7)	Monthly (8)	Cumulative (9)
1986 Nov.	(1,378)	(1,378)	0	0	14,155	14,155	12,776	12,776
Dec.	(1,051)	(2,429)	0	0	12,688	26,843	11,637	24,414
1987 Jan.	(4,977)	(7,406)	0	0	21,278	48,121	16,301	40,715
Feb.	906	(6,500)	0	0	21,910	70,030	22,815	63,530
Mar.	(2,682)	(9,182)	0	0	43,728	113,759	41,047	104,577
Apr.	5,615	(3,567)	0	0	38,037	151,795	43,652	148,228
May	(506)	(4,073)	0	0	39,579	191,375	39,073	187,302
June	394	(3,679)	578	578	36,959	228,334	37,931	225,233
July	1,599	(2,080)	1,995	2,573	22,741	251,075	26,335	251,568
Aug.	(626)	(2,706)	3,408	5,981	22,085	273,160	24,867	276,435
Sept.	(453)	(3,160)	4,307	10,288	18,522	291,682	22,375	298,810
Oct.	(701)	(3,860)	4,730	15,018	15,165	306,846	19,194	318,004
Nov.	2,307	(1,553)	4,440	19,458	7,592	314,438	14,339	332,343
Dec.	2,350	797	4,475	23,933	6,700	321,138	13,525	345,868
1988 Jan.	2,627	3,424	7,714	31,647	10,459	331,597	20,800	366,668

Feb.	8,945	12,369	8,446	40,093	10,154	341,751	27,546	394,214
Mar.	4,847	17,216	12,238	52,331	19,760	361,511	36,845	431,058
Apr.	7,159	24,375	15,406	67,737	18,461	379,971	41,026	472,084
May	5,504	29,879	17,456	85,193	16,759	396,730	39,718	511,802
June	10,009	39,888	17,711	102,904	14,276	411,006	41,996	553,799
July	11,314	51,202	20,548	123,453	8,768	419,774	40,631	594,429
Aug.	10,182	61,384	21,971	145,424	8,427	428,201	40,580	635,009
Sept.	12,075	73,459	20,122	165,546	6,946	435,148	39,144	674,153
Oct.	9,010	82,469	18,901	184,447	5,724	440,871	33,634	707,787
Nov.	7,161	89,630	17,969	202,416	4,286	445,158	29,416	737,204
Dec.	6,293	95,923	15,269	217,685	3,230	448,388	24,792	761,996
1989 Jan.	8,819	104,742	28,380	246,065	5,756	454,144	42,954	804,950
Feb.	7,952	112,693	30,629	276,694	6,171	460,314	44,751	849,701
Mar.	(12,404)	100,289	44,962	321,656	14,256	474,570	46,815	896,516
Apr.	(12,046)	88,243	44,368	366,024	14,053	488,624	46,375	942,891
May	(13,777)	74,466	43,289	409,312	13,708	502,331	43,219	986,110
June	(9,275)	65,192	38,353	447,665	12,144	514,476	41,223	1,027,333
July	(10,255)	54,937	42,336	490,001	5,002	519,478	37,082	1,064,415
Aug.	(12,283)	42,653	42,349	532,350	5,003	524,481	35,069	1,099,484
Sept.	(7,849)	34,804	35,952	568,302	4,248	528,729	32,351	1,131,835

Note: Numbers in parentheses indicate an increase in apprehensions due to INS enforcement in comparison with no change in policy.

Table 4.8 REDUCTION IN NON-LINEWATCH APPREHENSIONS DUE TO IRCA'S PROVISIONS, INCLUDING CHANGES IN INS ENFORCEMENT, SAWS LEGALIZATION, AND REMAINING IRCA EFFECTS

Month (1)	INS Enforcement		SAWs		Remaining IRCA Effect		Total	
	Monthly (2)	Cumulative (3)	Monthly (4)	Cumulative (5)	Monthly (6)	Cumulative (7)	Monthly (8)	Cumulative (9)
1986 Nov.	1,382	1,382	0	0	23,718	23,718	25,100	25,100
Dec.	1,502	2,883	0	0	20,108	43,826	21,610	46,709
1987 Jan.	(892)	1,991	0	0	30,461	74,286	29,568	76,278
Feb.	2,458	4,449	0	0	33,289	107,575	35,747	112,025
Mar.	2,844	7,293	0	0	45,161	152,736	48,005	160,030
Apr.	4,676	11,969	0	0	40,882	193,618	45,557	205,587
May	2,740	14,709	0	0	39,367	232,985	42,107	247,694
June	736	15,445	665	665	39,973	272,958	41,374	289,068
July	(1,480)	13,965	2,422	3,087	33,353	306,311	34,295	323,363
Aug.	(1,794)	12,172	3,881	6,968	30,209	336,520	32,296	355,659
Sept.	(2,261)	9,911	5,303	12,271	27,220	363,740	30,262	385,921
Oct.	(2,909)	7,002	6,417	18,688	24,403	388,143	27,911	413,833
Nov.	(1,940)	5,062	6,354	25,041	18,683	406,827	23,098	436,930
Dec.	(989)	4,073	6,014	31,055	15,423	422,250	20,448	457,379
1988 Jan.	(5,734)	(1,660)	9,778	40,833	22,625	444,875	26,669	484,048
Feb.	(5,956)	(7,616)	12,124	52,957	24,759	469,634	30,927	514,974

Mar.	(9,682)	(17,298)	17,008	69,964	27,497	497,131	34,823	549,797
Apr.	(7,206)	(24,504)	20,730	90,694	24,453	521,583	37,976	587,773
May	(8,225)	(32,729)	22,749	113,443	21,159	542,743	35,684	623,457
June	(5,334)	(38,064)	24,626	138,069	18,944	561,687	38,235	661,692
July	(6,014)	(44,078)	28,860	166,929	16,688	578,375	39,534	701,226
Aug.	(6,502)	(50,580)	29,228	196,157	15,021	593,396	37,747	738,973
Sept.	(6,655)	(57,235)	30,093	226,250	13,751	607,147	37,189	776,162
Oct.	(5,258)	(62,493)	29,033	255,284	11,446	618,592	35,221	811,383
Nov.	(4,360)	(66,852)	27,551	282,835	3,932	622,525	27,124	838,507
Dec.	(3,787)	(70,639)	22,969	305,804	2,851	625,376	22,034	860,541
1989 Jan.	(1,228)	(71,867)	33,417	339,221	3,948	629,323	36,137	896,678
Feb.	(1,261)	(73,128)	36,300	375,521	4,255	633,578	39,293	935,971
Mar.	(6,177)	(79,305)	45,736	421,258	1,809	635,388	41,368	977,340
Apr.	(11,986)	(91,291)	47,712	468,970	1,885	637,273	37,612	1,014,952
May	(10,367)	(101,658)	44,177	513,147	1,745	639,018	35,555	1,050,507
June	(8,668)	(110,327)	41,370	554,517	1,634	640,652	34,335	1,084,843
July	(10,226)	(120,553)	46,826	601,343	(5,136)	635,516	31,464	1,116,306
Aug.	(9,838)	(130,391)	43,877	645,220	(4,813)	630,704	29,226	1,145,532
Sept.	(8,598)	(138,990)	40,870	686,090	(4,483)	626,221	27,789	1,173,321

Note: Numbers in parentheses indicate an increase in apprehensions due to INS enforcement in comparison with no change in policy.

Table 4.9 COMPONENTS OF POST-IRCA CHANGES IN THE APPREHENSIONS
OF MEXICAN MALES AND OF MEXICAN FEMALES AND CHILDREN

| Group | Component | | |
	INS Resources and Effort	SAWs[a]	Remaining Effects of IRCA
Males	(279,375)	1,368,538	824,628
Females and children	(30,178)	55,528	202,640

Note: Numbers in parentheses indicate a negative number.
a. SAWs = special agricultural workers.

The increases in INS effort and resources that frequently characterized the three-year post-IRCA period have generated increased numbers of apprehensions. The SAWs variable and the variables reflecting
remaining IRCA effects have generated decreased numbers. The latter
are likely to reflect the influence of employer sanctions, whose introduction is likely to have made the prospect of undocumented
movement to the United States less attractive. Fears, even if not well-
founded, of more serious punishments than had been imposed in
the past would also be likely to decrease the number of attempts to
cross. A general decline in circulatory migration, including any increased tendency to remain in the United States among those who
had once entered illegally, would have a similar effect.

The results also lead to a number of policy implications concerning
the likely future impact of IRCA's provisions on the course of apprehensions. Because the enrollment period for the SAW program
expired in November 1988, there is little prospect for further monthly
changes in apprehensions as a result of this factor (although the
cumulative number averted will continue to increase). Should the
legalized SAW workers move out of the agricultural sector, however,
and should a need emerge for replenishment agricultural workers (a
need that IRCA requires the secretaries of Agriculture and Labor to
estimate), then further declines in apprehensions might be expected
if large numbers of such workers subsequently legalized.

Of particular policy interest is the question of how the employer
sanctions provisions of IRCA are working. On the one hand, these
penalties might be expected to lead to an additional drop in apprehensions as more employers learn about the proscriptions in the law
against hiring undocumented workers and as more potential migrants perceive any increased difficulties in finding employment,

associated perhaps with greater compliance with the law by business. On the other hand, if the enforcement of employer sanctions proves ineffective as a result of insufficient INS resources and personnel, or if employer compliance is weak, perhaps as a result of a continuing high demand for undocumented labor, the deterrent efficacy of employer sanctions might be expected to deteriorate over time (Espenshade et al., forthcoming). Available evidence on these alternative futures is contradictory. The positive (though statistically insignificant) coefficients on the YEAR2 and YEAR3 variables in table 4.5 imply that apprehensions increased from 1987 to 1989, everything else constant. This result may indicate that the negative effects of IRCA had begun to wear off by the third year of the reform period. Two years, however, may be an insufficiently long observation window for the effectiveness of employer sanctions to become apparent. But the fact that positive coefficients were also recorded for the second and third year summer and spring dummies suggests that the hypothesis of declining effects of sanctions must be taken seriously. In the case of non-linewatch apprehensions in particular, these are large enough (and in one instance statistically significant) to indicate an increase in apprehensions during the spring of the third year, all else equal.

The increases observed for women and children in table 4.4 are also particularly interesting. On the one hand, they may reflect a tendency for wives and children to come to the United States to join husbands who have legalized (Cornelius, 1989). On the other hand, they may reflect the social organization of undocumented Mexican migration, which involves households adopting a strategy of sending one or more members to the United States to work (Massey, Alarcón, Durand, and González, 1987). If employer sanctions have made it more difficult for undocumented Mexican males to find jobs, they may have had little effect on undocumented females. Female domestic work has not only had a long tradition in the Southwest, but it is also much more invisible and less subject to detection than most forms of male employment. Also, it is reasonable to think that any seasonal component associated with such work would coincide with the start of the school year around the end of August. Interestingly, the peak months for apprehensions for females are July and August. It would be an ironic twist if IRCA leads to decreased undocumented migration among males but increased migration of undocumented females. The pressures on Mexican households to send persons North to find work continue to exist. If it becomes more difficult to send males, then females may be sent instead. But if this is what is happening, the trend is not so large as to swamp traditional male migration. But it clearly is something to monitor closely in future research.

What do our results imply about the impact of IRCA on changes in the number of illegal border crossings? Stated differently, to what extent is it possible to infer changes in the number of illegal border crossings from changes in the number of linewatch apprehensions? We know from the data in tables 4.7 and 4.8 that an IRCA-dependent decline in illegal border crossings *not associated with changes* in INS effort and resources reduced linewatch and non-linewatch apprehensions by about 2.4 million between November 1986 and September 1989. Of this total, 1,254,000 apprehensions (or about 52 percent) are traceable to a smaller population at risk of attempting an illegal migration due to the effects of the SAW legalization program, which removed potential undocumented migrants from the pool of eligibles. Moreover, another 1,155,000 apprehensions (or 48 percent of the total) were averted because of IRCA's impact on the propensity of this at- risk population to undertake an illegal entry. If we now assume along with the INS that the probability of an undocumented migrant being apprehended at the border is roughly 0.30, then an estimate of the reduction in the number of illegal border crossings (or the "flow" of undocumented immigrants) due to IRCA may be developed from (2,409,000)/0.30, or roughly 8 million in the 35-month post-IRCA period.[21]

The fact that a model including variables that would be expected to influence the number of illegal border crossings gives such a high degree of fit to the data lends confidence to this estimate. In addition, the variables included in the model behave in a manner entirely consistent with prior expectations, including the variables measuring the seasonal pattern of apprehensions. Thus, for example, as the number of apprehensions increases, other things being equal, the higher the ratio of U.S.-to- Mexican wages. The model also includes numerous other variables that are plausibly related either to the size of the population at risk of migrating illegally or to the propensity to migrate in undocumented status.

Could a decline in circulation account for the change in apprehensions in the wake of IRCA not due to changes in INS effort? Our model explicitly accounted for SAWs agricultural legalization, a group whose residential tenure in the United States during this period could have been (even under the provisions of the law) quite limited. What about the remaining undocumented populations—those who resided in the United States and applied for legalization and those who did not—continuing instead in undocumented status? A reasonable estimate of the undocumented Mexican origin population resident in the United States in mid-year 1986 is about 2 million persons. This would be a snapshot or stock estimate based on Census Bureau calculations (Warren and Passel, 1987). It incorporates an enumerated 1980 Census undocumented population of about 1,131,000 with a 20 percent undercount, and a middle estimate for net annual growth of 100,000. Through January 1989 Mexican nationals had submitted 1,233,300 regular legalization applications and 1,054,000 SAW applications. Depending on how one views the SAW population, one can estimate that about as many undocumented migrants from Mexico as were enumerated in the 1980 Census participated in the legalization programs. The numbers are certainly consistent with the notion that about as many applied for the regular legalization program as had arrived by January 1982.

There is reason to be skeptical that change in the behavior of the regular legalization population alone could result in the post-IRCA effect. First, to the extent that these individuals were permanent settlers rather than temporary sojourners, they would not have been regularly crossing the border before IRCA, and their apprehensions would not have been counted among the earlier totals. Second, if they engaged in regular rates of crossing, they would not have met the requirements of the application, because these required that they be continuously resident in the United States. Third, we noticed no additional statistical power associated with the inclusion in our statistical model of the cumulative applications for regular legalization status. Fourth, and perhaps of most significance, the statistical results for the model are so clearly linked to demographic and economic conditions in the two countries that short-term sojourns by de facto residents of the United States should have reduced the predictive quality of the model, which does not appear to be the case. It seems, then, that although some change in behavior of the undocumented stock in the United States may have contributed to the shortfall, a substantial amount of the decline in apprehensions, especially in the year following IRCA, can probably be traced to a decreased propensity to migrate North among the pool of eligibles in Mexico, including new starts and experienced migrants.

Ultimately, however, the extent to which the number of illegal border crossings can be inferred from apprehensions data depends upon the probability of being apprehended and whether this probability remains relatively constant over time. Linewatch and non-linewatch hours and capital budget expenditures for enforcement are two factors that are linked to the probability of apprehension. We estimate that their joint effect on both kinds of apprehensions had only a small effect on post-IRCA apprehensions (an increase of about 104,000). In other words, an increased INS effort in the post-IRCA period to apprehend persons entering the United States illegally—reflected largely in an increase in Border Patrol officer hours—resulted in a higher probability of being apprehended in relation to FY 1986 and in more apprehensions than there would have been previously. Seen in combination with the other components, our results suggest that the post-IRCA change in apprehensions is due mostly to a decrease in the flow of undocumented persons across the border.

CONCLUSION

This paper has developed and estimated a statistical model to analyze the determinants of apprehensions at the southern U.S. border over the period 1977–89. The first part of the time span includes the late 1970s and early 1980s, when the number of Border Patrol apprehensions was relatively stable and the Mexican economy underwent a period of relative prosperity. The period also includes the mid-1980s, when apprehensions increased sharply as the Mexican economy deteriorated owing to the global collapse of oil prices in 1982. Finally, the series encompasses a three-year period after IRCA was signed into law on November 6, 1986. Our research devotes special attention to a quantitative assessment of the components of changes in apprehensions during this IRCA period and develops estimates of the amount of change associated with (1) enrollment in the SAW program, (2) changes in INS enforcement effort, and (3) several dummy variables designed to capture the remaining effects of IRCA.

The results show a substantial decline in apprehensions during the post-IRCA period resulting from the implementation of immigration reform. We estimate an overall net decline in the total of linewatch and non-linewatch apprehensions between November 1986 and September 1989 of about 2,300,000, or an amount about 47 percent below the level that would be anticipated in the absence of IRCA. But it is impossible to tell from this overall total alone whether IRCA is having its intended effect. Because IRCA aims to reduce the number of illegal border crossings and to raise the probability of being apprehended at the border, it is in principle possible for IRCA to be highly effective and at the same time for there to be a relatively small change in the aggregate number of linewatch apprehensions due to IRCA.[22] For this reason, it is necessary to disaggregate the "total IRCA effect" into its three separate components. Increases in INS enforcement effort raised apprehensions by about 104,000 from November 1986 through September 1989 over what they would have been without these changes. The remaining changes involved decreases. About 52 percent of this decrease is due to the agricultural legalization program, and about 48 percent is due to the remaining effects of IRCA. By these measures, IRCA has been considerably more successful in reducing illegal border crossings than it has in increasing the probability of being apprehended by the Border Patrol.

At the same time, the number of illegal border crossings of women and children and non-Mexicans appears to be increasing. In general, our results indicate that the flow of undocumented migrants across the U.S.- Mexican border is appreciably influenced by demographic, economic, and policy variables. The continued growth of the young Mexican population and the improvement of the U.S. economy relative to the Mexican economy act in tandem to increase the number of undocumented migrants attempting to enter the United States. Other factors that we have not been able to capture (for example, the growth of social networks and household survival strategies in Mexico) undoubtedly play a role in the determination of the migrant flow, too. To the extent that the pattern of apprehensions reflects the flow of undocumented immigrants into the United States, our results indicate that the new legislation has slowed the rate of undocumented migration across the southern border of the United States, especially male migration. But with the pressures for migration in general remaining unabated, the recent growth in the number and proportion of females (and children) may be more than a temporary phenomenon.

Notes

This research was carried out under the auspices of the Program for Research on Immigration Policy, a program of public policy research and assessment in the area of immigration involving The Urban Institute and the RAND Corporation. Core support for the program is provided by the Ford Foundation. Conclusions or opinions expressed in the program's publications are those of the authors and do not necessarily reflect the views of other staff members, officers, or trustees of The Urban Institute or the RAND Corporation; advisory groups; or any organizations that provide financial support to the program. We gratefully acknowledge the assistance of Michael D. Hoefer of the U.S. Immigration and Naturalization Service, Linda Peterson of the U.S. Bureau of the Census, and Sergio Peqa of the World Bank, who helped us acquire and interpret the data; Jane Mell and Julie Goldsmith, who provided research assistance; Keith Crane and Beth Asch, who provided comments on our work; and LaVonia Proctor and Terri Murray who typed the manuscript.

1. Parts of this chapter are adapted from White, Bean, and Espenshade (forthcoming) and Espenshade, White, and Bean (forthcoming). For a discussion of the other provisions of IRCA and their implementation, see Goodis (1986) and Bean et al. (1989).

2. A major premise behind the passage of IRCA was that undocumented immigration may have negative effects on the wages and employment prospects of native workers. Research has failed to find much evidence for this supposition. See Muller and Espenshade (1985); Bean, Telles, and Lowell (1987); and Bean, Lowell and Taylor (1988).

3. Overarching these immediate programmatic issues is the view that long-range solutions inevitably must concentrate on promoting more rapid economic growth and development in "sending" countries, together with steps to bring population and labor force growth into balance with labor demand (Espenshade, 1989).

4. Because the same individual may be apprehended more than once during any given time period, apprehension statistics refer to the number of events, not people.

5. For earlier efforts to analyze apprehensions data in a longitudinal framework, see Frisbie (1975), Davila (1986), and Borjas, Freeman, and Lang (1987).

6. The U.S. Border Patrol is responsible for the security of the land borders of the United States with Canada and Mexico. Immigration investigators, like Border Patrol agents, also have responsibility for locating persons in violation of the Immigration and Nationality Act, but they generally operate away from the border areas of the United States, typically in cities where they concentrate their activities on particular economic sectors where undocumented aliens are thought to be working (Levine, Hill, and Warren, 1985).

7. Apprehensions on patrol result from time spent patrolling highways and roads in areas removed from usual areas of linewatch operations, and usually involve Border Patrol agents assigned to backup stations. Farm and ranch check apprehensions result from time spent inspecting farms, ranches, and similar operations for illegal aliens. Another non-linewatch activity involves traffic checks and transportation checks, which are similar in their operations and result in similar number of apprehensions. Traffic checks refer to apprehensions stemming from time spent spot-checking and observing through traffic. This includes time spent maintaining permanent or temporary checkpoints on highways examining vehicles for deportable aliens. Transportation checks, on the other hand, include time spent checking bus depots, train stations, airports, and questioning persons in the terminals on arrival or departure. This also includes time spent checking freight trains or freight yards for undocumented migrants. In addition, the Border Patrol conducts city patrols, consisting of time spent checking industries, businesses, hotels, jails, institutions, construction work, and the like. Finally, there is a miscellaneous collection of other operations including boat patrols, crewmen, and stowaways, and aliens turned over to the Border Patrol by other governmental agencies.

8. For a related model, but one that pertains to illegal immigration rather than apprehensions, see Todaro and Maruszko (1987).

9. We single out Mexico's population for the at-risk group because statistics compiled between 1977 and 1989 from monthly Border Patrol field operation reports on deportable aliens suggest that more than 97 percent of all apprehensions of undocumented migrants crossing the border from Mexico to the United States were of persons

born in Mexico. Migrants from El Salvador are conspicuous among the non-Mexican population. Mexicans also comprise the majority of the population legalizing under IRCA. INS provisional legalization application statistics from May 1989 indicate that 70 percent of the nearly 1.8 million applicants for the regular legalization program are citizens of Mexico, and that 81 percent of the 1.3 million SAW applicants are Mexican citizens (U.S. Immigration and Naturalization Service, 1989). Finally, Warren and Passel (1987) estimate that Mexico was the source of 55 percent of an estimated 2.1 million resident undocumented aliens enumerated in the 1980 Census.

10. A grandfather clause in IRCA exempts employers of undocumented aliens as of November 1986 from the teeth of employer sanctions so long as the workers do not change jobs.

11. Doris Meissner has speculated that many potential undocumented migrants adopted a "wait and see" attitude immediately after IRCA, and that sufficient time has now elapsed that the flow northward has resumed (Suro, 1989).

12. We tried lagging these variables by one month and three months and obtained similar results.

13. An interesting account replete with photographs of the technology that INS now uses along the southern border is contained in Federation for American Immigration Reform (1989). In the time-series model, we lagged the CAPINV variable by 12 months.

14. We did investigate alternative specifications. Most of these involved different expressions for our measures of IRCA or of the economic characteristics. Our ordinary least squares estimates gave results broadly similar to those in table 4.5, but with a first-lag autocorrelation of 0.35.

15. Whereas reported unemployment rates are generally higher in the United States than in Mexico, variations in the ratio provide a reasonable index of relative employment opportunities. The ratio varies from a low of about 0.75 (September 1977) to a high of 2.7 (January 1982).

16. The relevant coefficients translate into reductions during the spring months of the first post-IRCA year of 40 percent for linewatch apprehensions and 63 percent for non-linewatch apprehensions. Because the coefficients reflecting these reductions are so large, the usual method of approximating the percentage change by the coefficient itself overstates the change. Instead, we had to calculate the change from the exponential form of the equation.

17. This residual influence of IRCA may be related largely, though perhaps not exclusively, to a generalized set of factors that serve to restrict the mobility of undocumented migrants in the post-IRCA period. Among other things, these factors could include employer sanctions, the grandfather clause in IRCA that creates incentives tying illegal workers to one employer, and the regular legalization program, eligibility for which is conditional upon continuous residence in the United States since January 1, 1982. These factors create additional disincentives for undocumented migrants to move in either direction between the United States and Mexico.

18. We also estimated the components when the variables are entered in different orders and found that the results did not change appreciably.

19. That is, we estimated that there were 138,990 more non-linewatch apprehensions as a result of past-IRCA increases in enforcement hours and expenditures than would have occurred otherwise. When combined with the 34,804 decline in linewatch apprehensions that occurred because of reductions in linewatch hours, we obtained a net effect of 104,086.

20. It should be noted that the SAWs coefficient is statistically significant at only a 10 percent level (one-tail test) in the linewatch equation.

21. The INS has maintained that, for every migrant apprehended, two or three get

away (Federation for American Immigration Reform, 1989; Suro, 1989). If we use 2.0 as the average number who get away for every one that is apprehended, the implied probability of being apprehended is $1 \div (1 + 2.0) = 0.333$.

22. In terms of the model in equation (4.1), IRCA's objectives are to reduce the quantity $P * m$ and to raise π. Because some of IRCA's consequences for Y, total linewatch apprehensions, may move in offsetting directions, it is impossible to gauge IRCA's success solely in terms of changes in Y.

References

Alba, Francisco, and Joseph E. Potter. 1986. "Population and Development in Mexico since 1940: An Interpretation." *Population and Development Review* 12: 47–75.

Bean, Frank D., B. Lindsay Lowell, and Lowell J. Taylor. 1988. "Undocumented Mexican Immigrants and the Earnings of Other Workers in the United States." *Demography* 25(1, Feb.): 35-52.

Bean, Frank D., Edward E. Telles, and B. Lindsay Lowell. 1987. "Undocumented Migration to the United States: Perception and Evidence." *Population and Development Review* 13(4, Dec.): 671–90.

Bean, Frank D., George Vernez, and Charles B. Keely. 1989. *Opening and Closing the Doors: Changing U.S. Immigration Patterns and Policies.* Santa Monica, Washington, D.C.: RAND and Urban Institute.

Borjas, George J., Richard B. Freeman, and Kevin Lang. 1987. "Undocumented Mexican-Born Workers in the U.S.: How Many, How Permanent?" Cambridge, Mass: National Bureau for Economic Research.

Cornelius, Wayne. Forthcoming. "Impacts of the 1986 U.S. Immigration Law on Emigration from Rural Mexican Sending Communities." *Population and Development Review* 15 (4, Dec.).

Davila, Alberto. 1986. "The Seasonality of Apprehensions of Undocumented Mexican Workers. *International Migration Review* 20(40, Winter): 986–91.

Espenshade, Thomas J. 1989. "Growing Imbalances between Labor Supply and Labor Demand in the Caribbean Basin." In *Mexican and Central American Population and U.S. Immigration Policy*, edited by Frank D. Bean, Jurgen Schmandt, and Sidney Weintraub, 113–60. University of Texas Press.

Espenshade, Thomas J., and J. Edward Taylor. 1988. "Undocumented and Seasonal Workers in the California Farm Work Force." In *Proceedings of the Fortieth Annual Meeting*, edited by Barbara D. Dennis, 182–91. Madison, Wis.: Industrial Relations Research Association.

Espenshade, Thomas J., Michael J. White, and Frank D. Bean. Forthcoming. "Patterns of Recent Illegal Migration to the United States." In *Future*

Demographic Trends in Europe and North America, edited by Wolfgang Lutz. Laxenburg, Austria: International Institute for Applied Systems Analysis.

Federation for American Immigration Reform. 1989. *Ten Steps to Securing America's Borders.* Washington, D.C.: Federation for American Immigration Reform.

Fix, Michael, and P.T. Hill. 1990. *Enforcing Employer Sanctions.* Santa Monica and Washington, D.C.: Program for Research on Immigration Policy.

Frisbie, Parker. 1975. "Illegal Migration from Mexico to the United States: A Longitudinal Analysis." *International Migration Review*, 9(1, Spring): 3-13.

Goodis, Tracy Ann. 1986. "A Layman's Guide to 1986 U.S. Immigration Reform." Urban Institute Working Paper PDS-86-4. Washington, D.C.: Urban Institute, December.

Hill, Ken. 1985. "Illegal Aliens: An Assessment." In *Immigration Statistics*, edited by D. Levine, K. Hill, R. Warren, pp. 225–50. Washington, D.C.: National Academy Press.

Hoefer, Michael. 1989. Personal communication.

Levine, Daniel B., K. Hill, and R. Warren, eds. 1985. *Immigration Statistics: A Study of Neglect.* Washington, D.C.: National Academy Press.

Massey, Douglas S. 1988. "Economic Development and International Migration in Comparative Perspective." *Population and Development Review* 14 (3, Sept.): 383–413.

Massey, Douglas S., and Felipe Garcia Espaqa. 1987. "The Social Process of International Migration." Science 237: 733–38.

Massey, Douglas S., Rafael Alarcoń, Jorge Durand, and Humberto González. 1987. *Return to Atzlan: The Social Process of International Migration from Western Mexico.* Berkeley and Los Angeles: University of California Press.

Mathews, Jay. 1988. "Using Fake Papers, Migrants Skirt Law." *Washington Post*, Nov. 3, Sec. A, p. 3.

McDonnell, Patrick. 1989. "Do Numbers Add Up on Illegal Entry?" *Los Angeles Times*, Nov. 12, Sec. 3, pp. 1, 6.

Mueller, Thomas and Thomas T. Espenshade. 1985. *The Fourth Wave: California's Newest Immigrants.* Washington, D.C.: Urban Institute Press.

New York Times. 1983. "Illegal Alien Captures at Record for Year." Sec. A, (Sept. 16): 13.

North, David. 1988. IRCA's Batting Averages (Memo #2). Transcentury Development Associates, Washington, D.C. Photocopy.

North, David, and Jennifer R. Wagner. 1981. "Enforcing the Immigration Law: A Review of the Options." In *U.S. Immigration Policy and The National Interest, Staff Report, Appendix E.* Washington, D.C.: Select Commission on Immigration and Refugee Policy, Apr.

Portes, Alejandro. 1983. "International Labor Migration and National Development." In *U.S. Immigration and Refugee Policy: Global and Domestic Issues,* edited by M.M. Kritz, 71–91. Lexington, Mass.: Lexington Books.

Portes, Alejandro, and Robert Bach. 1985. *Latin Journey: Cuban and Mexican Immigrants in the United States.* Berkeley and Los Angeles: University of California Press.

SAS Institute, Inc., 1984. SAS/ETS User's Guide, Version 5 Edition. Cary, N.C.: SAS Institute.

Select Commission on Immigration and Refugee Policy. 1981. *U.S. Immigration Policy and the National Interest: The Staff Report of The Select Commission on Immigration and Refugee Policy.* Washington, D.C.: U.S. Government Printing Office.

Suro, Roberto. 1989. "1986 Amnesty Law is Seen as Failing to Slow Alien Tide." *New York Times,* Sec. 1, (June 18): 1.

Todaro, Michael P., and Lydia Marusko. 1987. "Illegal Migration and U.S. Immigration Reform: A Conceptual Framework." *Population and Development Review* 13(1, Mar.): 101–15.

U.S. Immigration and Naturalization Service. 1989. *Provisional Legalization Application Statistics.* Washington, D.C.: Statistical Analysis Branch, Office of Plans and Analysis, U.S. Immigration and Naturalization Service, May 12.

Warren, Robert, and Jeffrey S. Passel. 1987. "A Count to the Uncountable: Estimates of Undocumented Aliens Counted in the 1980 U .S. Census." *Demography* 24(3, Aug.): 375–93.

White, Michael J., Frank D. Bean, and Thomas J. Espenshade. Forthcoming. "The U.S. 1986 Immigration Reform and Control Act and Undocumented Migration to the United States." *Population Research and Policy Review.*

Chapter Five

UNDOCUMENTED MIGRATION TO THE UNITED STATES: EVIDENCE FROM A REPEATED TRIALS MODEL

Thomas J. Espenshade

"Since everybody agrees that undocumented workers are likely to attempt their crossings several times until successful, we can see that, even as a proxy, the number of apprehensions is of little use."—José Alberro

Among students of undocumented immigration to the United States, it has become customary to express regret over the absence of direct evidence on the volume of this migration, to acknowledge the limitations of using data on the number of arrests or apprehensions of illegal migrants as a proxy for the undocumented flow, and then to proceed to use apprehensions data in quantitative studies of the determinants of U.S. undocumented migration on the grounds that superior alternatives do not exist (Frisbie, 1975; Jenkins, 1977; Blejer, Johnson, and Porzecanski, 1978; Fogel, 1982; Davila, 1986; and Borjas, Freeman, and Lang, 1987). Limitations of data on the level of apprehensions center not on the quality of the data per se, but on their suitability as a proxy for the undocumented flow. Criticisms include, first, that many illegal migrants to the United States escape detection by the U.S. Immigration and Naturalization Service (INS); second, that less fortunate ones may be apprehended several times within a given time interval; and, third, that the volume of apprehensions depends not only on the flow of undocumented migrants but also on the level of effort the INS expends in trying to stem this flow.

A partial solution to some of these difficulties is to include the size of the U.S. Border Patrol budget or some other measure of INS effort as an explanatory variable in time-series regressions of variations in the level of Border Patrol apprehensions (Jenkins, 1977; Fogel, 1982; and Borjas et al., 1987). A superior approach, however, is to develop explicit models of the apprehension process that recognize that the observed number of apprehensions in a given time period depends on the size of the population at risk of undertaking an undocumented migration, on the rate of undocumented migration, and on the probability of being apprehended by the INS. The preceding chapter four, by Bean, Espenshade, White, and Dymowski, and related work by these authors illustrate this research strategy (Espenshade, White, and Bean, forthcoming; White, Bean, and Espenshade, forthcoming). Although the immigration research literature often recognizes that data on apprehensions refer to the number of events and not to the number of separate persons apprehended, and that illegal migrants who are apprehended crossing into the United States are likely to keep on trying until they are successful (Cornelius and Diez-Canedo, 1976; Todaro and Maruszko, 1987; Massey et al., 1987; and Cornelius, forthcoming), no quantitative study of the determinants of undocumented migration to the United States has adequately dealt with the phenomenon of repeaters.

This chapter extends the analysis in chapter four by developing a repeated trials model of undocumented migration. In the next section, INS monthly time-series data on the number of total apprehensions and on the number of repeaters are combined to construct a data series on the monthly flow of undocumented immigrants to the United States across the U.S.-Mexican border. Following that, the economic, demographic, and policy determinants of this flow are examined. Aided by the results from a time-series regression model, the text then turns to the question of how the 1986 Immigration Reform and Control Act (IRCA) has affected this flow. Finally, these results are discussed and briefly compared with findings from related studies.

REPEATED TRIALS MODEL

The rationale for adopting a repeated trials model of undocumented migration is clearer if one has some perspective on the social process of illegal alien apprehension. Part of the story relates to the chronic underfunding of the INS and to the understaffing of the U.S. Border Patrol (Federation for American Immigration Reform, 1989). In the years surrounding IRCA, the task of guarding the approximately 6,000 miles of U.S. land borders with Canada and Mexico was assigned to 3,600 Border Patrol agents (Bean et al., 1989). Despite this vast expanse of territory, however, fewer than 200 miles of southern border, frequently near major U.S. cities, account for 90 percent of all illegal alien apprehensions. This fact is attributable both to the economic disparities between the United States and Mexico and to the fact that most of the southern border is virtually impenetrable desert and mountains. In fiscal year 1987, for example, 60 percent of total apprehensions occurred along just 60 miles of border south of El Paso, Texas, and San Diego (Federation for American Immigration Reform, 1989).[1]

The Social Process of Illegal Alien Apprehension

Most aliens arrested by the U.S. Border Patrol for being in the United States illegally are apprehended either as they cross over the U.S.-Mexican border or shortly thereafter. Data compiled from INS administrative reports of field operations between January 1977 and September 1988 indicate that two-thirds of all apprehensions along the southern border occur at the point of entry into the United States. Another one-quarter result from migrants apprehended within the first three days of their arrival. Only 1 in every 10 apprehensions is of a migrant who is arrested after being in the country for four days or longer. Likewise, more than 60 percent of all arrests of illegal aliens arise from Border Patrol linewatch activities. Linewatch apprehensions are those resulting from time spent guarding the border against smuggling and illegal entry of aliens, and include such functions as surveillance, tower watch, and patrolling along the border on foot, horseback, or in some kind of vehicle. Nearly every linewatch apprehension (roughly 98 percent) consists of a person apprehended as he or she is trying to enter the United States illegally. Finally, five out of every six apprehensions are adult male Mexican citizens. When Mexican women and their minor children are added in, Mexican nationals comprise almost 98 percent of all illegal alien apprehensions along the southern U.S. border. Taken together, these data imply that the typical undocumented migrant is a young adult Mexican male who comes across the southern border near a major U.S. city and who, unless he manages to escape detection altogether, is in the United States for a few hours or days at most before being apprehended by the Border Patrol.[2]

For the vast majority of illegal migrants, being apprehended entails little financial or psychic cost (Blejer et al., 1978). According to current practice, there is virtually no penalty levied against persons apprehended while illegally entering the United States. Instead of receiving fines or detention, apprehended illegal Mexican migrants are generally given a free meal and a short bus ride back across the border (Federation for American Immigration Reform, 1989).[3] Experienced observers of the U.S. Border Patrol argue that inadequate funding for INS has lowered the morale of Border Patrol officers and encouraged reluctant acceptance of a new era of "revolving door" immigration enforcement. They claim, "With no deterrent measures, nearly all apprehended illegal aliens will try again and again until at last they get through undetected" (Federation for American Immigration Reform, 1989: 26). It should come as no surprise, then, that most illegal migrants view being apprehended simply as "bad luck" or as "just another nuisance" in pursuit of work in the United States (Cornelius and Diez-Canedo, 1976; Cornelius, forthcoming). One migrant who has been coming to work in this country every summer since 1970 said that since IRCA, "It's harder to cross, but we do get across, if not on the first try, then on the second, third or fourth. . . .They can't close the border to us, no matter how hard they try" (Rohter, 1988: A6).

However suggestive these anecdotes may be, viewing the process of undocumented migration as a sequence of repeated attempts to enter the United States illegally until one is successful also has a straightforward underlying economic rationale. Todaro and Maruszko (1987) argue that the cost of migrating is one determinant of the rate of illegal migration and that reductions in this cost will increase incentives to migrate. If migrants residing in a traditional rural sending community in Mexico have already decided that an undocumented trip to the United States entails likely benefits that exceed the costs of such a move, and they now find themselves deposited a few hundred yards inside their home country, having recently been apprehended on their first attempted crossing by the U.S. Border Patrol, the costs of making a second attempt now are much less than they were initially when the move originated farther from the border. In other words, if a first attempt makes economic sense, then subsequent attempts do as well. For most migrants, it will be easier to try to reenter the United States than to go home. In the case of Mexican illegal aliens, home may be several hundred miles away, whereas a job in Orange County may be just a few miles up the road (Federation for American Immigration Reform, 1989).

A Formal Model of the Apprehension Process

The process just described of INS apprehensions of undocumented workers may be modeled in the following way. Imagine a new cohort of undocumented migrants from Mexico arriving at the U.S.-Mexican border on the first day of every month t. Call the size of this cohort F_t. In addition, suppose that each person in F_t faces an independent probability p_t of being apprehended on the U.S. side on each attempt to cross the border during month t. Alternatively, p_t may be viewed as the fraction of individuals crossing the border at any one time who are apprehended. Those who are apprehended are taken back to the Mexican side and are assumed to try again to enter the United States. This process continues throughout the month until all members of the original cohort have successfully entered the United States.

The situation is described more formally in table 5.1, where, for convenience, subscripts have been ignored. F is the size of the cohort making a first attempt at the start of a month. A fraction p of this cohort is apprehended, implying that $F(1-p)$ manage to evade detection by the INS and enter the United States without apprehension, leaving a number Fp to make a second attempt. On this second attempted crossing Fp^2 are apprehended and $Fp(1-p)$ successfully enter the United States, having been apprehended only once. This process continues throughout the month. The model implies that everyone will eventually get into the United States if they keep trying and that they will be able to do so within a month. The latter assumption requires some justification. INS officials believe that, for every undocumented entrant apprehended, two or three get away (Dillin, 1986; Federation for American Immigration Reform, 1989). This estimate suggests that the per-attempt probability of being apprehended is about 0.3. If one now makes the conservative assumption that a typical illegal alien is capable of making at least seven attempts per month, then just $(0.3)^7$, or about 2 per 10,000, would still be left trying at the end of the month.[4]

The column sums in table 5.1 are of special interest. The total

Table 5.1 REPEATED TRIALS MODEL

Attempt Number (1)	Size of Group Making the Attempt (2)	Number Apprehended on This Attempt (3)	Number Entering U.S. Successfully on This Attempt (4)
1	F	$F \cdot p$	$F \cdot (1 - p)$
2	$F \cdot p$	$F \cdot p^2$	$F \cdot p(1 - p)$
3	$F \cdot p^2$	$F \cdot p^3$	$F \cdot p^2(1 - p)$
⋮	⋮	⋮	⋮
i	$F \cdot p^{i-1}$	$F \cdot p^i$	$F \cdot p^{i-1}(1 - p)$
⋮	⋮	⋮	⋮
Column sums[a]	$F/(1 - p)$	$Fp/(1 - p) = A$	F

a. The sum of column (2) equals the monthly number of illegal border crossings; the sum of column (3) equals the total monthly number of apprehensions; the sum of column (4) equals the total monthly number of persons entering the United States.

number of illegal border crossings each month is given by the sum of numbers in column 2. The sum of column 3 equals the total monthly number of apprehensions. The INS routinely gathers monthly data on this variable for the nine Border Patrol sectors along the U.S.-Mexican border. It is these data, in fact, that researchers have frequently used as a proxy for the flow of illegal immigrants into the country. But it is clear that monthly apprehensions (A) and the monthly flow of illegal aliens (F) will be perfectly correlated only if the per-attempt probability of being apprehended (p) is constant from one month to the next. Substantial monthly variations, however, both in the number of Border Patrol officer hours devoted to apprehension activities and in the expenditure on physical capital employed in the apprehension effort (including sensors, imaging devices, and transportation vehicles) suggest that the assumption of a time-invariant p is not tenable (Bean et al., chapter four, this volume; Espenshade et al., forthcoming; and and White et al., forthcoming). Finally, the sum of column 4 equals the total monthly number of persons successfully entering the U.S. interior, or simply F, the original monthly cohort size.

Table 5.1 also contains information on the monthly number of "repeaters" (R), that is, on the number of instances in which someone has been apprehended two or more times. R corresponds, therefore, to the sum of numbers in column 3 beginning with the second row, or to $Fp^2/(1-p)$. In addition to total apprehensions, the INS also collects monthly data on the number of repeaters. Data on both these variables are generated by individual Border Patrol officers, who complete an arrest record (Report of Deportable Aliens Located, INS form I-213) whenever an apprehension is made. Information from these records, which contain demographic and socioeconomic details about the migrants in addition to data on conditions surrounding the arrest (including whether the alien has previously been apprehended), is compiled and aggregated to the individual Border Patrol sector level and then forwarded monthly to the INS Central Office in Washington, D.C.

Time-series estimates of F and p may then be constructed from INS information on total apprehensions and on repeaters, as follows. The ratio

$$R/A = \{Fp^2/(1-p)\}/\{Fp/(1-p)\} = p. \tag{5.1}$$

Furthermore, from the sum of column 3 in table 5.1,

$$F = A(1-p)/p. \tag{5.2}$$

From equation (5.1) one sees that the month-specific per-attempt probability of being apprehended in the United States is given simply by the repeater fraction. This probability may then be used in conjunction with the total number of apprehensions in equation (5.2) to construct a series on the monthly flow of undocumented migrants (F_t). This flow not only represents the size of the cohort of illegal immigrants moving up to the U.S.-Mexican border each month from Mexico (and, incidentally, from other parts of Central America), but it also corresponds to the gross number of undocumented migrants who successfully enter the United States each month.

INS time-series data on repeaters and on total apprehensions for the period 1977–88 have been combined as in the preceding equation (5.1) to form the monthly series on the per-attempt probability of apprehension (p_t) shown in figure 5.1. This series has a mean value of 0.317 and exhibits substantial variation ranging from a minimum of 0.211 in May 1980 to a maximum of 0.396 in August 1982. Two extended periods with abnormally low apprehension probabilities occurred in 1980 and again in 1988. Beginning in spring 1980 and continuing throughout much of the remainder of the year, U.S. Border Patrol efforts to apprehend undocumented migrants were reduced, partly through a "gentlemen's agreement" with the U.S. Bureau of the Census, so as to maximize cooperation of the Hispanic community with the bureau's decennial census count in April 1980, and partly because Border Patrol personnel were reassigned to guard detention centers created in the southeastern states to cope with the influx of Mariel Cuban and Haitian boat people (Vialet, 1989). Between fiscal years 1987 and 1988, total Border Patrol hours allocated to linewatch activities declined by almost 20 percent as Border Patrol agents were increasingly being used in such nonborder activities as drug interdiction, investigating criminal aliens, and informing employers about their new responsibilities under IRCA (Bean et al., 1989).[5]

These figures on apprehension probabilities were then combined, using the formula in equation (5.2), with information on the monthly number of total apprehensions to generate estimates of F_t, the monthly flow of undocumented migrants into the United States across the U.S.-Mexican border. Constructed data on the size of this monthly flow between January 1977 and September 1988 are shown in figure 5.2. This graph exhibits both seasonal and secular influences. With few exceptions, the flow is at a minimum in the late winter months of November and December, when many migrants return home to Mexico for the Christmas holidays and the annual town fiestas (Cor-

Figure 5.1 PROBABILITY OF BEING APPREHENDED ON EACH ATTEMPT

All southern border sectors

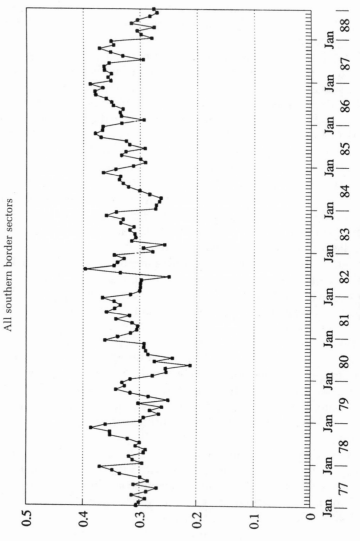

Month and Year

Figure 5.2 MONTHLY FLOW OF UNDOCUMENTED IMMIGRANTS

All southern border sectors

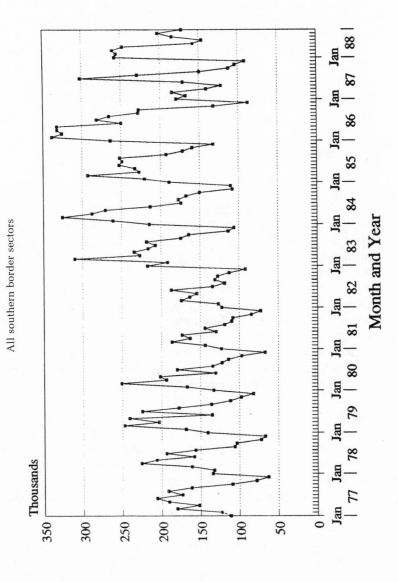

nelius, 1989). It resumes again after the start of the new year and peaks in the late spring and early summer months, forming a cycle that closely corresponds to the planting and harvesting seasons in California agriculture (Taylor and Espenshade, 1987).[6] The secular trend in the flow stays roughly level or declines slightly until 1982, when the drop in world oil prices forced Mexico into its worst economic crisis since the 1910 Revolution (Massey, 1988). There is evidence of accelerated emigration from Mexico after 1982 until November 1986, when IRCA's passage apparently altered both the secular and seasonal flow pattern that had existed in the preceding four years.

A Preliminary Examination of IRCA's Effects

An important policy question dominating much of the discussion in this volume is whether IRCA has had an effect on the flow of undocumented immigration. Table 5.2 provides some insight into this issue by comparing monthly estimates of the undocumented flow following IRCA's adoption with flow values in the pre-IRCA period. INS officials routinely engaged in such "before and after" comparisons after November 1986, to argue that IRCA was successful in reducing the flow (Mathews, 1988).[7] There is little difference between the average flow values in the post-IRCA period and the entire pre-IRCA period (January 1977 to October 1986). When the post-IRCA levels are compared with values in the period immediately prior to IRCA, however, IRCA appears to be working as its supporters hoped it would. The estimated average flow in the 22 months following IRCA is about 28 percent less than the average in the 22 months prior to November 1986. A somewhat stronger impact is suggested when fiscal year 1986 is used as a reference point.

The problem with this sort of before and after analysis, of course, is that none of the many other influences that might arguably affect the flow of illegal aliens has been held constant. As a result, one cannot confidently attribute reduced levels of the flow after IRCA to the new policy reforms, because they might just as well have been due to other factors. The kinds of comparisons needed for this analysis were between the flow in the post-IRCA period and hypothetical values of what the flow would have been during the same period had IRCA never been adopted. This approach allowed other factors to be held constant. Before proceeding to make these comparisons, however, it was first necessary to develop a statistical model of the

Table 5.2 AVERAGE MONTHLY VALUES OF THE UNDOCUMENTED FLOW IN PRE-IRCA AND POST-IRCA PERIODS

Item	Pre-IRCA			Post-IRCA	Percentage Deviation of Post-IRCA Values from Pre-IRCA Values		
	Jan. '77–Oct. '86 (118 mos.)	Jan. '85–Oct. '86 (22 mos.)	Oct. '85–Sept. '86 (FY '86)	Dec. '86–Sept. '88 (22 mos.)	Jan. '77–Oct. '86 (118 mos.)	Jan. '85–Oct. '86 (22 mos.)	Oct. '85–Sept. '86 (FY '86)
Monthly flow of undocumented immigrants	175,100	246,000	256,500	178,300	+1.8	−27.5	−30.5

Note: The Immigration Reform and Control Act was signed into law on Nobember 6, 1986.

determinants of the month-to-month variations in the undocumented flow apparent in figure 5.2.

DETERMINANTS OF THE UNDOCUMENTED MIGRANT FLOW

The statistical model used here is a modification of the one developed in chapter four and elsewhere (Espenshade et al., forthcoming; White et al., forthcoming). To begin, the monthly flow of undocumented migrants is assumed to be the product of the size of the population at risk of undertaking an illegal migration to the United States (P_t) and the monthly rate of illegal migration (m_t), or

$$F_t = P_t \cdot m_t, \tag{5.3}$$

by the definition of a demographic rate. Taking natural logarithms of both sides and assuming that $\ln(P_t)$ and $\ln(m_t)$ are both linear functions of a set of explanatory variables, yields the following specification for F_t:

$$\ln F_t = \beta_0 + \beta_1 X_{1t} + \beta_2 X_{2t} + \dots + u_t. \tag{5.4}$$

The particular variables chosen for the right side of equation (5.4) depend upon our understanding of the determinants of the size of the at-risk population and of the rate of undocumented migration.

Using arguments similar to those advanced in the preceding chapter, it is assumed that the two principal factors affecting P are the population of young adults living in Mexico (MEXPOP) and the cumulative number of agricultural workers applying for the special agricultural worker (SAWS) legalization program. The monthly rate of illegal migration is assumed to depend on relative economic conditions between the United States and Mexico (UNEMPRATIO and WAGERATIO), a series of monthly dummy variables (JAN–NOV) designed to capture the cyclical nature of the planting and harvest season in southwestern agriculture, and another set of dummy variables (POSTIRCA, YEAR2, SPRING, SUMMER, SPRING2, and SUMMER2) reflecting secular and seasonal impacts of IRCA's adoption. The full set of explanatory variables used in the regression analysis is listed in table 5.3.

Equation (5.4) was estimated with a technique that corrects for first-order serial correlation in the error terms, using 141 monthly observations from January 1977 to September 1988.[8] Results are shown

Table 5.3 VARIABLE NAMES, DEFINITIONS, SOURCES OF DATA, AND
EXPECTED SIGNS OF ESTIMATED COEFFICIENTS

Variable Name	Definition	Data Source	Expected Sign of Coefficient
Dependent Variable			
FLOW	Natural log of monthly flow of undocumented immigrants across U.S.-Mexican border	U.S. Border Patrol reports of field operations	N/A[a]
Explanatory Variables			
MEXPOP	Mexican population 15–34 years of age (in millions)	International Division, U.S. Bureau of the Census	+
SAWS	Cumulative number of SAWs applications (in millions)	U.S. Immigration and Naturalization Service (INS)	−
UNEMPRATIO	Ratio of U.S. male unemployment rate (percentage) to Mexican male unemployment rate (percentage)	U.S. Bureau of Labor Statistics, Employment and Earnings; International Labor Office, Bulletin of Labor Statistics; World Bank	−
WAGERATIO	Ratio of hourly wage rate in U.S. nonagricultural sector (in Mexican pesos) to hourly earnings in Mexican manufacturing sector (in pesos)	U.S. Bureau of Labor Statistics, Employment and Earnings; International Labor Office, Bulletin of Labor Statistics; World Bank	+
JAN–NOV	Monthly dummy variables for seasonal labor demand (December omitted)	Each monthly dummy = 1 for that month and 0 elsewhere	+
POSTIRCA	Deterrent effect of IRCA	Dummy variable (= 1 for NOV 1986 and all subsequent months)	−
YEAR2	Altered IRCA effect in second year of post-IRCA period	Dummy variable (= 1 for NOV 1987 and all subsequent months)	?

(Continued)

Table 5.3 VARIABLE NAMES, DEFINITIONS, SOURCES OF DATA, AND
EXPECTED SIGNS OF ESTIMATED COEFFICIENTS (Continued)

Variable Name	Definition	Data Source	Expected Sign of Coefficient
SPRING	Spring effect in post-IRCA period	Dummy variable (= 1 March–June months of post-IRCA period)	–
SUMMER	Summer effect in post-IRCA period	Dummy variable (= 1 in July–Oct. months of post-IRCA period)	?
SPRING2	Altered spring effect in year 2 of post-IRCA period	SPRING*YEAR2	?
SUMMER2	Altered summer effect in year 2 of post-IRCA period	SUMMER*YEAR2	?

a. N/A = not applicable.

in table 5.4, suggesting that demographic, economic, and immigration policy variables are important determinants of variations in the undocumented migrant flow. The flow is increased by Mexican population growth, by an improvement in economic conditions in the United States relative to those in Mexico, and by the unfolding of the planting and harvesting season in agriculture. On the other hand, the adoption of IRCA led to a decline of almost 50 percent in the undocumented flow, as indicated by the magnitude of the POSTIRCA coefficient, and this underlying negative effect was further strengthened during the spring of 1987. There is also a strong suggestion that IRCA's impact on the northward illegal flow may have waned somewhat during the second year of IRCA's operation. The coefficient on YEAR2 is positive with a p-value of .0505, but in the absence of an a priori hypothesis to warrant a one-tail test, the YEAR2 coefficient is narrowly insignificant at the 5 percent level. The SAWS variable has the expected sign but is the only variable in the list about which there is a prediction that is not statistically significant at the 5 percent level.

IRCA'S IMPACT ON THE UNDOCUMENTED FLOW

One is now in position to evaluate IRCA's effects on the flow of illegal migrants to the United States. The aggregated results, sum-

Table 5.4 REGRESSION COEFFICIENTS FOR THE LOGARITHM OF THE
MONTHLY FLOW OF UNDOCUMENTED IMMIGRANTS, 1977–88

Variable	$\hat{\beta}$	Variable	$\hat{\beta}$
MEXPOP	0.050**	SEP	0.520**
	(3.003)		(8.155)
SAWS	−0.472	OCT	0.403**
	(−0.898)		(6.415)
UNEMPRATIO	−0.137*	NOV	0.183**
	(−2.522)		(3.383)
WAGERATIO	0.072**	POSTIRCA	−0.486**
	(2.945)		(−4.739)
JAN	0.695**	YEAR2	0.366
	(12.761)		(1.976)
FEB	0.770**	SPRING	−0.375**
	(12.558)		(−3.050)
MAR	1.073**	SUMMER	0.166
	(16.944)		(1.161)
APR	0.934**	SPRING2	0.226
	(14.833)		(1.088)
MAY	0.906**	SUMMER2	−0.033
	(14.319)		(−0.117)
JUN	0.787**	INTERCEPT	10.042**
	(12.385)		(37.741)
JUL	0.832**	RHO(1)	−0.262**
	(13.056)		(−2.955)
AUG	0.711**	R^2	0.882
	(11.152)		
		N	141

Note: T-statistics are in parentheses.
* p ≤ .05, two-tail test.
** p ≤ .01, two-tail test.

marized in table 5.5, are obtained from the regression equation in
table 5.4 by calculating the expected monthly flow between November
1986 and September 1988 in the absence of IRCA. This computation was performed by assigning the value zero to all six IRCA-
related dummy variables and to the SAWS variable in table 5.4. The
estimated flow presented in column 2 of table 5.5 corresponds to the
flow data shown earlier in figure 5.2. According to the repeated trials
model estimate, the total number of undocumented migrants to the
United States across the southern border from November 1986 to
September 1988 inclusive was somewhat larger than 4 million, or
roughly 175,000 each month.

Table 5.5 IMPACT OF IRCA ON THE FLOW OF UNDOCUMENTED MIGRANTS
TO THE UNITED STATES

Period (1)	Estimated Flow[a] (2)	Counterfactual Flow[b] (3)	Change due to IRCA[c] (4)	Percentage Reduction due to IRCA (5)
TOTALS				
Two-year post-IRCA				
period (Nov. '86–Sep. '88)	4,054,185	6,492,605	– 2,438,420	37.6
Year 1 (Nov. '86–Oct. '87)	1,976,780	3,522,625	– 1,545,845	43.9
Year 2 (Nov. '87–Sep. '88)	2,077,405	2,969,980	– 892,575	30.1
MONTHLY AVERAGES				
Two year post-IRCA				
period (Nov. '86–Sep. '88)	176,269	282,287	– 106,018	37.6
Year 1 (Nov. '86–Oct. '87)	164,732	293,552	– 128,820	43.9
Year 2 (Nov. '87–Sep. '88)	188,855	269,998	– 81,143	30.1

a. Calculated from total apprehensions and repeaters data as $A(1 - p)/p$.
b. Expected flow in the absence of IRCA. Calculated from regression equation in Table 4 by setting values for SAWS and all IRCA-related dummy variables (POST-IRCA, YEAR2, SPRING, SUMMER, SPRING2, and SUMMER2) equal to zero in the post-IRCA period.
c. Column (2) minus column (3).

It should be emphasized that this figure is an estimate of the gross or one-way inflow of undocumented migrants during this time and does not incorporate illegal migrants who left the country in the same period. Other estimates of the *net* influx of undocumented immigrants suggest that the annual increment to the stock of illegal aliens resident in the United States is much smaller. The best estimates put the figure somewhere between 100,000 and 300,000 per year between 1980 and 1986, with 200,000 being the generally accepted figure (Passel and Woodrow, 1987; Woodrow, Passel, and Warren, 1987; U.S. Bureau of the Census, 1989). This net flow is believed to have been cut to between 100,000 and 200,000 per year since IRCA's passage (U.S. Immigration and Naturalization Service, 1989).

The so-called counterfactual flow in column 3 of table 5.5 is an estimate of what the flow would have been in the absence of IRCA's passage. An estimated total of 6.5 million undocumented migrants would have crossed the southern U.S. border. Thus, IRCA had the effect of reducing the gross undocumented flow by an amount somewhere between 2.4 million and 2.5 million migrants in the first two years following its passage. This absolute decline equates to a relative decline of 38 percent from the counterfactual flow. Table 5.5 also divides IRCA's two-year impact into its annual components. There apparently was a greater effect of IRCA in the first year following adoption than during the second; the proportionate reductions in the undocumented flow are 43.9 and 30.1 percent, respectively.

DISCUSSION

This chapter has developed a repeated trials model of undocumented migration to the United States across the U.S.-Mexican border and then applied the model to INS data on the monthly number of total Border Patrol apprehensions and on the number of repeaters, to generate time-series estimates of the monthly probability of apprehension and the flow of undocumented migrants into the country. The repeated trials model captures the phenomenon that, once arrested by the U.S. Border Patrol and taken back across the Mexican border, most undocumented migrants are likely to keep trying to enter the United States until they succeed. The model's results and those of the estimated regression equation suggest that IRCA's passage in October 1986 was subsequently associated with a decline of approximately 38 percent in the number of undocumented migrants crossing the U.S.-Mexican border into the United States between November 1986 and September 1988. In the two years following IRCA's adoption, the estimated undocumented flow across the U.S. southern border totaled slightly more than 4 million, whereas the results here suggest that the comparable figure would have been closer to 6.5 million, or almost 2.5 million greater, had IRCA not been passed. It is worth reiterating that these figures are estimates of the gross, or one-way, influx of undocumented migrants to the United States and do not take into account the number who doubtless leave during the same interval. The net growth in the stock of illegal aliens resident in the United States is therefore substantially less than the numbers suggested by our data.

Regardless of the congruence between the repeated trials model and the underlying social phenomena it is designed to reflect, the dependability of the model in producing reasonable estimates of monthly probabilities of apprehension and flows of illegal immigrants to the United States is conditional upon the quality of Border Patrol data on total apprehensions and on the number of repeaters.

Despite substantial improvements in the past decade, lingering doubts remain in the demographic research community about the quality of INS data generally (Levine, Hill, and Warren, 1985). Referring specifically to the INS form I-213, the record of deportable aliens located, and the source of information on total apprehensions and on repeaters, the National Academy of Sciences panel charged with evaluating immigration statistics noted that a considerable amount of information of "uncertain quality" is collected and recommended that the INS "process and tabulate data on a regular basis from at least a substantial sample of I- 213 forms, and put more emphasis on the quality of the basic data collected" (Levine et al., 1985: 136).

Previous authors who have used apprehensions data in their analyses of undocumented migration to the United States have raised few questions about the quality of information on total apprehensions. As noted at the beginning of this chapter, the accuracy of the reports has usually been accepted at face value, and doubts have typically centered, instead, on the appropriateness of these data as a proxy for the undocumented flow. Moreover, so far as this author is aware, there exists no systematic attempt to evaluate the quality of the INS repeater data and therefore no direct evidence either supporting or questioning their use. Alternatively, this discussion relies on some indirect evidence.

If the repeater data are flawed for whatever reason, these inaccuracies should give a flawed series for p_t in figure 5.1, because the monthly apprehension probabilities are formed by dividing the number of repeaters by the total number of apprehensions. For example, if the repeater series showed essentially no variation, so that it was constant from month to month, then p_t should vary inversely with the number of total apprehensions. In particular, p_t should exhibit a strong seasonal cycle with a maximum in December and a minimum in the spring and summer months when total apprehensions are the greatest.[9] Alternatively, if the number of repeaters were simply a constant fraction of total apprehensions, then the series for p_t would be flat. Figure 5.1 shows that neither of these scenarios is correct. The series for p_t fluctuates substantially, ranging almost by a multiple of two, from 0.21 to nearly 0.40. In addition, the variation clearly fails to exhibit strong seasonality and therefore to conform to the inverse of fluctuations in total apprehensions. Nor, however, is the variation in probabilities of apprehension totally arbitrary or random. As noted earlier, the lows in these probabilities during 1980 and again in 1988 correspond with unique events in Border Patrol activities in those years.

Furthermore, the variation in p_t is used to convert the A series on total apprehensions into an F series on an estimated undocumented flow by applying equation (5.2). If the p_t series possessed considerable noise or other nonsystematic variation, these limitations would be transmitted to the F series, and we would then not expect to find systematic relations between the undocumented flow and explanatory variables. The fact that these systematic relations have been found in table 5.4 and that, as noted below, they are generally *stronger* than corresponding regression coefficients in equations relying on apprehensions as the dependent variable lends additional credibility to the underlying repeater data.

The results presented in this chapter are most directly comparable with those given by White et al. (forthcoming), who examine the determinants of linewatch apprehensions at the southern U.S. border between January 1977 and September 1988, the same time period used here, with a similar set of explanatory variables. The signs of the regression coefficients, their levels of statistical significance, and even in some cases the magnitudes of the estimated coefficients are remarkably similar in the two analyses. For example, an increase of 1 million persons in the Mexican population between 15 and 34 years of age is estimated to raise the flow of undocumented migrants by 5.0 percent and the number of linewatch apprehensions by 4.8 percent. Likewise, an increase of one unit in the ratio between U.S. and Mexican unemployment rates lowers the illegal flow by 13.7 percent and the number of linewatch apprehensions by 12.3 percent.

In most instances, however, using the estimated flow of undocumented workers as a dependent variable instead of the number of linewatch apprehensions of illegal migrants amplifies the magnitudes of the explanatory variables' effects. For example, according to table 5.4, the month of March is typically associated with an increase of 107 percent over the previous December figure in the number of arriving undocumented migrants. The March effect on linewatch apprehensions is 72 percent. Moreover, the POSTIRCA effect on the flow of illegal immigrants is a negative 48.6 percent versus a negative 27.0 percent in the case of linewatch apprehensions. Finally, the YEAR2 influence is much stronger when the dependent variable is the undocumented flow rather than the number of apprehensions—36.6 and 7.2 percent, respectively.

White et al. (forthcoming), also examine what their results imply about the impact of IRCA on changes in the number of illegal border crossings. IRCA can affect illegal border crossings in two ways: (1) through the SAW program by reducing the population at risk of migrating in undocumented status and (2) by lowering the propensity of the at-risk population to migrate illegally. These two channels of effects accounted for a reduction of 618,000 in the number of line-watch apprehensions between November 1986 and September 1988. If one assumes that there is a 0.3 probability of being apprehended at the border, then the IRCA-related reduction in linewatch apprehensions in the 23-month post-IRCA period translates into a decline of 2.06 million in the flow of undocumented migrants (White et al., forthcoming). This estimate is about 16 percent less than the 2.44 million reduction implied by the repeated trials model.

In sum, evidence from a repeated trials model is broadly consistent with studies of the determinants of illegal alien apprehensions. Both point to the importance of the same demographic, economic, and policy variables in determining variations in the flow. But the results also suggest that reliance on proxy indicators rather than on direct estimates of the gross number of illegal migrants entering the United States each month may systematically understate the quantitative importance of both economic and policy determinants and under-estimate IRCA's impacts on the undocumented migrant flow.

Notes

This chapter is a revised version of a paper entitled, "If at First You Don't Succeed. . . : A Repeated Trials Model of Undocumented Migration to the United States," presented at the annual meeting of the Population Association of America, Toronto, May 3–5, 1990. Research for this project was conducted during summer 1989 when the author was a visiting scholar in the Statistics Division of the U.S. Immigration and Natural-ization Service. Support was also received from the Program for Research on Immi-gration Policy, a program of public policy research on immigration being carried out jointly by The Urban Institute and the RAND Corporation. Core support for the pro-gram is provided by the Ford Foundation. Conversations with Frank D. Bean, Michael D. Hoefer, Denise Hopkins, Lorenzo Moreno, Jeffrey S. Passel, Germán Rodríguez, Robert Warren, and Michael J. White; the comments of seminar participants at the University of North Carolina at Chapel Hill, the U.S. Immigration and Naturalization Service, and The Urban Institute; and the technical assistance of Robert F. Dymowski and Diane Van Houten are all gratefully acknowledged.

1. The U.S. border with Mexico consists of nine Border Patrol sectors stretching 1,900 miles from San Diego in the west to McAllen, Texas on the Gulf of Mexico. The length of a Border Patrol sector often bears little relation to its importance as an illegal alien crossing point. San Diego is the shortest of all sectors (66 miles), yet it records over 40 percent of all apprehensions along the southern border. And although the Marfa sector is the longest on the southern border (365 miles), it registers the fewest apprehensions. As an exceptional example, the Chula Vista Border Patrol station in the San Diego sector

covers only 1 mile of border, but it records more illegal alien apprehensions than any other station. One out of every seven apprehensions along the southern border arises in this one-mile strip (Federation for American Immigration Reform, 1989).

2. Information in this paragraph is summarized from Espenshade et al. (forthcoming).

3. Under current practice, the small number of non-Mexican and non-Canadian illegal aliens are generally flown back to the capitals of their home country. This interior repatriation has been shown to reduce substantially the chances of returning to the United States (U.S. Immigration and Naturalization Service, 1977).

4. The assumption that every member of every monthly cohort of illegal migrants will eventually be able to enter into the United States if he or she simply keeps on trying to bypass the INS contrasts with the approach taken by Todaro and Maruszko (1987), who assume that the "effective capture rate" is nonnegligible.

5. Further discussion of the quality of the repeater data and the resulting probability estimates is contained in the concluding section of this chapter.

6. The undocumented inflow in figure 5.1 reached a minimum of 62,800 in December 1977 and a maximum of 338,300 in February 1986. It is impossible using INS data alone to gauge the extent of the reverse flow back to Mexico. Borjas et al. (1987) show that a seasonal pattern in the flow is likely to have existed at least since 1958, but its shape has changed over time. Between 1967 and 1985, alien apprehensions reached a peak in March and a minimum in December of each year. The peaks were typically located much later, between July and October, however, in the 1958–64 period.

7. INS spokespersons argued their case, however, on the basis of data on the apprehensions and not on the actual flow of illegal immigrants.

8. The software package (SAS) used to calculate these estimates contains an autoregressive program that can compute estimates using one of four estimation methods: the default method—labeled Yule-Walker (YW); iterated YW; nonlinear least-squares (NLS); and maximum likelihood (ML). The default YW method is the fastest computationally and was used here (SAS Institute, 1984).

9. Data on the cyclical nature of total apprehensions are graphed in chapter four in this volume.

References

Alberro, José. 1982. "Commentary." In *The Gateway: U.S. Immigration Issues and Policies*, edited by B.R. Chiswick, 229–37. Washington, D.C.: American Enterprise Institute for Public Policy Research.

Bean, Frank D., Georges Vernez, and Charles B. Keely. 1989. *Opening and Closing the Doors: Evaluating Immigration Reform and Control*. Santa Monica, Calif., and Washington, D.C.: RAND and Urban Institute.

Bean, Frank D., Thomas J. Espenshade, Michael J. White, and Robert F. Dymowski. 1990. "Post-IRCA Changes in the Volume and Composition of Undocumented Migration to the United States: An Assessment Based on Apprehensions Data." In: *Undocumented Migration to the United States: IRCA and the Experience of the*

1980s, edited by Frank D. Bean, Barry Edmonston, and Jeffrey S. Passel. Washington, D.C.: The Urban Institute.

Blejer, Mario I., Harry G. Johnson, and Arturo C. Porzecanski. 1978. "An Analysis of the Economic Determinants of Legal and Illegal Mexican Migration to the United States." In Research in Population Economics: An Annual Compilation of Research, vol. 1, edited by J.L. Simon, 217–31. Greenwich, Conn.: JAI Press.

Borjas, George J., Richard B. Freeman, and Kevin Lang. 1987. "Undocumented Mexican-Born Workers in the U.S.: How Many, How Permanent?" Cambridge, Mass.: National Bureau for Economic Research.

Cornelius, Wayne A. Forthcoming. "Impacts of the 1986 U.S. Immigration Law on Emigration from Rural Mexican Sending Communities." Population and Development Review 15(4, Dec.).

Cornelius, Wayne A., and Juan Diez-Canedo. 1976. "Mexican Migration to the United States: The View from Rural Sending Communities." Cambridge, Mass.: Massachusetts Institute of Technology, Center for International Studies.

Davila, Alberto. 1986. "The Seasonality of Apprehensions of Undocumented Mexican Workers." International Migration Review 20(4, Winter): 986–91.

Dillin, John. 1986. "Illegal Aliens Flood across U.S. Border." Christian Science Monitor, Feb. 21.

Espenshade, Thomas J., Michael J. White, and Frank D. Bean. Forthcoming. "Patterns of Recent Illegal Migration to the United States." In Future Demographic Trends in Europe and North America, edited by Wolfgang Lutz. Laxenburg, Austria: International Institute for Applied Systems Analysis.

Federation for American Immigration Reform. 1989. Ten Steps to Securing America's Borders. Washington, D.C.: Federation for American Immigration Reform.

Fogel, Walter. 1982. "Twentieth-Century Mexican Migration to the United States." In The Gateway: U.S. Immigration Issues and Policies, edited by B.R. Chiswick, 193–221. Washington, D.C.: American Enterprise Institute for Public Policy Research.

Frisbie, Parker. 1975. "Illegal Migration from Mexico to the United States: A Longitudinal Analysis." International Migration Review 9(1, Spring): 3–13.

Jenkins, J. Craig. 1977. "Push/Pull in Recent Mexican Migration to the U.S.." International Migration Review 11(2, Summer): 178–89.

Levine, Daniel B., Kenneth Hill, and Robert Warren, eds. 1985. Immigration Statistics: A Story of Neglect. Washington, D.C.: National Academy Press.

Massey, Douglas S. 1988. "Economic Development and International Migration in Comparative Perspective." Population and Development eview 14(3, Sept.): 383–413.

Massey, Douglas S., Rafael Alarcón, Jorge Durand, and Humberto González.

1987. *Return to Aztlan: The Social Process of International Migration from Western Mexico.* Berkeley and Los Angeles: University of California Press.

Mathews, Jay. 1988. "Using Fake Papers, Migrants Skirt Law." *Washington Post*, Nov. 3, Sec. A, p. 3.

Passel, Jeffrey S., and Karen A. Woodrow. 1987. "Change in the Undocumented Alien Population in the United States, 1979–1983." *International Migration Review* 21(4): 1304–34.

Rohter, Larry. 1988. "Immigration Law is Failing to Cut Flow from Mexico." *New York Times*, June 24, p. A1, A6.

SAS Institute, Inc. 1984. *SAS/ETS User's Guide, Version 5 Edition.* Cary, N.C.: SAS Institute.

Taylor, J. Edward, and Thomas J. Espenshade. 1987. "Foreign and Undocumented Workers in California Agriculture." *Population Research and Policy Review* 6(3): 223–39.

Todaro, Michael P., and Lydia Maruszko. 1987. "Illegal Migration and U.S. Immigration Reform: A Conceptual Framework." *Population and Development Review* 13(1, Mar.): 101–114.

U.S. Bureau of the Census. 1989. "Population Growth in the United States." In *The President's Comprehensive Triennial Report on Immigration.* Washington, D.C.: U.S. Immigration and Naturalization Service, January.

U.S. Immigration and Naturalization Service. 1977. *An Evaluation of the Cost Effectiveness of Repatriating Aliens to the Interior of Mexico.* Washington, D.C.: U.S. Immigration and Naturalization Service, Office of Plans and Analysis, July.

U.S. Immigration and Naturalization Service. 1989. "International Migration to the United States." In *The President's Comprehensive Triennial Report on Immigration.* Washington, D.C.: U.S. Immigration and Naturalization Service, January.

Vialet, Joyce. 1989. "Brief History of United States Immigration Policy." *Immigration and Nationality Act (as amended through January 1, 1989) with Notes and Related Laws.* Committee on the Judiciary of the House of Representatives, Committee Print, April 1989, 101st Cong., 1st sess., serial no. 2, 8th ed., 413–33. Washington, D.C.: U.S. Government Printing Office.

White, Michael J., Frank D. Bean, and Thomas J. Espenshade. Forthcoming. "The U.S. 1986 Immigration Reform and Control Act and Undocumented Migration to the United States." *Population Research and Policy Review.*

Woodrow, Karen A., Jeffrey S. Passel, and Robert Warren. 1987. "Preliminary Estimates of Undocumented Immigration to the United States, 1980–86: Analysis of the June 1986 Current Population Survey." In *Proceedings of the Social Statistics Section of the American Statistical Association.* Washington, D.C.: American Statistical Association.

Chapter Six

EFFECTS OF THE IMMIGRATION REFORM AND CONTROL ACT OF 1986: PRELIMINARY DATA FROM MEXICO

Douglas S. Massey, Katherine M. Donato, and Zai Liang

The 1986 Immigration Reform and Control Act (IRCA) has been called "the most sweeping revision of the nation's immigration laws since 1965" (Goodis, 1986: 1). Although the bill is complex and balances many competing interests, its main purpose was to curb the flow of undocumented migrants into the United States. To accomplish this goal, it enacted penalties against employers who knowingly hire undocumented workers and allocated additional resources to the U.S. Immigration and Naturalization Service for border enforcement (Espenshade et al., 1990).

IRCA's employer sanctions require employers and job applicants to fill out an I-9 form, on which employers state that they have seen one or more documents that confirm the applicant's right to work. On this form the applicant also pledges that he is eligible to work in the United States. Employers do not have to authenticate the documents or file the I-9 form with the government; they simply keep a copy of the form for three years, or for one year after the employee leaves. Employers who do not complete and retain the form may be fined from $100 to $1,000 for each offense, and those who knowingly hire undocumented workers may be fined from $250 to $2,000 per alien for the first offense; $2,000 to $5,000 per alien for the second offense; and $3,000 to $10,000 per alien for the third offense. Employers convicted of a "pattern and practice" of hiring undocumented aliens may be imprisoned for up to six months and fined another $3,000 per alien (Goodis, 1986).

The IRCA legislation authorized a supplement of $422 million to the U.S. Immigration and Naturalization Service (INS) to increase border enforcement in 1987, followed by an additional $419 million in 1988; these initiatives were intended to increase U.S. Border Patrol personnel by 50 percent. The bill also set aside $35 million in contingency funds for use in "immigration emergencies" (Goodis, 1986). As a result of these measures, the number of linewatch hours along the Mexico-U.S. border increased markedly during 1987 and 1988 (White, Bean, and Espenshade, 1989).

These measures to deter undocumented migration were accompanied by others intended to deal humanely with illegal aliens already in the United States, and to assuage growers' fears that IRCA would disrupt their labor supply (Espenshade et al., 1990; Martin and Taylor, 1988). In recognition of the legitimate claims of many long-term undocumented aliens for U.S. residence, IRCA offered a general amnesty for those able to demonstrate continuous residence in the United States after January 1, 1982. These former undocumented aliens received Temporary Worker Cards and after one year could apply for permanent resident status; but they were barred from all public cash assistance programs for five years after legalization (Martin and Taylor, 1988). About 1.7 million persons applied for the general amnesty, 87 percent of them Mexican (Hoefer, 1989).

To mollify growers, the new law also established the Special Agricultural Workers, or SAW, program. Although formally a part of IRCA's amnesty, the SAW program is essentially a temporary worker program whose explicit purposes are to facilitate the widespread entry of Mexicans into the United States for seasonal farm labor and to encourage return migration rather than permanent settlement. To qualify for the SAW amnesty, workers had to prove that they had performed at least 90 days of farm labor in the United States during each of the three previous years (1984 to 1986). Also those who worked for 90 days or more in agriculture in 1986 could qualify for temporary status and obtain permanent residence after two years. SAW participants were then issued Temporary Worker Cards, but were prohibited from applying for permanent resident aliens for three years. Moreover, unlike individuals in the general amnesty, SAW participants could leave and enter the United States freely during their time in temporary status, and were eligible to receive food stamps and some Medicaid benefits. SAW recipients were not required to demonstrate proficiency in English or to show a knowledge of U.S. history, both of which are requirements of the general amnesty program (Martin and Taylor, 1988). Although the U.S. Congress anticipated only about 350,000 applicants under the SAW provisions, some 1.2 million workers eventually applied, with about 83 percent coming from Mexico (Martin and Taylor, 1988; Hoefer, 1989).

This chapter takes advantage of two unique datasets to evaluate the impact of IRCA's amnesty and enforcement provisions. The first dataset is a survey of two Mexican communities conducted in the winter of 1987–88, during the initial phase of IRCA's implementation. Using retrospective data on U.S. migration, we computed the annual probability of making an undocumented trip to the United States, to discern whether IRCA has had any impact in deterring illegal migration. We also made use of detailed information on the conditions of border-crossing, in an effort to detect the impact of IRCA's tougher enforcement measures.

The second dataset was compiled from an earlier survey of four Mexican communities conducted during the winter of 1982–83. Although this survey cannot be used to assess the impact of IRCA directly, it provides detailed information on the use of U.S. social services by documented and undocumented migrants. By estimating multivariate models to predict the probability of using various social services, and including legal status as an explanatory variable, we infer the likely long-term impact that legalization will have on the demand for U.S. social services as a result of the amnesty.

Our results suggest that IRCA has not deterred Mexicans from entering the United States illegally, and has not greatly increased the difficulty of crossing the U.S.-Mexican border without documents. Moreover, our models indicate that legal status is the most powerful predictor of service utilization among Mexican migrants to the United States, and that by giving legal papers to a large number of relatively poor, uneducated people, IRCA's amnesty could significantly increase the demand for U.S. social services.

The following section describes the data sources used in the analysis and discusses the weaknesses inherent in evaluating policy changes so soon after their implementation. We then conduct a systematic analysis of undocumented migration before and after IRCA, followed by a parallel analysis of the cost and difficulty of illegal border-crossing. The next section examines service utilization that attempts to measure the impact of legal status on service usage net of other confounding factors. A short conclusion considers the lessons to be gleaned from this preliminary analysis of Mexican survey data and suggests areas for future research.

DATA SOURCES

The effect of IRCA's employer sanctions and border enforcement measures are assessed in this chapter using data obtained from two surveys conducted in 1987–88, the year after IRCA's passage, as part of a larger analysis of Mexican migration to the United States. Starting in 1987 several communities have been studied annually using a combination of survey and ethnographic methods. During a five-year period a multilevel data file containing individual, household, and community-level information will be constructed. The data file will contain information on over 5,000 households located in at least 25 communities, and is anticipated to cover some 3,000 persons with U.S. migrant experience, both legal and illegal.

The present data come from two surveys of Mexican communities conducted during the first year of this larger project. The first community is San Francisco del Rincón, a small city of about 70,000 inhabitants, and the second is León, Mexico's sixth largest urban area (with a population of just over 1 million). Both are located in the state of Guanajuato, a primary source of migration to the United States (Dagodag, 1975; North and Houstoun, 1976). Although agriculture still dominated the economy of San Francisco del Rincón as late as 1970, the community experienced strong industrial growth thereafter and today houses many small factories and workshops manufacturing shoes, hats, clothes, and leather goods. León is similarly an important center for nondurable goods manufacture, and is famous throughout western Mexico for its shoes and leather apparel. Both communities also contain large commercial and construction sectors.

Since it is impossible to conduct an in-depth ethnographic survey of an entire metropolitan area, the study focused on specific working class neighborhoods in each place. In San Francisco del Rincón, a working-class neighborhood of 780 dwellings was demarcated and within it a representative sample of 200 households was selected, yielding a sampling fraction of .256. A similar neighborhood of 997 dwellings was identified in León and another sample of 200 questionnaires was administered, producing a sampling fraction of .232. Nonresponse was more of a problem in León, owing to suspicions aroused by urban politics and the upcoming presidential elections; the response rate was only 88 percent in León compared to 97 percent in San Francisco del Rincón. Whenever a refusal or vacant dwelling was encountered, another household was selected randomly and incorporated into the sample to reach the desired sample size of 200 households.

The sample was gathered from December through February in 1987–88, a time of year when seasonal migrants are most likely to be in Mexico. Thus, we have complete reports on migratory behavior during 1987, but in most cases little information on 1988. Moreover, this analysis is based on data gathered from migrants who had returned to Mexico by the end of 1987, excluding those who have settled abroad. Although the study will eventually include interviews with out-migrants who live in the United States, these data were not available in machine-readable form at the time of this analysis. The age-period-cohort analyses we report here therefore underestimate the likelihood of migration to the United States. This bias can be expected to increase as one moves from the past to the present, since those who left recently are most likely to be in the United States at the survey date. Thus, to the extent that the likelihood of illegal migration is expected to decline after IRCA's passage in 1987, the bias is conservative.

The questionnaire was applied using ethnosurvey methods (elaborated in Massey, 1987a) and was modelled on a format used in an earlier study of four Mexican migrant communities (briefly discussed here and covered in detail in Massey et al., 1987). The questionnaire had three sections. The first collected basic social, demographic, and economic information on all household members, including whether or not each person had ever migrated to the United States. All migrants were asked a series of questions about their first and most recent trips to the United States, including the date, duration, destination, occupation, wage, and documentation. In the second phase, a life history was compiled for all household heads, focusing on histories of marriage, fertility, employment, business ownership, and property ownership. Finally, in the third phase, all household heads with experience in the United States were asked about their border-crossing activities and their experiences during the last U.S. trip.

Our analysis of IRCA's impact on undocumented migration draws on data about migrants' first trip to the United States and their experience crossing the U.S. border. Using the technique of age-period-cohort analysis, we estimate probabilities of making a first trip to the United States by year, focusing on the period from 1975 to the present. Likewise, from the border-crossing questions we tabulate information on the number of apprehensions and the cost of being smuggled across the border over the same time period.

The period 1975 to 1988 can be divided into three distinct phases corresponding to different sets of conditions in Mexico and the United States. The first phase, from 1975 to 1982, corresponds to an era of economic growth in Mexico and stagflation in the United States; the second phase, from 1983 through 1986, represents an era of deepening economic crisis and hyperinflation in Mexico but economic growth and recovery in the United States; the third phase covers the years 1987 and 1988, which correspond to the post-IRCA period when employer sanctions and stronger border enforcement were being phased in within the United States.

During the first period (1975–82), therefore, conditions generally predicted relatively low rates of out-migration to the United States and low costs of border-crossing, followed in the second period (1983– 86) by rising rates of out-migration and escalating costs of illegal entry (as the demand for U.S. entry grows). If IRCA has had any impact at all, we expected to see a reversal, or at least a dampening of illegal out- migration during the third phase, in 1987 and 1988, and a further rise in the costs of illegal entry.

This period-by-period analysis represents a classic time series experiment (see Campbell and Stanley, 1966) in which a base trend of performance is established, some policy change is introduced, and changes in the trend are then documented and attributed to the new policy. In this case, the trend can be established over the periods 1975–82 and 1983–86, and the effects noted in the years 1987 and 1988. The major threat to the internal validity of any time-series study, of course, is the confounding of experimental variables (e.g., the implementation of IRCA) with other concurrent events that represent extraneous sources of variation (e.g., the Mexican political crisis). That is, even if we discern a clear break in the trend of illegal out-migration following IRCA's passage in 1986, this trend may be attributed to other historical changes that occurred about the same time (such as the political instability that followed the Mexican presidential elections). Competing explanations may be dismissed as less plausible, but they cannot be eliminated by design.

The interpretability of results in a time-series experiment depends primarily on the number and stability of data points before and after the experimental manipulation, in this case, the implementation of IRCA. Although we have ample information prior to IRCA's implementation, the inclusion of only two data points subsequent to IRCA (in addition, the data for 1988 only partially cover the first two months of that year) represents a major design flaw, but one that is intrinsic to any attempt to evaluate the impact of a policy so soon after its implementation.

Possible long-term impacts of IRCA's legalization program were assessed by us using extant data gathered from four Mexican migrant communities during 1982–83. These data have been reported in detail elsewhere and are described only briefly here (see Massey, 1985, 1986, 1987a; Massey et al., 1987). The four samples include two urban and two rural communities located in the states of Michoacán and Jalisco, Mexico's two other major migrant-sending states (Dagodag, 1975). One rural community was a traditional agrarian town of small landholders, and the other was a commercialized farming center of landless day laborers. Of the two urban communities, one was a factory town just south of Guadalajara, and the other was a working-class neighborhood of Guadalajara itself.

Using ethnosurvey methods, a simple random sample of 200 households within each community was interviewed during the winter of 1982–83. These community samples were followed by a nonrandom survey of some 60 out-migrant households residing in the United States. The questionnaire was similar to that described previously, and the data for our analysis came from the third phase (1987 and 1988), which asked detailed questions about use of social services in the United States. Prior work with these data has established that undocumented migrants are very unlikely to draw upon U.S. social welfare programs such as food stamps, the Aid to Families with Dependent Children (AFDC) program, or unemployment composition, but that the propensity to use these services increases with U.S. experience and rises greatly with the acquisition of legal documents (Massey, 1985; Massey et al., 1987).

These results, however, were based only on simple cross-tabulations and did not control for a variety of confounding factors that might affect the likelihood of service utilization, such as age, occupation, education, and family composition (see Blau, 1984; Simon, 1984; Tienda and Jensen, 1986; Jensen, 1988; Borjas and Trejo, 1989). In the present analysis, we specify and then estimate a multivariate model of service utilization for documented and undocumented migrants from the four sample communities, controlling for confounding variables and including legal status as an explicit explanatory variable. By comparing probabilities of service utilization between documented and undocumented migrants, we can infer the impact that IRCA's legalization will have on future demand for social services in the United States.

SHORT-TERM IMPACT ON UNDOCUMENTED MIGRATION

IRCA's primary purpose, of course, was to reduce the flow of undocumented migrants into the United States; and in the months subsequent to its passage, reports in the media made much of sharp declines in the number of border apprehensions, heralding these as harbingers of the law's impact. After rising to a peak during the summer of 1986, apprehensions fell precipitously through the fall of 1986, when IRCA was passed, and remained low during the ensuing year. The number of apprehensions for 1987 was 31 percent below the figure for 1986 (U.S. Immigration and Naturalization Service, 1988). Apprehensions per shift fell from a high of 4.0 in the 12 months immediately prior to IRCA's passage to 2.8 during the year immediately following it (Espenshade et al., 1990).

It is very difficult to interpret these trends, however, much less to attribute them to IRCA. The limitations of apprehensions statistics as indicators of undocumented migration are well-known (see Levine, Hill, and Warren, 1985); but even if we accept them as rough indicators of the gross undocumented migration, they do not provide a good test of IRCA's enforcement impact. The problem is that the level of undocumented migration within any year reflects several distinct processes: (1) the propensity for those without prior U.S. experience to attempt a first illegal entry; (2) the propensity of experienced migrants to attempt an additional undocumented trip; and (3) the propensity for undocumented migrants based in the United States to circulate back and forth.

To a considerable extent, the falloff in apprehensions indicates a change in the third component. IRCA gave legal documents to nearly 3 million people, some of whom would have circulated in and out as undocumented migrants and in so doing, would have been apprehended. Legalizing these persons effectively removed from the undocumented flow, undoubtedly accounting for a large part of the drop in border apprehensions. Of greater interest in evaluating the impact of IRCA's enforcement measures is whether it affected the first two components of the migration process—namely, the propensity for Mexicans to undertake new and repeat trips; however, these quantities are unknowable from apprehensions statistics.

This analysis focuses on the first component of the migration process—the propensity for Mexicans without prior U.S. experience to undertake an initial trip to the United States. Using retrospective data gathered from males in San Francisco del Rincón and León, we estimated the probability of undertaking a first trip to the United States using the technique of age-period-cohort analysis (Mason et al., 1973, 1976). Employing a discrete- time approach that takes person-years as units of observation (Fineberg and Mason, 1978; Allison, 1982, 1984), we began at birth and coded each year of a man's life as 0 if he had never migrated and 1 if he migrated for the first time in that year. All years subsequent to the one in which he first migrated were excluded.

Probabilities may be estimated using a maximum-likelihood logit procedure that regresses this 0–1 variable on dummies for age, period, and birth cohort. Such a model is underidentified unless one makes some a priori restrictions on the parameters (since by knowing age and period one can logically derive cohort). Fortunately, the characteristic age-curve of migration makes this task straightforward; initial specifications of the model assumed constant migration rates below age 20 and above 40, with five-year age intervals in between. Period was specified in terms of 17 dummy variables: 1945–54 (roughly the first half of the U.S.-sponsored Bracero Program), 1955–64 (the second half of the program), 1965–74 (the period immediately after the 1965 amendments to the U.S. Immigration and Nationality Act), and single years from 1975 through 1988 (which establish trends before and after IRCA); years prior to 1945 comprise the reference period. As in earlier studies of Mexican migration, the cohort coefficients proved insignificant in early specifications of the model and were eliminated; technical details about the model are discussed at length in Massey (1985).

Results of the age-period analysis for San Francisco del Rincón are presented in table 6.1. The columns on the left show coefficients for an equation estimating the probability of migrating to the United States in any legal status, and those on the right show coefficients estimating the probability of migrating to the United States without documents. Given that the vast majority of migrants were undocumented, the equations are quite similar and interpretation focuses on undocumented migration, which was the primary target of IRCA's enforcement measures.

The coefficients for age behave in expected fashion, with a peak value in the interval 20–24 (.888), falling gradually through ages 25–29 (.540) and 30–34 (.302) before becoming progressively negative across intervals 35–39 (−.042) and 40+ (−.841). The period measures display a series of peaks and valleys that correspond to increases and decreases in the propensity to migrate illegally to the United States during the period 1975 to 1988. Peaks occurred during the years 1975, 1980, and 1987, and valleys in the years 1977 and 1984, but the probability of illegal out-migration was generally quite high after 1977.

Although estimates of coefficients and standard errors are within acceptable bounds and appear to be relatively stable, the estimate of the intercept is both large and unreliable. The standard error is quite large compared to the estimate itself, and the intercept is not statistically different from 0 (in the undocumented migration model it is

Table 6.1 AGE-PERIOD ANALYSIS OF THE PROBABILITY THAT MALES WILL
LEAVE SAN FRANCISCO DEL RINCÓN, GUANAJUATO, ON A FIRST
TRIP TO THE UNITED STATES

Age and Period	Any U.S. Migration			Undocumented Migration		
	B	SE	p	B	SE	p
Age						
Less than 20 years	—a	—	—	—	—	—
20–24 years	0.876**	0.086	0.000	0.888**	0.094	0.000
25–29 years	0.575**	0.113	0.000	0.540**	0.125	0.000
30–34 years	0.431**	0.140	0.002	0.302*	0.166	0.069
35–39 years	0.245	0.188	0.193	−0.042	0.260	0.873
40+ years	−0.179	0.188	0.342	−0.841**	0.360	0.020
Period						
Before 1945	—	—	—	—	—	—
1945–54	0.387*	0.204	0.058	0.102	0.336	0.762
1955–64	0.009	0.215	0.966	−0.212	0.336	0.528
1965–74	0.115	0.191	0.547	0.208	0.274	0.446
1975	0.511**	0.245	0.038	0.785**	0.308	0.011
1976	0.233	0.281	0.408	0.503	0.337	0.136
1977	−0.585	0.528	0.268	−0.312	0.560	0.578
1978	0.496**	0.238	0.048	0.769**	0.303	0.011
1979	0.596**	0.228	0.009	0.823**	0.298	0.006
1980	0.747**	0.214	0.001	1.025**	0.284	0.000
1981	0.499**	0.238	0.036	0.780**	0.302	0.010
1982	0.360	0.255	0.158	0.640**	0.316	0.043
1983	0.486**	0.239	0.042	0.640**	0.316	0.043
1984	0.281	0.266	0.291	0.565*	0.325	0.082
1985	0.592**	0.227	0.009	0.831**	0.298	0.005
1986	0.424*	0.246	0.084	0.646*	0.316	0.041
1987	0.861**	0.206	0.000	1.125**	0.279	0.000
1988	0.591**	0.228	0.010	0.885**	0.295	0.003
Intercept	−2.743	2.642	0.299	−4.367	3.875	0.260
Chi-square	90.610**			83.580**		
Person-years	20,701			19,532		

a. Dash (—) = excluded category.
* $p < .10$.
** $p < .05$.

−4.367 with a standard error of 3.876, yielding a p-value of .260).
This result suggests that the intercept is not readily estimable from
the data. Since this term is quite large relative to other coefficients
in the model, it will have a sizable impact in estimating specific
probabilities of U.S. migration and must be interpreted with some
caution.

Given the oscillation of yearly migration probabilities before IRCA's passage in 1986 and the presence of only two data points afterward, it is difficult to draw any firm conclusions about the impact of IRCA, but there is certainly no evidence that it had any impact in reducing the likelihood of illegal out-migration from San Francisco del Rincón. The year after IRCA's passage, 1987, showed the highest probability of out-migration in any year since 1975, and the probability of migration during 1988 was also very high, even though it was a severely truncated period (i.e., data were only collected during the first two months of that year).

Table 6.2 presents the results of another age-period analysis that incorporates the data from León. Out-migration from this large metropolitan area was less frequent than from San Francisco del Rincón. A few periods lacked any reported migration at all and the outcome variable was quite skewed, creating problems for maximum likelihood estimation. We therefore pooled the León data with the San Francisco data and estimated a single age-period model for this combined sample.

The age and period coefficients essentially replicate the pattern observed for San Francisco alone. The age coefficients are virtually identical except for the oldest age interval, and the period coefficients show the same pattern of peaks and valleys. The period coefficients from the combined sample, however, are universally lower than those from San Francisco, reflecting the generally lower probability of out-migration from León. As in the earlier model, the intercept (.263) carries a very large standard error (2.967) and is not significantly different from 0, but it is opposite in sign from the earlier estimate.

In spite of the difficulty in reliably estimating the intercept, both models reveal the most significant period for undocumented migration to be 1987, the year after IRCA; and in both cases, 1988 also displayed a high probability of migration even though it only included two months of exposure to the risk of migration. In other words, based on the time trend displayed by the period coefficients, we reached the same conclusion from both models: there is little evidence that IRCA has deterred undocumented Mexican migration to the United States.

Table 6.3 provides a more concrete illustration of the relative magnitude of out-migration before and after IRCA, by showing predicted migration probabilities for years from 1975 to 1988, calculated using the equation estimates in tables 6.1 and 6.2. For each model, the table presents the predicted probability that a male aged 20–24 left on a first trip to the United States without documents between 1975

194   *Undocumented Migration to the United States*

Table 6.2 AGE-PERIOD ANALYSIS OF THE PROBABILITY THAT MALES WILL
LEAVE EITHER SAN FRANCISCO DEL RICÓN OR LEÓN,
GUANAJUATO, ON A FIRST TRIP TO THE UNITED STATES

Age and Period	Any U.S. Migration			Undocumented Migration		
	B	SE	p	B	SE	p
Age						
Less than 20 years	—[a]	—	—	—	—	—
20–24 years	0.755**	0.078	0.000	0.803**	0.088	0.000
25–29 years	0.571**	0.097	0.000	0.554**	0.116	0.000
30–34 years	0.415**	0.124	0.001	0.312**	0.152	0.040
35–39 years	0.295*	0.160	0.066	0.012	0.232	0.959
40+ years	0.049	0.137	0.718	−0.358*	0.214	0.094
Period						
Before 1945	—	—	—	—	—	—
1945–54	0.075	0.164	0.648	−0.243	0.293	0.407
1955–64	−0.372**	0.178	0.037	−0.473*	0.279	0.089
1965–74	−0.098	0.144	0.499	0.071	0.211	0.737
1975	0.266	0.195	0.174	0.416*	0.261	0.083
1976	0.072	0.216	0.741	0.270	0.280	0.334
1977	−0.986*	0.514	0.055	−0.642	0.535	0.230
1978	0.189	0.195	0.335	0.483*	0.248	0.052
1979	0.340*	0.179	0.057	0.649**	0.233	0.005
1980	0.521**	0.164	0.002	0.703**	0.229	0.002
1981	0.123	0.201	0.541	0.470*	0.248	0.058
1982	−0.083	0.226	0.723	0.266	0.269	0.324
1983	0.095	0.202	0.639	0.331	0.261	0.204
1984	−0.032	0.217	0.882	0.250	0.269	0.352
1985	0.276	0.180	0.125	0.472*	0.244	0.053
1986	0.059	0.201	0.769	0.298	0.261	0.253
1987	0.435**	0.166	0.008	0.766**	0.222	0.001
1988	0.227	0.183	0.215	0.548**	0.237	0.021
Intercept	2.429	1.980	0.219	0.263	2.967	0.929
Chi-square	118.100**			97.080**		
Person-years	40,241			38,365		

a. Dash (—) = excluded category.
* p < .10.
**p < .05.

and 1988 (generated by applying a one to the relevant coefficients
and zeros to all others), along with the cumulative probability that
a man will have migrated illegally by his 40th birthday, given the
migration rates prevailing in each period (generated by using predicted probabilities for each age interval, to construct a single dec-
rement life table, following Massey, 1985). In both cases, a three-
year moving average was computed to smooth year-to-year fluctuations.

Table 6.3 PREDICTED PROBABILITIES THAT A 20–24-YEAR-OLD MALE WILL MIGRATE ILLEGALLY TO THE UNITED STATES AND THAT A MALE WILL MIGRATE ILLEGALLY BY AGE 40 GIVEN PERIOD RATES: SAN FRANCISCO DEL RINCÓN AND LEÓN, GUANAJUATO, 1975–88

	Mexican Oil Boom								Economic Crisis				Post-IRCA	
	1975	'76	'77	'78	'79	'80	'81	'82	'83	'84	'85	'86	'87	'88
San Francisco del Rincón, Guanajuato														
Probability that male 20–24 will migrate illegally	.06	.05	.02	.06	.07	.08	.06	.06	.06	.05	.07	.06	.09	.07
Three-year moving average	.06	.04	.04	.05	.07	.07	.07	.06	.06	.06	.06	.07	.07	.08
Probability that male will migrate illegally by age 40	.18	.14	.07	.18	.19	.23	.18	.16	.16	.15	.19	.16	.25	.20
Three-year moving average	.16	.13	.13	.15	.20	.20	.19	.17	.16	.17	.17	.20	.20	.23
San Francisco del Rincón and León, Guanajuato														
Probability that male 20–24 will migrate illegally	.78	.75	.54	.78	.81	.82	.78	.74	.76	.74	.78	.75	.83	.79
Three-year moving average	.77	.69	.69	.71	.80	.80	.78	.76	.75	.76	.76	.79	.79	.81
Probability that male will migrate illegally by age 40	.99	.99	.94	.99	.99	.99	.99	.99	.99	.99	.99	.99	.99	.99
Three-year moving average	.99	.97	.97	.97	.99	.99	.99	.99	.99	.99	.99	.99	.99	.99

The instability of the intercept created major problems in estimating predicted probabilities. The model based on the San Francisco data yielded an estimated intercept of −4.367, whereas the combined datasets generated a figure of 0.263; neither was significantly different from 0. To be conservative in our estimates, we used the large negative intercept to compute migration probabilities from San Francisco, and assumed the intercept to be 0 in predicting migration probabilities using the combined sample.

As one would expect, shifting the constant from −4.367 to 0 had a very strong impact on predicted out-migration probabilities. In San Francisco, the estimated probability that a 20–24-year-old-male will migrate to the United States fluctuated between .02 and .09, yielding lifetime migration probabilities (i.e., cumulative probabilities by age 40) ranging from .07 to .25. In contrast, when the same probabilities were estimated from the combined sample, the figures varied from .54 to .83, yielding lifetime migration probabilities that approached 1.0. Given the lack of statistical significance of any of the estimated intercepts, the most appropriate assumption about the intercept was that it is 0. If this assumption is correct, then the probability of out-migration from Mexico was very high both before and after IRCA.

No matter what the specific level of assumed out-migration, however, in each case the smoothed probabilities depicted a rising trend in the likelihood of illegal out-migration from 1976 to 1980, followed by a slight decline and a leveling-off between 1981 and 1985, and then a resumption of the upward trend in 1986, 1987, and 1988. The unsmoothed probabilities indicated that in 1987, the year after IRCA's passage, when its tougher enforcement measures were being implemented, the probability of out-migration to the United States reached a 15-year peak. Assuming a very low intercept, the probability of out-migration among 20 year-olds reached .09, and assuming an intercept of 0, then it reached .83. The lifetime migration probabilities range from .25 to nearly 1.0.

Whatever the true level of out-migration, preliminary figures from two Mexican communities suggest that IRCA did not have a significant impact in discouraging undocumented migration to the United States. In the year after its passage, rates of out-migration were higher than at any time during the past decade, and this upward trend appeared to continue into 1988. If IRCA had any impact at all, it was to keep migration probabilities from rising higher than they might otherwise have done, which is a very weak outcome and clearly not what the U.S. Congress intended.

This conclusion is reinforced by limited information we gathered on illegal border-crossings into the United States. In the questionnaire, undocumented migrant household heads were asked about the methods they used to gain entry to the United States, the number of times they were apprehended, and the amount they paid to "coyotes" (smugglers) to transport them across the frontier. If tighter border enforcement were really making itself felt, we would expect the use of coyotes to increase, since they are specialists in the trafficking of human cargo and are in a better position to guarantee successful arrival. We might also expect an increase in the number of apprehensions and an inflation of their fees, as demand for coyotes increases in the face of greater risks.

Although small numbers of cases require some caution in drawing conclusions, the data in table 6.4 suggest that the cost and difficulty of crossing the border did not increase measurably after 1986. Whereas migrants were more likely to use a coyote in attempting a crossing (with the proportion using a coyote jumping from 70 percent before

Table 6.4 METHOD THAT UNDOCUMENTED MIGRANTS USED TO CROSS THE U.S.-MEXICO BORDER, THE NUMBER OF APPREHENSIONS THEY EXPERIENCED, AND THE FEE PAID TO COYOTES, BY PERIOD, 1975–88: MIGRANTS FROM SAN FRANCISCO DEL RINCÓN AND LEÓN, GUANAJUATO

	Mexican Boom Years	Mexican Crisis Years	Post-IRCA Years
	1975–82	1983–86	1987–88
Method of U.S. Border-Crossing			
With coyote (%)	68.5	70.6	85.7
With family	9.5	0.0	0.0
With friends	12.5	11.8	0.0
With others	0.0	5.8	14.3
Alone	9.5	11.8	0.0
Number of Apprehensions			
0 (%)	71.9	70.6	100.0
1	15.6	17.6	0.0
2	12.5	0.0	0.0
3 +	0.0	11.8	0.0
Mean fee paid to coyote for crossing			
1988 dollars	330	285	303
Number of migrants	32	17	7

IRCA to 86 percent afterward), the cost of a coyote's services did not increase. In real terms, the cost of a coyote was $330 during the years 1975–82, falling to $285 in 1983–86, and increasing slightly to $303 during the years 1987–88. In other words, the cost of gaining entry to the United States after IRCA was below that which prevailed during the late 1970s. Across all periods, the most common figure cited by migrants for being smuggled across the U.S. border was $300, which was the average in 1987–88.

Thus, IRCA's only impact seems to have been that of increasing the efficiency of illegal entry. As undocumented migrants turned to coyotes in larger numbers, the proportion who reported at least one apprehension fell to 0 after fluctuating around 30 percent during the years 1975–82 and 1983–86. Moreover, IRCA's tougher enforcement did not seem to deter those who were apprehended. Our survey found that the number of entries was *always* one greater than the number of apprehensions, a pattern so uniform that we eventually dropped the question on attempted entries from the questionnaire. In other words, our data suggest that statements such as "for every three undocumented migrants that are apprehended, one gets in" are meaningless (see Lesko Associates, 1975). According to our information, all migrants who attempt undocumented entry into the United States eventually get in, and IRCA has not changed this basic fact.

LONG-TERM IMPACT ON USE OF SOCIAL SERVICES

IRCA's second major policy component, aside from its tougher enforcement package, was the legalization of undocumented migrants with at least six years of continuous residence in the United States, or those who worked in U.S. agriculture during 1986. As a result of these amnesty programs, nearly 3 million former undocumented migrants achieved temporary legal status and the chance ultimately to become legal resident aliens. In establishing these amnesty programs, however, the U.S. Congress was mindful of the potential burden to states facing large numbers of newly eligible immigrants with strong needs for social services. It therefore prohibited the 1.7 million recipients of the general amnesty from receiving any form of cash assistance for five years after legalization; for the same period it restricted the 1.2 million SAW recipients to receiving food stamps and some Medicaid benefits and barred them from other cash assistance programs (Martin and Taylor, 1988; Espenshade et al., 1990).

Earlier work has established that undocumented workers are unlikely to use U.S. social services (see Massey and Schnabel, 1983)
but that the propensity to do so rises with time spent in the United
States (Blau, 1984; Massey, 1985; Tienda and Jensen, 1986; Jensen,
1988); it also increases greatly when migrants move from undocumented to documented status (Massey et al., 1987). Indirect evidence
furthermore suggests that recent cohorts of immigrants to the United
States are more prone to become dependent than earlier generations
of immigrants (Borjas and Trejo, 1989). In this section, therefore, we
consider the potential long-term impact of the legalization program
by estimating a multivariate model of lifetime service usage that
directly compares documented and undocumented migrants.

The survey asked 346 migrant male household heads whether they
had ever used four kinds of social services while in the United States:
AFDC, food stamps, unemployment compensation, and public education. We estimated the propensity to use these services as a function of migrants' basic social, demographic, and economic
characteristics. Our independent variables included age (coded into
four dummy variables corresponding to different intervals); occupation (four dummy variables corresponding to different occupational groups); education (two dummy variables indicating whether
or not the respondent had attended or finished primary school);
English language ability (1 if he understands English and 0 otherwise); rural origin (1 if rural, 0 otherwise), whether his spouse or
children were in the United States (1 if so, 0 otherwise); whether
other family members were in the United States (1 if so, 0 otherwise);
whether the respondent had children born in the United States (1 if
so, 0 otherwise); total years of U.S. migrant experience; years since
acquiring legal documents; period of first trip to the United States
(specified as a series of dummy variables corresponding to three
periods); and, of course, the main explanatory variable, legal status
(where 1 indicates a permanent resident alien and 0 otherwise).

Table 6.5 presents the results of logit models estimated to predict
the probability of ever receiving AFDC, food stamps, unemployment
compensation, or any one of the three. The dependent variable was
coded as 1 if migrants reported ever using the service and 0 otherwise; it was regressed on the independent variables just described,
using maximum likelihood techniques. These regressions generally
confirm the standard findings of earlier research. The propensity to
use social services is highest during younger ages and falls thereafter,
with the age coefficient becoming statistically negative after age 35;
it also tends to fall as education rises, although the effect of schooling

Table 6.5 LOGISTIC REGRESSION ANALYSIS OF THE PROBABILITY OF EVER USING SELECTED SOCIAL SERVICES: MIGRANTS FROM FOUR MEXICAN COMMUNITIES, 1982

Variable	AFDC		Food Stamps		Unemployment Compensation		Any Social Services	
	B	SE	B	SE	B	SE	B	SE
Age								
Less than 20 years	—ᵃ	—	—	—	—	—	—	—
20–24 years	-2.052	1.443	-1.268	1.058	-0.234	0.812	-0.683	0.761
25–29 years	-3.102*	1.660	-2.147	1.180	-0.051	0.806	-0.779	0.776
30–34 years	-1.434	1.438	-1.132	1.094	-0.528	0.921	-0.813	0.855
35+ years	-6.971**	2.457	-3.957**	1.397	-0.365	0.804	-1.109	0.773
Occupation								
Professional-technical	—	—	—	—	—	—	—	—
Skilled	-0.104	1.304	-0.260	0.946	0.646	0.729	1.254*	0.715
Unskilled	0.830	1.423	-1.518	1.326	0.216	0.814	0.254	0.803
Service	0.241	1.363	-1.979	1.333	-0.584	0.820	-0.650	0.837
Farmworker	0.246	1.356	-1.549	1.019	-0.612	0.682	-0.402	0.677
Education								
0 years	—	—	—	—	—	—	—	—
1–5 years	-1.335	1.118	-0.771	0.954	-0.379	0.628	-0.258	0.628
6+ years	-4.940**	1.781	-1.488	1.048	-0.911	0.720	-0.821	0.705
English Ability								
Understands English	0.141	1.145	-0.313	0.972	0.313	0.537	0.351	0.513
Origin								
Rural	-0.104	1.304	0.589	0.885	-0.259	0.552	0.030	0.533

Social Connections in United States								
Immediate family	0.079	0.131	0.160	0.111	0.028	0.071	0.016	0.072
Other family	0.011	0.029	−0.023	0.027	0.011	0.014	0.013	0.013
U.S.-born children	−0.216	1.054	0.212	0.977	2.440**	0.547	2.486**	0.561
Migrant Experience								
Years of U.S. experience	0.157**	0.061	0.105**	0.042	0.032	0.027	0.040	0.027
Years since documents acquired	−0.051	0.047	−0.099*	0.052	−0.006	0.025	−0.016	0.026
Legal Status								
Documented	4.693**	1.564	3.170**	1.150	1.696**	0.636	1.844**	0.633
Period of Trip								
Before 1960	—	—	—	—	—	—	—	—
1960–69	2.302	1.633	1.115	1.124	0.600	0.857	1.359	0.842
1970–79	3.269*	1.853	0.380	1.255	1.166	0.787	1.389*	0.813
1980–82	4.337**	1.984	1.324	1.318	1.065	0.868	1.389	0.893
Intercept	−7.040**	2.383	−2.907	1.409	−3.299**	1.103	−3.410**	1.095
Chi-square	44.800**		47.08**		159.700**		169.850**	
Number of migrants	346		346		346		346	

a. Dash (—) = excluded category.
* p < .10.
** p < .05.

is only significant in the AFDC model. Service usage is also directly related to the length of U.S. experience, an effect that is highly significant in the AFDC and food stamps models. There is also some evidence to support Borjas and Trejo's (1989) claim that recent immigrants are more likely to become dependent than earlier cohorts—the likelihood of using AFDC increases steadily across cohorts from the 1960s through the 1980s.

Other variables that were included as controls—occupation, rural origin, English language ability, and U.S. family connections—are generally not relevant in determining the likelihood of using U.S. social services, with the exception of having U.S.-born children, which strongly increases the likelihood of receiving unemployment compensation. The strongest variable across all models, however, is legal status. The acquisition of legal papers greatly increases the likelihood that a migrant will make use of U.S. social services, an effect that holds no matter how much time has elapsed since the documents were obtained (see the marginal and generally insignificant coefficients in table 6.5 for years since the documents were obtained).

Table 6.6 reaffirms the importance of legal status by showing estimates for equations predicting the propensity to send children to public schools in the United States. The columns on the left predict whether or not migrants had children in primary schools, and those on the right predict whether or not they had children in any school (primary, secondary, or university). Virtually the only significant variable in these models is legal status. Surprisingly, whether or not a migrant had children born in the United States has no impact on the likelihood of school usage, and years of U.S. experience has no strong effect.

Thus, legal status is the primary determinant of the propensity to use social services among Mexican migrants to the United States, at least in the four communities in our 1982–83 survey. These results strongly suggest that by conferring legal status on nearly 3 million former undocumented migrants, the ultimate burden to U.S. social service agencies will be significantly increased, despite the restrictions enacted by Congress.

Of course, migrants not only draw upon social services; they also contribute to the provision of those services through the payment of taxes. Table 6.7 therefore presents the results of an analysis of tax withholding, using the same set of predictor variables but changing the outcome to a dichotomous variable that equals 1 when the migrant reported having taxes deducted from his paycheck and 0 oth-

Table 6.6 LOGISTIC REGRESSION ANALYSIS OF THE PROBABILITY OF
HAVING CHILDREN IN U.S. SCHOOLS: MIGRANTS FROM FOUR
MEXICAN COMMUNITIES, 1982

	Primary School			Any U.S. School		
Variables	B	SE	p	B	SE	p
Age						
Less than 20 years	—[a]	—	—	—	—	—
20–24 years	0.943	1.292	0.465	0.431	1.033	0.676
25–29 years	0.891	1.347	0.508	−0.133	1.124	0.906
30–34 years	0.464	1.396	0.740	−0.613	1.175	0.602
35+ years	0.784	1.299	0.546	0.216	1.005	0.830
Occupation						
Professional-technical	—	—	—	—	—	—
Skilled	0.035	1.086	0.974	−0.357	1.012	0.724
Unskilled	−0.722	1.336	0.589	−0.125	1.138	0.913
Service	−0.024	1.133	0.983	−0.809	1.083	0.455
Farmworker	−0.785	1.048	0.454	−1.344	0.967	0.165
Education						
0 years	—	—	—	—	—	—
1–5 years	0.641	0.887	0.470	0.163	0.749	0.828
6+ years	1.207	1.058	0.254	0.873	0.948	0.357
Origin						
Rural	−0.529	0.642	0.409	−0.638	0.625	0.307
Social Connections						
in United States						
Immediate family	0.160	0.124	0.196	0.273**	0.117	0.019
Other family	−0.002	0.020	0.911	−0.006	0.021	0.779
U.S.-born children	−0.348	1.007	0.730	0.089	1.041	0.932
Migrant Experience						
Years of U.S.						
experience	0.067	0.042	0.111	0.076*	0.041	0.090
Years since						
documents acquired	−0.008	0.025	0.752	−0.037	0.027	0.173
Legal Status						
Documented	1.493**	0.740	0.044	2.370**	0.731	0.001
Period of Trip						
Before 1960	—	—	—	—	—	—
1960–69	−0.251	0.988	0.799	−1.146	0.936	0.221
1970–79	0.192	0.895	0.830	−0.402	0.811	0.620
1980–82	−0.947	1.117	0.397	−1.543	1.009	0.126
Intercept	−4.391**	1.714	0.010	−2.536*	1.326	0.056
Chi-square	36.220**			56.520**		
Number of migrants						
with children	272			272		

a. Dash (—) = excluded category.
*p <.10.
**p <.05.

Table 6.7 LOGISTIC REGRESSION ANALYSIS OF THE PROBABILITY OF
HAVING TAXES WITHHELD FROM PAYCHECK: MIGRANTS FROM
FOUR MEXICAN COMMUNITIES, 1982

Variables	B	SE	p
Age			
Less than 20 years	—[a]	—	—
20–24 years	1.176*	0.677	0.082
25–29 years	1.460**	0.696	0.036
30–34 years	3.078**	0.953	0.001
35+ years	1.059**	0.650	0.050
Occupation			
Professional-technical	—	—	—
Skilled	0.601	0.966	0.543
Unskilled	8.253	22.751	0.717
Service	−0.090	1.018	0.929
Farmworker	0.310	0.933	0.740
Education			
0 years	—	—	—
1–5 years	−0.624	0.509	0.220
6+ years	−0.636	0.673	0.345
Origin			
Rural	−1.432**	0.462	0.002
Social Connections in United States			
Immediate family	0.084	0.139	0.546
Other family	0.026	0.024	0.270
U.S.-born children	0.769	1.327	0.562
Migrant Experience			
Years of U.S. experience	0.054	0.052	0.300
Years since documents received	0.006	0.025	0.806
Legal Status			
Documented	−1.100	1.047	0.293
Period of Trip			
Before 1960	—	—	—
1960–69	0.869	0.588	0.139
1970–79	1.336**	0.545	0.014
1980–82	2.532**	0.943	0.007
Intercept	−0.331	1.133	0.770
Chi-squared	81.570**		
Number of migrants	333		

a. Dash (—) = excluded category.
*p <.10.
**p <.05.

erwise. The results of this analysis suggested that legal status is not a significant determinant of tax payment. The withholding of income taxes is determined primarily by age, rural origin, and period. Reported withholding increases with advancing age and has grown markedly in recent years; and migrants from rural areas are significantly less likely to have taxes withheld than those from urban areas. Legal status, however, had no significant impact on the probability of having taxes withheld once other factors were controlled. In general, the rate of tax withholding is very high among undocumented Mexican migrants (Massey, 1985, 1987b), and the model suggests that legalization will not significantly raise it (indeed, the coefficient, although not significant, is negative).

Thus, the tax contributions are unlikely to be altered by the amnesty, but rates of service utilization are likely to increase substantially. To get an idea of the magnitude of the ultimate demand, we used the equations in tables 6.5 and 6.6 to predict probabilities of ever using specific services. These probabilities, shown in table 6.8, were calculated by assuming the case of a rural origin male aged 30–34 with some primary education who began migrating during the 1970s, holds an unskilled occupation, and has immediate family in the United States, including U.S.-born children. To simulate the long-run impact of IRCA, we compared legal and undocumented migrants with the same characteristics, but we systematically varied the years of U.S. experience from 0 to 25 and assumed that all migrants obtained legal documents in year 5.

The probabilities predicted for illegal migrants indicate the level of service usage that might be expected in the absence of any legalization program. In the short run, the likelihood of ever using a U.S. social service is quite low among undocumented migrants. After 10 years of U.S. experience, the probability is .247 for AFDC, .019 for food stamps, .496 for unemployment, and .075 for public schools. After 20 years in the United States, these probabilities rise to .487, .020, .561, and .107, respectively. In the absence of an amnesty, then, the burden to U.S. social service agencies would not be especially large.

Legalization, however, changes the picture completely. After 10 years of U.S. experience, and 5 years after legalization, the probability of ever receiving AFDC is .973 for legal migrants, and the probabilities of using food stamps, unemployment compensation, and public schools are .318, .843, and .466, respectively. These probabilities are from 2 to 30 times higher than those for undocumented migrants with the same amount of U.S. experience. IRCA, of course, bars migrants from receiving AFDC and unemployment compensation for

Table 6.8 PREDICTED PROBABILITY OF USING SELECTED SOCIAL SERVICES BY YEARS OF U.S. EXPERIENCE AND YEARS SINCE RECEIVING DOCUMENTS: MIGRANTS FROM FOUR MEXICAN COMMUNITIES, 1982–83

Years of Experience in U.S.	Years Since Receiving Documents	AFDC		Foodstamps		Unemployment		Public Schools	
		Illegal	Legal	Illegal	Legal	Illegal	Legal	Illegal	Legal
0	0	0.081	0.906	0.011	0.211	0.425	0.801	0.044	0.329
5	0	0.162	0.955	0.019	0.311	0.463	0.825	0.063	0.418
10	5	0.247	0.973	0.019	0.318	0.496	0.843	0.075	0.466
15	10	0.359	0.984	0.020	0.324	0.528	0.859	0.090	0.514
20	15	0.487	0.990	0.020	0.331	0.561	0.874	0.107	0.562
25	20	0.618	0.994	0.021	0.337	0.592	0.888	0.127	0.610

Note: Predicted probabilities are for a rural origin migrant aged 30–34 with less than a primary education who began migrating during the 1970s, holds an unskilled job, and has immediate family in the United States, including U.S.-born children.

5 years, so the cumulative probabilities do not apply to them. But these high probabilities suggest that when the 5-year moratorium on service usage expires, there will be strong pent-up demand for services, which could significantly increase the burden on states.

SAW applicants are eligible for food stamps upon legalization, and all amnesty recipients can immediately send their children to U.S. public schools, so the predicted probabilities provide a direct simulation of their experience. If migrants receiving amnesty under the provisions of IRCA behave like Mexican migrants in our earlier samples, then legalization will translate into a much higher demand for education and food stamps in the short run. After five years of U.S. experience, some 30 percent of the SAW workers can be expected to have applied for food stamps, and 42 percent of all amnesty recipients will have children in U.S. public schools. Given that the number of amnesty recipients is in the millions and that they are highly concentrated in a few states (California has 55 percent, Texas 18 percent, and Illinois and New York 7 percent—see Hoefer, 1989), local demands for food stamps, public education, and Medicaid probably will soon increase as a result of IRCA, whereas the demand for AFDC and unemployment compensation can be expected to increase sharply after 1992, when the five-year moratorium expires.

SUMMARY AND CONCLUSION

The study described in this chapter used data from two Mexican community surveys to consider selected impacts of IRCA. To assess the short-run effect of the law's tougher enforcement measures on undocumented migration, we employed data from men interviewed during 1987–88 in two sending communities, San Francisco del Rincón and León, both in the state of Guanajuato. Age-period analyses of the likelihood of illegal migration revealed no discernable impact of IRCA. In 1987, the year following IRCA's passage, the probability of undocumented migration was higher than at any time during the past 15 years, and partial data suggest that it could be even higher in 1988. The only discernable effect that IRCA had was to increase the use of "coyotes" in crossing the border, which lowered the apprehension rate but did not affect the real cost of using a coyote.

The long-term impact of IRCA's legalization program was evaluated by estimating a multivariate model that predicted the use of U.S. social services by legal and illegal migrants after various lengths of time in the United States. Data were taken from an earlier survey of four Mexican migrant communities conducted in 1982–83. Analyses of the propensity to use AFDC, food stamps, unemployment compensation, and public education all showed that legal status was the most important single determinant of service usage, but was unrelated to tax contributions. By moving from undocumented to legal status, therefore, the likelihood of ever using services increased from two to 30 times. If our analysis is correct, demand is probably now growing for food stamps and public education as a result of IRCA, and after five years, load levels in AFDC and unemployment programs can be expected to move sharply upward.

Although these results are suggestive, at least two caveats must be borne in mind. First, data come from a small number of migrant sending communities, making it difficult to generalize specific levels to other settings. However, if prior work on such communities is any guide, the analyses are correct in indicating the basic processes involved; that is, service usage is driven primarily by legal status and length of experience, and illegal migration has continued to rise in spite of IRCA's passage, although the specific probabilities of use and undocumented migration may vary from community to community. Second, our analyses display weaknesses inherent to any policy evaluation so soon after implementation. In the case of the model of out-migration, we have only two data points after IRCA's passage in 1986, and in the case of service usage, we are making inferences about future trends primarily from past patterns of behavior.

As mentioned at the outset, however, the data used in the present analyses represent part of a more extensive project, and over subsequent years we will collect additional information from a much larger sample of communities and migrants. When the complete data file has been compiled, it will contain information through the year 1992 on several thousand migrants located in more than 25 communities. Replication of our analyses on this larger set of data should provide a more definitive evaluation of IRCA's continuing impacts on American society.

References

Allison, Paul D. 1982. "Discrete-Time Methods for the Analysis of Event Histories." In *Sociological Methodology 1982*, edited by S. Leinhardt. San Francisco: Jossey-Bass.

_____. 1984. *Event History Analysis: Regression for Longitudinal Event Data*. Beverly Hills and London: Sage.

Blau, Francine D. 1984. "Use of Transfer Payments by Immigrants." *Industrial and Labor Relations Review* 37:222–39.

Borjas, George J., and Stephen J. Trejo. 1989. "Immigrant Participation in the Welfare System." Paper presented at the annual meeting of the Population Association of America, Baltimore.

Campbell, Donald T., and Julian C. Stanley. 1966. *Experimental and Quasi-Experimental Designs for Research*. Chicago: Rand-McNally.

Dagodag, W. Tim. 1975. "Source Regions and Composition of Illegal Mexican Immigration to California." *International Migration Review* 9:499–511.

Espenshade, Thomas J., Frank D. Bean, Tracy Ann Goodis, and Michael J. White. 1990. "Immigration Policy in the United States: Future Prospects for the Immigration Reform and Control Act of 1986." In *Population Policy: Contemporary Issues*, edited by Godfrey Roberts, 59–84. New York: Praeger.

Fineberg, Stephen F., and William M. Mason. 1978. "Identification and Estimation of Age-Period-Cohort Models in the Analysis of Discrete Archival Data." In *Sociological Methodology 1979*, edited by Karl F. Schuessler. San Francisco: Jossey-Bass.

Goodis, Tracy Ann. 1986. "A Layman's Guide to 1986 U.S. Immigration Reform." *Impacts of Immigration in California Policy*. Discussion Paper PDS-86-4. Washington, D.C.: Urban Institute.

Hoefer, Michael D. 1989. "Characteristics of Aliens Legalizing Under IRCA." Paper presented at the annual meeting of the Population Association of America, Baltimore, March 29.

Jensen, Lief I. 1988. "Patterns of Immigration and Public Assistance Utilization, 1970–80." *International Migration Review* 22:51–83.

Lesko Associates. 1975. *Final Report: Basic Data and Guidance Required to Implement a Major Illegal Alien Study during Fiscal Year 1976*. Washington, D.C.: U.S. Immigration and Naturalization Service.

Levine, Daniel B., Kenneth Hill, and Robert Warren, eds. 1985. *Immigration Statistics: A Story of Neglect*. Washington, D.C.: National Academy Press.

Martin, Philip L., and J. Edward Taylor. 1988. "Harvest of Confusion: SAWs, RAWs, and Farmworkers." Working Paper PRIP-UI-4. Washington, D.C.: Urban Institute.

Mason, Karen O., William M. Mason, Haliman H. Winsborough, and William K. Poole. 1973. "Some Methodological Issues in Cohort Analysis of Archival Data." *American Sociological Review* 38:242–58.

Mason, William M., Karen O. Mason, and Haliman H. Winsborough. 1976. "Reply to Glenn." *American Sociological Review* 41:904–5.

Massey, Douglas S. 1985. "The Settlement Process among Mexican Migrants to the United States: New Methods and Findings." In *Immigration*

Statistics: A Story of Neglect, 255–92. Washington, D.C.: National Academy Press.

————. 1986. "The Settlement Process among Mexican Migrants to the United States." *American Sociological Review* 51:670–85.

————. 1987a. "The Ethnosurvey in Theory and Practice." *International Migration Review* 21:1498–1522.

————. 1987b. "Understanding Mexican Migration to the United States." *American Journal of Sociology* 92:1372–1403.

Massey, Douglas S., and Kathleen M. Schnabel. 1983. "Background and Characteristics of Undocumented Hispanic Migrants to the United States." *Migration Today* 11(1):6–13.

Massey, Douglas S., Rafael Alarcón, Jorge Durand, and Humberto González. 1987. *Return to Aztlan: The Social Process of International Migration from Western Mexico*. Berkeley and Los Angeles: University of California Press.

North, David S., and Marion F. Houstoun. 1976. *The Characteristics and Role of Illegal Aliens in the U.S. Labor Market: The U.S. Bracero Experience*. Washington, D.C.: Litton.

Simon, Julian. 1984. "Immigrants, Taxes, and Welfare in the United States." *Population and Development Review* 10:55–79.

Tienda, Marta, and Lief I. Jensen. 1986. "Immigration and Social Program Participation: Dispelling the Myth of Dependency." *Social Science Research* 15:372–400.

U.S. Immigration and Naturalization Service. 1988. *1987 Yearbook of the Immigration and Naturalization Service*. Washington, D.C.: U.S. Government Printing Office.

White, Michael J., Frank D. Bean, and Thomas J. Espenshade. 1989. "The Effects of IRCA on the Pattern of Apprehensions at the Border." Paper presented at the Conference on the International Effects of the Immigration Reform and Control Act of 1986, Guadalajara.

Chapter Seven

UNDOCUMENTED MIGRATION FROM MEXICO TO THE UNITED STATES: PRELIMINARY FINDINGS OF THE ZAPATA CANYON PROJECT

Jorge A. Bustamante

This chapter constitutes the second research report of the Zapata Canyon Project, which, since 1986, has sought to document the flow of illegal migration from Mexico to the United States.[1] The purpose of the current study is to present new data to facilitate an evaluation of the effects of the Immigration Reform and Control Act of 1986 (IRCA), now that the act's legalization program for undocumented immigrants has ended and its sanctions on employers who hire un-documented immigrants have fully begun. The first section of this study explains some of the main provisions of the IRCA legislation. The second section discusses the paradox of a law that aims to restrict immigration even though demographic patterns in the United States point to a greater demand for foreign labor. The third section briefly explains the measurement of migrant flows used in the Zapata Canyon Project. The fourth section discusses the project's findings, and the last section draws some conclusions based on the data presented.

REFORM OF U.S. IMMIGRATION LAWS

The passage of IRCA in October 1986 was fueled primarily by the perception that the country had "lost control of its borders."[2] Diverse ideological factions worked to maintain a fear among the U.S. public that the presence of undocumented immigrants was a "serious danger."[3] The power of these ideological factions drowned out the voice of the experts who maintained that undocumented immigration did more good than harm for the U.S. economy (Bustamante, 1987, note 7). The principal objective of the new reforms was to eliminate the illegal entry of foreigners into the United States. To achieve this goal, the new legislation (IRCA) included various provisions, the most well-known and controversial of which was the imposition of sanctions on employers who hired undocumented immigrants. This provision abolished the 1952 reforms, or the Walter-McArran Act, which, with the Texas proviso, had made the United States the only country that expressly authorized employers to hire foreigners entering the country in violation of its own immigration laws (Bustamante, 1987, note 9).

Another provision, known in the United States as "amnesty," allowed for undocumented immigrants to legalize their immigration status. The new legislation offered two main routes to legalization. One was "regular legalization," which was open to those undocumented immigrants who could prove continuous residency in the United States since January 1, 1982. At the end of the application period for this program, which lasted from May 5, 1987 to May 4, 1988, the U.S. Immigration and Naturalization Service (INS) reported that it had received 1.8 million applications, of which it estimated 90 percent would be approved (Espenshade et al., 1990). This figure was lower than the 2 million applications the INS had estimated it would receive at the beginning of the legalization program.

The other route to legalization was for "special agricultural workers." This was open to foreigners who could prove that they had worked in perishable agriculture in the United States for a minimum of 90 days during each of the three years before the passage of the law, or a minimum of 90 days in agriculture during the 12 months preceding May 12, 1986. Within this route, a subcategory was opened that granted temporary work authorization for one year, with the option to legalize permanently, so long as the work was exclusively in agriculture. After this period qualifying individuals could apply for legalization as special agricultural workers. At the end of the last extension of the application period, on November 30, 1988, the INS reported that it had received over 1 million applications. Since undocumented immigrants who came to the United States after January 1982 were not eligible for the "regular legalization" program, the majority of undocumented Mexicans could not qualify, since their migration pattern included entering and returning to Mexico to visit relatives. This meant that the majority of undocumented Mexicans would try to qualify as special agricultural workers. The INS had reported that many of the applicants in this category had presented fraudulent documents, so it was expected that in contrast to regular legalization, there would be a high percentage of denied applications in the special agricultural workers category (see Martin and Taylor, 1988).

In theory, the undocumented immigrants who did not legalize through one of the routes created by the new legislation would have to return to their country of origin. In reality, this does not appear to be occurring. The principal reason is that U.S. employers have not stopped hiring undocumented workers.[4] This has resulted not only in the continued presence of undocumented immigrants who did not qualify for legalization but also in the increased entry of new undocumented immigrants, data on which are presented next.

A PARADOX

It is paradoxical that legislation as restrictive as IRCA could pass in the same year in which, because of changes in U.S. demographic patterns, the demand for foreign labor increased. In effect, in 1986, the year IRCA was passed, there was a turnaround in the labor force population dynamics of the United States, marking the beginning of a shortage in the entry of young male workers into the labor market. The U.S. Department of Labor has estimated that by the year 2000 there will be a 6 percent decrease in the number of young men between the ages of 16 and 24 entering the labor market and a 15 percent decrease in those between the ages of 24 and 34 entering the labor market. Young men constituted 23 percent of the labor market in 1972, whereas in 1986 they comprised 20 percent. By the year 2000 it is estimated that this percentage will decrease to 16. In the meantime, the proportion of workers over age 35 will increase from 51 percent in 1986 to 61 percent by the year 2000 (Fullerton, 1987). If the preceding data do not convince one of the relationship between these demographic changes and an increase in the demand for undocumented immigrant labor, one can also consider recent projections of the composition of the labor force in the United States.[5] Silvestri and Lukasiewics (1987), of the U.S. Department of Labor's Office of Labor Statistics, found that among the occupations for which there will be the greatest demand between 1986 and the year 2000 are: waiters and waitresses; grocery store clerks; cleaners of houses, offices, and public places; cooks' assistants and restaurant cooks; bartenders; service employees in private clubs; and security guards. These are occupations in which more than half the undocumented population works, as is shown later in this chapter. Silvestri and Lukasiewics (1987) also reported that the service sector, which includes the preceding occupations, is the sector that will grow the fastest between now and the end of the century, expanding from 17.5 million in 1986 to nearly 30 million in the year 2000. Given the growth patterns of the age groups that will be working between now and the end of the century, the working-age population in the United States cannot possibly meet the demand for more than 5 million employees in jobs with lower level salaries and qualifications. Unless in the coming years new labor-saving technologies enable jobs to be performed less expensively than they can be done by undocumented workers, the U.S. economy will be threatened with an economic slowdown. Such a slowdown can be avoided only by "importing" the foreign workforce necessary to fill the shortages created by the aging of the U.S. working population.

THE MEASUREMENT OF MIGRANT FLOWS ACROSS THE BORDER

The previous discussion underscores the necessity to scientifically address whether the IRCA reforms have produced the effects intended. At the Colegio de la Frontera Norte, we responded to this question by using two methods to observe the northward flow of undocumented immigrants. The first was based on a short questionnaire administered to a select sample of about 25 persons a day, three days a week, in cities where the Colegio de la Frontera Norte has permanent research offices along the border (Tijuana, Mexicali, Nogales, Ciudad Juárez, Nuevo Laredo, and Matamoros). These questionnaires were designed to be given in less than three minutes to undocumented immigrants in the parts of each city that have the most crossings of undocumented immigrants into the United States. The questionnaires have been administered, with interruptions, since September 1987.

The other method of observation was based on photographs taken at regular time intervals in border areas in the United States between Tijuana and San Diego at which the most crossings of undocumented immigrants occur. Three photographs a day were taken at 1-hour intervals, using the sunset as the reference point. The first photograph was taken 2 hours and 10 minutes before sunset, the second one was taken 1 hour and 10 minutes before sunset, and the third one was taken 10 minutes before sunset. These time intervals were chosen because our previous research revealed that in this geographic area, the greatest number of undocumented immigrants crossed the border during the 2 hours before sunset.

The photographs were taken daily in one of two places in Tijuana—Zapata Canyon and "el bordo." The photographs vary in the number of people sighted at various times. The area known in Tijuana as "el bordo" parallels the Mexican-U.S. border along part of the road leading to the scenic highway that stretches from Tijuana to Ensenada. This site joins the four areas of "el bordo" that are systematically focused upon in the two daily photographs, taken within one-hour intervals before sunset. On the south side of the road is the old part of Tijuana known as the "northern zone." The proximity of "el bordo" to where undocumented immigrants gather before leaving on their clandestine journey to the United States means that they remain there for a shorter time period waiting for it to get dark than those who cross by the Zapata Canyon. For this reason, only two shots were taken there daily, also at one-hour intervals.

Taken together, the photographs shot daily in both the Zapata Canyon and in "el bordo" cover 90 percent of the entire border over which undocumented immigrants cross between Tijuana and San Diego. This is important in light of the fact that, according to the findings of surveys conducted by the National Population Council (CONAPO, 1986), about 50 percent of all undocumented immigrants who cross the Mexican border into the United States do so through Tijuana. To count and classify the migrants, the photographs are projected backward in the form of a transparency on a screen. On the other side of the screen the right side of the picture appears on a grid that facilitates counting the people that appear in the transparency and their electronic recording in terms of spatial coordinates. Each month three types of graphs are produced—one for the total number of people; one for men; and one for women. These graphs represent the greatest number of undocumented immigrants appearing in the three daily shots of the Zapata Canyon and the two daily shots of "el bordo."

Both sets of statistics comprise data for the Zapata Canyon Project, so named in honor of the place where our systematic measures began. These measures now cover five border cities through which 93 percent of all undocumented immigrants cross into the United States. Some of the most important findings of this project have been published bimonthly since the end of 1987, in *El Correo Fronterizo*, the official publication of the Colegio de la Frontera Norte.

SOME PRELIMINARY FINDINGS

Figures 7.1 and 7.2 provide a comparison of the greatest number of undocumented immigrants found on a daily basis in the three photographs taken daily in December in the Zapata Canyon in the years 1986, 1987, and 1988. The peaks correspond to the weekends. It is important to note the difference in the daily flow of male and female migrants. The proportion of migrants who are women varies between one-third and one-fifth of the total flow. These proportions are among the largest observed along the Mexican-U.S. border, due to the larger market for women in the service sector and textile industry in the state of California. Equally as important as the data on proportions are the differences in the fluctuations in the lines of the graphs with respect to each gender, indicating a certain independence in the migration patterns of the women with respect to the men, corresponding to the different labor markets for each gender.

Figures 7.3 and 7.4 provide a wider comparison of the differences in the migration patterns of the two sexes, suggesting the need for further examination of the separate migration patterns of undocu-

Figure 7.1 ZAPATA CANYON PROJECT: GREATEST NUMBER OF UNDOCUMENTED IMMIGRANTS PER DAY, A COMPARISON OF DECEMBER 1986–88 (WOMEN ONLY)

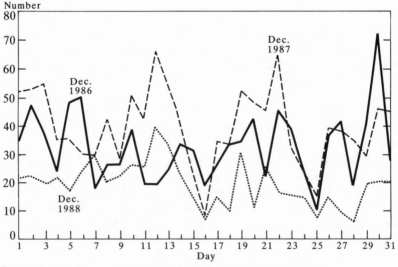

Source: Zapata Canyon Project, El Colegio de la Frontera Norte, Tijuana.

Figure 7.2 ZAPATA CANYON PROJECT: GREATEST NUMBER OF
UNDOCUMENTED IMMIGRANTS PER DAY, A COMPARISON OF
DECEMBER 1986–88 (MEN ONLY)

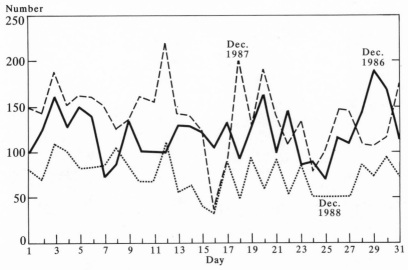

Source: Zapata Canyon Project, El Colegio de la Frontera Norte, Tijuana.

mented men and women. In these graphs there is a marked pattern
in the decrease of the migrant flow around December, a decrease that
serves as the most dramatic difference among the four recorded months
from 1986 to 1988. Although these four months represent too short
a period to make definitive conclusions about a decrease in the level
of flows of undocumented immigrants since IRCA was signed into
law in November 1986, the data on men for the months of September,
October, and November appear to support the view that such a decrease occurred. Nevertheless, for women, the year 1987 shows higher
volumes of undocumented immigrant entries than the previous year
(in the same months).

On the other hand, the December data on men in 1986 compared
with 1987 show a change in the pattern from previous months. This
pattern continues through several months in 1988, and then the flow
decreases again, at least in comparison to the same months in the
previous year. The fact that the differences for both men and women
are not very great in the month of December for the three recorded
years suggests it would be helpful to evaluate 1989 data before making final conclusions about migrant flows. In any case, there does

Figure 7.3 MONTHLY AVERAGES OF THE GREATEST NUMBER OF
UNDOCUMENTED IMMIGRANTS PER DAY IN THE ZAPATA
CANYON (MEN ONLY)

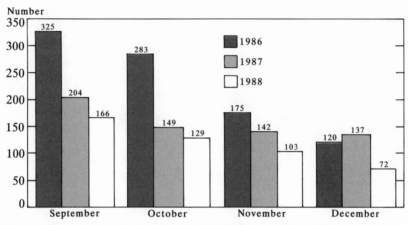

Source: Zapata Canyon Project, El Colegio de la Frontera Norte, Tijuana.

Figure 7.4 MONTHLY AVERAGES OF THE GREATEST NUMBER OF
UNDOCUMENTED IMMIGRANTS PER DAY IN THE ZAPATA
CANYON (WOMEN ONLY)

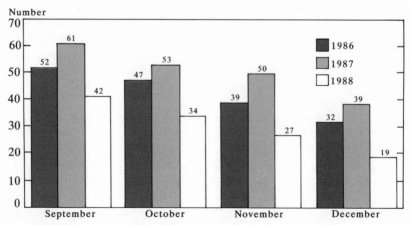

Source: Zapata Canyon Project, El Colegio de la Frontera Norte, Tijuana.

not appear to be sufficient empirical evidence to prove that IRCA is reducing the flow of undocumented immigrants. Furthermore, factors other than U.S. legislation could be inhibiting Mexican migration to the United States—for example, the financial costs of leaving one's place of origin to reach the U.S.-Mexican border.

Figures 7.5, 7.6, and 7.7 illustrate the importance of considering the cost of migration in explaining migrant flows to the north. The data in these graphs represent the sum of all the principal expenses (food, tickets, lodgings, a "coyote" or "*pollero*" [an individual who takes undocumented immigrants across the border for a price], and police extortions or robberies) reported by emigrants who were interviewed. The regions of origin that appear in the figures are those that produced more than four migrants a month, with the exception of figures 7.5 and 7.6, where the northwest region in Tijuana (figure 7.5) and the south region in Ciudad Juárez (figure 7.6), produced less than four migrants a month. The number of individuals interviewed per month in the cities on each graph varied by city. The monthly average was 230 cases for Tijuana, 75 for Ciudad Juárez, and 320 for

Figure 7.5 IMMIGRANTS' TOTAL EXPENSES FROM THEIR REGIONS OF ORIGIN
TO THE BORDER (TIJUANA)

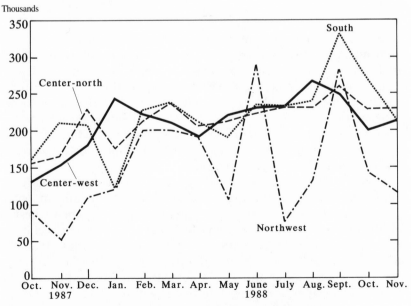

Source: Zapata Canyon Project, El Colegio de la Frontera Norte, Tijuana.

Figure 7.6 IMMIGRANTS' TOTAL EXPENSES FROM THEIR REGIONS OF ORIGIN
TO THE BORDER (CIUDAD JUÁREZ)

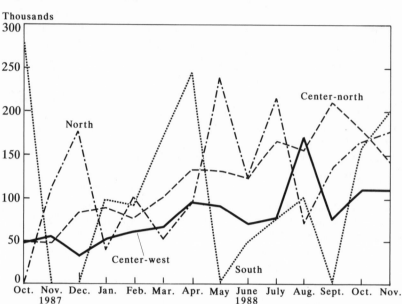

Source: Zapata Canyon Project, El Colegio de la Frontera Norte, Tijuana.

Nuevo Laredo and Matamoros combined. The regions of origin referenced in figures 7.5, 7.6, and 7.7 include the following federal divisions: "South" refers to Oaxaca, Chiapas, and Quintana Roo; "Gulf" refers to Veracruz, Tabasco, and Tamaulipas from Tampico south; "North" refers to border states; "Center-north" refers to Zacatecas, Durango, San Luis Potosí, Aguascalientes, and Querétaro; "Northwest" refers to Sinaloa, Baja California Sur, and Nayarit; "Center-west" refers to Colima, Jalisco, Michoacán, Guanajuato, Guerrero, Distrito Federal, Hidalgo, Tlaxcala, and Pueblo.

Since of all the cities surveyed Tijuana is the part of the northern border farthest from the usual places of origin of undocumented immigrants, the cost of getting to Tijuana is naturally the highest of all the cities included in figures 7.5, 7.6, and 7.7. The average inflation rate in the data for figure 7.5 (43 percent) was less than the official rate for Mexico in 1988 (55 percent). For the data in figure 7.5, the average inflation rate (74 percent) was greater than the national rate for the same period; in the case of the data for figure 7.7, it was much lower (22 percent) than the national rate. My hypothesis

Figure 7.7 IMMIGRANTS' TOTAL EXPENSES FROM THEIR REGIONS OF ORIGIN
TO THE BORDER (NUEVO LAREDO AND MATAMOROS)

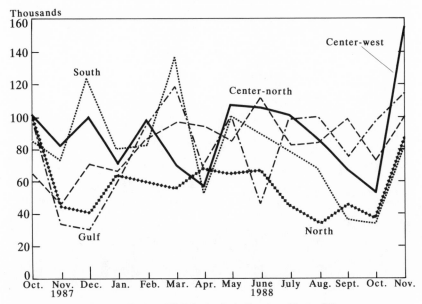

Source: Zapata Canyon Project, El Colegio de la Frontera Norte, Tijuana.

is that these differences in cost are due to the proportion of migration
expenses that are partially or totally financed by dollars sent by
relatives or friends from the United States. In any case, the costs of
migration rose in 1988 significantly less than they did in the two
previous years.

Figures 7.8, 7.9, and 7.10 illustrate the dynamic of the education
level of undocumented immigrants. The most important finding here
is the higher level of education for female undocumented immigrants
than for men, as can be seen in figures 7.8 and 7.9. Another important
finding is the significant difference between the education level of
the immigrants who crossed the border from Tijuana and those who
crossed the border from Nuevo Laredo and Matamoros. There appears to be a relationship between education level and the probability
of getting to Tijuana. In any case, here we find evidence that the
socioeconomic level of undocumented immigrants varies in relation
to the part of the border from which they cross into the United States.
Also interesting are the low levels of education in figure 7.10, in
comparison with the data in figure 7.9. In figure 7.10, there is a clear

Figure 7.8 EDUCATION LEVEL OF UNDOCUMENTED IMMIGRANTS WHO
CROSSED THROUGH TIJUANA FROM OCTOBER 1987 TO
SEPTEMBER 1988 (WOMEN ONLY)

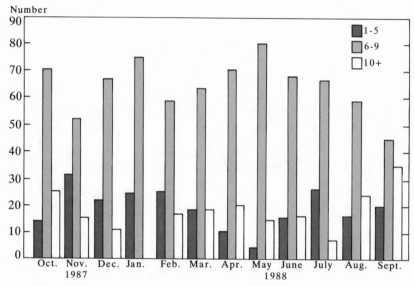

Source: Zapata Canyon Project, El Colegio de la Frontera Norte, Tijuana.

increase between October 1982 and September 1988 in the relative number of people with low levels of education, whereas in the case of Tijuana, the opposite is true, both for men and women immigrants. In this case, the flow of human capital through emigration seems to be greater through Tijuana than through the northwest. Certainly, these are not the immigrants of the past, who were predominantly of rural origin, poor, and illiterate. These are people with on average three to four more years of education than the national average.

CONCLUSIONS

Based on the findings of the Zapata Canyon Project through 1988, the following conclusions can be drawn:

1. The continued flow of undocumented immigrants to the United States confirms that IRCA is not completely achieving its prin-

Figure 7.9 EDUCATION LEVEL OF UNDOCUMENTED IMMIGRANTS WHO
CROSSED THROUGH TIJUANA FROM OCTOBER 1987 TO
SEPTEMBER 1988 (MEN ONLY)

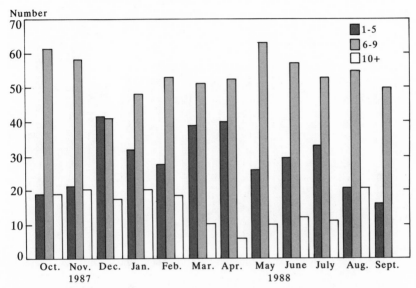

Source: Zapata Canyon Project, El Colegio de la Frontera Norte, Tijuana.

cipal goal of stopping the entry of undocumented immigrants.
IRCA was not created to end undocumented immigration, so much
as to respond politically to the ideological reasons behind the
most restrictive provisions, such as those reflected in the phrase,
"We have lost control of our borders." A country that had truly
lost control of its borders would be concerned enough to indicate
officially the exact location of the border at the most important
crossing point between the two countries, namely the Zapata Canyon. There is no official indication of the location of the international border in this area.

2. It appears that IRCA's legalization programs were designed disproportionately to favor non-Mexican undocumented immigrants, by creating a condition for permanent residency that is
contrary to the practice of Mexican immigrants who come and go
between Mexico and the United States every year. On the other
hand, it appears that IRCA's legislators wanted Mexican migrants
exclusively for agricultural labor, because they designed requirements most likely to be filled by Mexicans rather than by other

Figure 7.10 EDUCATION LEVEL OF UNDOCUMENTED IMMIGRANTS WHO
CROSSED THROUGH NUEVO LAREDO FROM OCTOBER 1987 TO
SEPTEMBER 1988 (MEN ONLY)

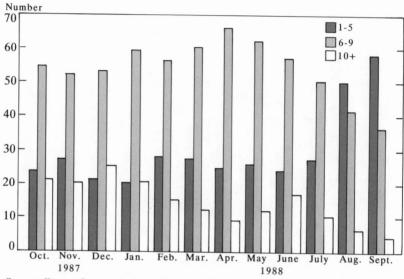

Source: Zapata Canyon Project, El Colegio de la Frontera Norte, Tijuana.

nationalities. This could be interpreted as an interesting twist in the design of categories selected for the legalization programs.

3. The data up to December 1988, more than two years after the passage of IRCA, suggest that the legislation was designed so as to maintain the flow of those undocumented immigrants who made salaries lower than the immigrants who became legal. This hypothesis is reinforced by the data indicating that the number of violations of the minimum wage law in California has tripled since IRCA was passed, according to information cited in Silvestri and Lukasiewics (1987).

4. The data collected to date appear to reinforce the hypothesis that IRCA was designed as a precautionary instrument for times of economic recession, during which it would be necessary to take drastic measures to diminish the stock of undocumented immigrants, and that in times of economic expansion the law could function with a maximum of flexibility, bordering on ineffectiveness.

5. Finally, the data strengthen the hypothesis that IRCA was a more convenient alternative to bilateral or multilateral negotiations, because negotiations would have raised the value of foreign labor.

A unilateral measure, as legislation is by definition, allows greater control over migrant flows and over the labor market in which undocumented immigrants participate.

In short, six factors contribute to IRCA's ineffectiveness: (a) The law was not created to limit the flow of undocumented immigrants, but to respond to political pressure from ideological factions that demanded the legislation; (b) IRCA was designed to favor non-Mexican undocumented immigrants who immigrate in a more permanent manner; (c) The law was designed to channel undocumented Mexicans into agriculture; (d) It was designed to provide a cheap labor force in which the continued presence of undocumented immigrants is a necessary element to lower the overall value of the labor force of legalized immigrants; (e) It was designed to easily get rid of undocumented immigrants in case of an economic recession; (f) It was designed as an alternative to bilateral negotiations that might have increased the value of the labor force and facilitated the organization of migrant workers.

Notes

1. For the first research report of the Zapata Canyon Project, see Bustamante (1987).

2. The phrase, "We have lost control of our borders," was coined on the eve of the presidential contest between Ronald Reagan and Jimmy Carter. Through a dramatic ad campaign on U.S. national television, the Republicans were trying to show President Carter's weakness in dealing with the more than 200,000 Cubans entering Florida. When the furor over the "Mariel invasion" died down, the phrase, which had captured the imagination of television watchers, was used by the proponents of IRCA to refer to the Mexican border situation.

3. In a public opinion poll conducted in California in 1985, 87 percent of those interviewed felt that undocumented migration from Mexico was at that time "a serious thing" or "very serious" (see Muller and Espenshade, 1985, p. 201). This book, one of the few that casts doubt on the negative effects of undocumented migration, was written shortly before the passage of IRCA.

4. Ned Sullivan, director of the Los Angeles office of the U.S. Department of Labor, confirmed that the number of employers who pay less than minimum wage has increased since the passage of IRCA (in Weinstein, 1989). Anthony Mischel, a lawyer in the Office for Legal Aid in Los Angeles, said that the number of cases (violations of the minimum wage law) formally opened has tripled between 1986 and 1988 (in Weinstein, 1989). According to these observers, the majority of these cases pertain to undocumented immigrants, for which specific examples are given.

5. See Silvestri and Lukasiewics (1987).

References

Bustamante, Jorge A. 1987. "Undocumented Migration." El Cotidiano, Spec. Ed. 1: 13–29. (Mexico D. F.: Metropolitana University, Azcapotzalco Division).

CONAPO, National Population Council. 1986. *Survey on the Northern Border of Undocumented Workers Deported by the Authorities in the United States of America: Statistical Results*. Mexico, D.F.: CONAPO.

Espenshade, Thomas J., Frank D. Bean, Tracy Ann Goodis, and Michael J. White. 1990. "Immigration Policy in the United States: Future Prospects for the Immigration Reform and Control Act of 1986." *Population Policy: Contemporary Issues*, edited by Godfrey Roberts, 59–84. New York: Praeger.

Fullerton, Howard N., Jr. 1987. "Labor Force Projections: 1986 to 2000." *Monthly Labor Review* 110 (9): 19–21.

Martin, Philip L., and J. Edward Taylor. 1988. "SAWs, RAWs, and California's Farm Labor Market." Paper prepared for Department of Agricultural Economy, University of California, Davis.

Muller, Thomas, and Thomas J. Espenshade. 1985. *The Fourth Wave: California's Newest Immigrants*. Washington, D.C.: Urban Institute.

Silvestri, George T., and John M. Lukasiewics. 1987. "A Look at Occupational Employment Trends to the Year 2000." *Monthly Labor Review* 110(9): 49–63.

Weinstein, Henry. 1989. "Illegal Immigrants Vulnerable." *Los Angeles Times*, Jan. 16.

Chapter Eight

IMPACTS OF THE 1986 U.S. IMMIGRATION LAW ON EMIGRATION FROM RURAL MEXICAN SENDING COMMUNITIES

Wayne A. Cornelius

This chapter focuses on the ways in which the U.S. Immigration Reform and Control Act of 1986 (IRCA) has affected traditional labor-exporting communities in Mexico. Specifically, it examines the ways in which IRCA has altered perceptions of the U.S. labor market, the propensity to migrate, settlement patterns in the United States, and the economies of migrant families and their home communities. Of particular importance to residents of rural "sending" communities in Mexico was the Special Agricultural Workers (SAW) program, which offered legalization to those claiming at least 90 days of employment as farmworkers in the United States in the 12-month period ending May 1, 1986.

Migrants' communities of origin constitute an especially crucial vantage point for assessing the impacts of the major changes in U.S. immigration law enacted under IRCA. What is happening at the border, and in the interior of the United States, is important, of course. But for IRCA to have the kinds of long-term consequences that its proponents intended, the law will have to change well-established perceptions, behavior patterns, and socialization processes in the principal source areas for unauthorized migration to the United States. Expectations about finding well-paid work in the United States—with or without legal entry documents—will have to be lowered, especially among would-be, first-time migrants.

METHODOLOGY

This article is based on data gathered through a total of 945 sample survey interviews conducted in 1988–89 in three rural communities located in west-central Mexico, a region with a 100-year tradition of sending workers to the United States (see Jones, 1984; Dagodag, 1984;

and Alarcón, Cárdenas, and Vega, forthcoming). A binational field research team, assembled by the Center for U.S.-Mexican Studies at the University of California, San Diego, and several Mexican universities interviewed 586 randomly selected household heads; 233 recent (post-January 1, 1982) migrants to the United States; and 126 prospective first-time migrants—persons aged 14 or older who had no history of work in the U.S. and who identified themselves as likely to migrate in the future.[1]

In each of the three communities, a simple random sample of 200 households was drawn from a sampling frame compiled through a complete household census conducted by our research team. In May 1988, according to our census, the research communities contained 299, 400, and 691 households, respectively. Our interviews with recent migrants to the United States and with prospective first-time migrants were done within the same set of households. Thus the number of interviews conducted per household ranged from one to three. Interviews with household heads averaged about 2 hours in duration; those with recent migrants to the United States averaged 1.5 hours; and interviews with prospective first-time migrants lasted about 1 hour.

The universe for this study is defined as all households maintaining a residence in the three Mexican sending communities studied. To be included in the sampling frame, a household did not need to occupy a dwelling in the community on a year-round basis. Indeed, in all three communities, numerous dwelling units are occupied for only a few weeks each year (usually in December, January, and early February, when migrant families traditionally return from the United States) or are occupied for most of the year by renters or housesitters (14.4 percent of the houses in the three communities, combined).

To prevent underrepresentation of residents who spend most of the year working in the United States, we took several steps. First, the field interviewing was divided into two principal periods: July–August 1988 and December–January 1988–89. The latter period was timed to coincide with the habitual return of migrants from the United States for the Christmas holidays and annual town fiestas. Some interviewing was also conducted in the interim months, as families returned from the United States. If an entire household was found to be absent both in July–August 1988 and in December–January 1988–89, it was replaced with a household that was also absent in July–August 1988, but had returned to the community by December–January 1988–89. Finally, nine interviews with household heads (1.5 percent of the total) were conducted in various California cities, where these individuals were located in the fall of 1988. The level of cooperation was quite high; the refusal rate among sampled household heads in the three communities ranged from 2.5 to 4.0 percent.

The research communities are located in the states of Jalisco, Michoacán, and Zacatecas. All three are predominantly agricultural (73 percent of the economically active adult males were principally employed in agriculture). U.S.-bound migration from all three communities began in the first decades of this century, was briefly interrupted in the 1930s by the Great Depression, and became a mass movement in the 1940s and 1950s, when many residents participated in the Bracero Program of contract labor importation. In numerous families having homes in these communities, members of three different generations have worked in the United States. All three communities had been studied in depth by members of our research team prior to the enactment of IRCA.[2]

It could be argued that a better test of the efficacy of IRCA would be provided by communities that only recently had begun to send migrants to the United States. Presumably it should be easier to deter new undocumented emigration from communities recently incorporated into the migratory stream, and considerably more difficult to do so with respect to communities having well-established migrant networks linking them to the United States.[3] With additional time and financial resources, we would have chosen to study both types of sending communities. We opted to study communities with a longer migratory history because of the availability of "baseline" (pre-IRCA) data on their migratory patterns.

Finally, in an effort to better assess how IRCA has affected the social and economic linkages between sending areas in Mexico and Mexican immigrant communities in the United States, several members of the research team conducted unstructured interviewing and ethnographic observation among a "snowball" sample of U.S.-based emigrants from the communities we had studied in Mexico.[4] These informants reside, more or less permanently, in northern California—primarily in the San Francisco Bay area, the Sacramento area, and the city of Watsonville.

Since the research communities were selected purposively, we make no claim that our findings are statistically representative of the entire universe of Mexican communities—now including large cities as well as rural localities—that send migrants to the United States. Our research sites are, however, quite typical of the small rural communities of west-central Mexico that have contributed heavily to the U.S.-bound migratory flow since the 1920s.[5] The representativeness of our research communities, within their regional context, is also suggested by the striking similarities noted, in the section following, between our findings concerning the impacts of IRCA on migratory behavior, perceptions, and remittances, and those of researchers who have conducted recent survey studies of other traditional labor-exporting communities in the same region of Mexico.

Knowledge and Perceptions of IRCA

We found a very high level of knowledge about IRCA among residents of the research communities (see table 8.1). By January 1989, 75 percent of all household heads, 91 percent of recent migrants to the United States (those who had migrated at least once since 1982), and 83 percent of recent *undocumented* migrants knew something about IRCA. Among the prospective first-time undocumented migrants in our research communities—those who had never gone to the United States, but hoped to do so in the near future—the knowledge level was only slightly lower.

Awareness of specific elements of the law was equally high. For example, 95 percent of recent migrants to the United States knew how employer sanctions are supposed to work—i.e., they knew what IRCA compels employers to do. Nine out of 10 household heads knew that using false documents to get a job in the United States is illegal under IRCA. Levels of knowledge about the legalization programs established by IRCA were also quite high. For example, 66 percent of the household heads and 83 percent of recent migrants to the United States knew something about the SAW legalization program. Knowledge of the general amnesty program was lower (47 percent among household heads; 71 percent among recent migrants).

Awareness of the employer-sanctions component of the law has affected migrants' perceptions of the difficulty of getting work in the United States, if one does not have papers. Eight-three percent of the household heads and recent migrants to the United States whom we interviewed believed that it is more difficult to get work now in the United States, because of employer sanctions. An even higher proportion of the would-be migrants in our research communities—87 percent—perceived greater difficulty in getting a U.S. job.[6]

In sum, the vast majority of sending community residents are knowledgeable about the new U.S. immigration law. The high level of information concerning IRCA in places with long traditions of U.S.-bound migration is not surprising. Communication between each town and its several "sister" communities of emigrants in the United

Table 8.1 KNOWLEDGE AND PERCEPTIONS OF IRCA

Item	All Household Heads (N = 586) (%)	Recent (1982–89) Migrants to U.S. (N = 233)ᵃ (%)	Post-IRCA (1987–89) Undocumented Migrants (N = 64) (%)	Prospective Migrants to U.S. (N = 126) (%)
Has heard something about IRCA	75	91	83	82
Knows about SAWs legalization program	66	83	81	53
Among those who know about IRCA:				
Knows how employer sanctions work	78	95	81	78
Knows that using false documents to get job in U.S. is illegal	89	91	77	96
Believes it is more difficult to get work now in U.S. because of employer sanctions	83	83	84	87

Source: Center for U.S.-Mexican Studies (University of California, San Diego) survey of three rural communities, 1988–89.

a. Persons who migrated to the United States at least once between January 1, 1982, and January 31, 1989.

States is continuous. Informants tell us that news and gossip fly rapidly between all these places. Telephoned reports of conditions in the U.S. are constantly reinforced by the testimony of returning migrants, and massively so at times like the Christmas holidays. Among all interviewees in the research communities, 14 percent said that they regularly got news about conditions in the United States from relatives based there, through letters and telephone conversations. Another 30 percent obtained such information from relatives and friends returning from the United States.

PROPENSITY TO MIGRATE

But how has this knowledge affected the propensity to migrate? The framers of IRCA assumed that awareness of a new, potentially significant obstacle to employment (i.e., employer sanctions) would "demagnetize" the U.S. job market, effectively deterring new undocumented immigration. In our research communities, however, the translation of IRCA-related knowledge into deterrence of emigration is far from complete.

Among our recent (1987–89) unauthorized-immigrant interviewees—none of whom had secured amnesty under IRCA—nearly two-thirds had thought of going to the United States during the 12 months preceding the interview (see table 8.2). Half of them had actually gone to the United States during the same period. Of those who had not gone, only 30 percent of the recent undocumented migrants gave an IRCA-related reason for not going. Among our sample of would-be, first-time migrants, 47 percent had thought about going to the United States during the preceding 12 months. Asked why they had not gone yet, only one out of five mentioned some IRCA-related concern, while 39 percent cited family-related circumstances (most frequently, "my parents—or my spouse—wouldn't let me go"), and 15 percent mentioned financial constraints. Similarly, among the nearly 27 percent of community residents who told us that they were considering permanent emigration to the United States in the near future, only 13 percent mentioned "lack of documents" as the reason why they had not yet left (44 percent cited family reasons, and another 12 percent, lack of money to finance the move).[7]

Our respondents' perceptions of the U.S. opportunity structure under IRCA were distinctly ambivalent. On the one hand, as already noted, most believed it was more difficult to find work in the United

Table 8.2 PROPENSITY TO MIGRATE

Item	All Household Heads (N = 586) (%)	Recent (1982–89) Migrants to U.S. (N = 233) (%)	Post-IRCA (1987–89) Undocumented Migrants (N = 64) (%)	Prospective Migrants to U.S. (N = 126) (%)
Has considered going to U.S. in last 12 months	39	74	63	47
Among those who have considered going:				
Actually went to U.S. in last 12 months	47	64	50	—
Among those who have not gone:				
Cites IRCA or lack of papers as main reason for not going[a]	25	22	30	20
Believes it is still possible to get job in U.S. without papers[b]	—[c]	48	59	71
Among those who believe it is still possible:				
Mentions bogus documents as way to get job in U.S.	—	27	37	21
Believes it is more difficult to cross border clandestinely now than before	—	28	30	40

Source: Center for U.S.-Mexican Studies (University of California, San Diego) survey of three rural communities, 1988–89.

a. Mentioned one of the following: the new U.S. immigration law; lack of legal-entry papers; fear of U.S. immigration authorities; fear of not being able to get work in the United States.

b. Question was: "From what you know, at present, are people still getting jobs in the U.S., even if they don't have papers?"

c. Question not asked.

States, because of the new U.S. immigration law. On the other hand, 48 percent of the recent (post-January 1, 1982) migrants to the United States in our research communities believed that it was still possible to find work in the United States as an unauthorized migrant (see table 8.2). This perception of continued access to the U.S. labor market was strongest among the prospective first-time migrants to the U.S., 71 percent of whom believed that unauthorized immigrants could still get jobs in the United States. Three out of five recent (1987–89) unauthorized migrants in our sample believed it was still possible to get a job in the U.S. without papers. When asked how, 37 percent of the recently experienced unauthorized migrants explicitly mentioned *papeles chuecos* (bogus documents), while 21 percent of the prospective first-time migrants mentioned the same option.[8] Most of the remainder expressed the belief that U.S. employers would continue to hire Mexicans regardless of their immigration status, or that networks of relatives and friends would continue to find jobs for new arrivals.

The proliferation of bogus documents and their use to gain employment in the United States is one of the most conspicuous features of the post-1986 IRCA implementation experience. Such documents—typically counterfeit "green cards" or *micas* (permanent legal immigrant credentials) and U.S. Social Security cards—are readily available for purchase, in communities of origin in Mexico as well as in Mexican and U.S. border cities (most such documents are produced in the United States). Informants in the research communities told us that the supply of such documents has increased rapidly in the post-IRCA period, and that their price has dropped.[9] Unauthorized migrants can often obtain them at little or no cost, through their social networks (especially relatives and friends based in the United States). Among recent (post-January 1, 1982) migrants interviewed in our Mexican research communities, 25 percent admitted that they had used false documents to gain employment during their most recent trip to the United States, paying a median price of (U.S.) $50 for them.[10] Undoubtedly, this figure is an underreport of actual behavior, because many of our interviewees made it clear that they consider the use of bogus documents to be an unsavory business. Moreover, as already reported here, the majority of interviewees were aware that they are subject to criminal penalties under IRCA if they attempt to use such documents to gain employment in the United States.

Stepped-up border enforcement by U.S. immigration authorities was not perceived by residents of our Mexican research communities as a very potent threat to gaining entry into the United States. Only

32 percent of our interviewees (excluding "don't knows") thought that it was more difficult to cross the border clandestinely now than before IRCA. Among recent, experienced unauthorized migrants, 30 percent believed it was harder; 40 percent of those who had not yet tried it—the prospective first-time migrants—thought it would be more difficult to cross the border now than before. As with employer sanctions, stepped-up border enforcement tends to be viewed by residents of our research communities not with fear but rather as just another nuisance that must be endured in pursuit of their goal: work in the United States.

For most prospective migrants to the United States, the most important source of confidence about their ability to gain employment there are the well-established immigrant networks—relatives and friends already living in the United States. As reported in chapter eight, 91 percent of the prospective first-time migrants interviewed in our research communities had relatives living in the U.S. destination where they were most likely to seek work.[11] If anything, these networks have been strengthened by IRCA, which has legalized many of the networks' U.S.-based members and given these people a greater sense of security and stability in their jobs. This may lead to a greater willingness and capacity to help relatives and friends to migrate.

Finally, it is important in this context to differentiate between the *quality* of jobs available to unauthorized migrants in the post-IRCA period (i.e., the perceived range of available job opportunities) and the difficulty of finding *employment in general*. Our informants in the research communities often stressed this distinction. As one interviewee recently returning from the United States observed, "To get a job in a big company, that may be hard. But a common, ordinary job? That's easy." Thus there is a widely shared perception in the sending communities that IRCA may have reduced the range of employment options available to unauthorized migrants to the United States; but there is an equally widespread notion that work of some sort—paying much more than any locally available job—can still be readily obtained in *El Norte*. It is the latter belief that continues to tempt "first-timers" to try their luck.

EFFECTS OF LEGALIZATION PROGRAMS

By far the most important effects of IRCA upon Mexican sending communities to date have flowed from the legalization components of the law, rather than employer sanctions. Participation in the "amnesty" programs created by IRCA was extensive among residents of the communities we have studied.[12] Forty-four percent of the households surveyed had at least one legalization applicant. Applicants for the SAW program outnumbered those for the general amnesty program. The mean number of persons per household who applied for SAW status was 0.55, while the mean number of general-amnesty applicants was 0.40 per household. Among survey respondents with a history of recent (post-1982) migration to the United States, 53 percent had applied for legalization, under either the general amnesty or the SAW program. The number of legalization applicants in our samples is biased downward, since some of those who did apply were likely to be in the United States during our periods of fieldwork in their home communities. This is especially true of SAW applicants.

Among the prospective, first-time migrants whom we interviewed, 42 percent told us that they were *thinking* about applying for amnesty, at the time of the interview. Of course, none of these would-be migrants could have qualified for amnesty because they had no previous U.S. work history. Nevertheless, they believed that by obtaining a letter from some employer in the U.S., they could gain legal status.

The SAW program proved to be an easy-to-qualify-for legalization option, attracting over 1.3 million applicants (82 percent of them Mexicans)—far more than the 250,000 applicants that the framers of IRCA had anticipated. The SAW program was also attractive because it provided (unintentionally) a fast track to permanent legal-immigrant status, without the costs, difficulties, English language, and U.S. civics requirements of the general amnesty program. There is evidence that a significant minority of SAW applicants did not actually meet the eligibility criteria for the SAW program. Many were minors, and even more were persons whose previous history of agricultural employment in the United States was limited or nonexistent. A computer-aided review of the work histories of 100 SAW applicants in our three-community sample of post-1982 migrants to the United States suggests that 76 percent could actually have qualified for SAW status. The remainder consisted of 10 percent who had worked sporadically in U.S. agriculture but not for the required minimum, and 14 percent who had never worked in U.S. agriculture. However, the SAW eligibility rate varied greatly from one sending community to another. In Gómez Farías, whose migrants to the U.S. work mostly in agriculture, 92 percent of SAW applicants actually qualified; in Tlacuitapa and Las Animas, which send migrants mainly into non-agricultural U.S. sectors, only 54 percent and 42 percent, respectively, of SAW applicants met eligibility requirements.[13]

In 1988, there was probably more emigration from our research communities (and similar labor-exporting communities of west-central Mexico) to the United States than in any previous year.[14] A large part or the 1988 migration surge—which included many first-timers, women, and children—consisted of people trying to take advantage of the IRCA-mandated legalization options, especially the SAW program. In our research communities, 39 percent of all household heads and 41 percent of recent (post-January 1, 1982) migrants to the United States acknowledged having relatives who had gone to the United States *principally* to legalize themselves under one of the IRCA amnesty programs.

Now that the application period for the SAW program has closed, would-be migrants to the United States who are still living in the research communities—as well as unauthorized migrants already working in the U.S. who did not qualify or make application for the earlier IRCA amnesty programs—are awaiting implementation of the Replenishment Agricultural Workers (RAW) program authorized by the 1986 immigration law. Under the RAW program, a still-to-be-determined number of migrant farm workers, to be chosen by lottery among the registrants, may be authorized to work in the United States on a short-term basis in the four fiscal years from October 1989 through September 1993, if the federal government determines that a shortfall in agricultural labor exists.[15]

The legalization programs created by IRCA appear to have induced substantial numbers of people in our research communities who had not previously sought work in the United States to enter the migratory stream. Many of these first-timers probably would have migrated anyway, as undocumented entrants, without the inducement of an opportunity to *arreglar papeles* (regularize documents). For others, however, this inducement was both a necessary and sufficient motive for migration.

So many Mexicans legalized themselves through IRCA that the drop in apprehensions of illegal entrants at the U.S.-Mexico border in 1987, 1988, and the first quarter of 1989 can be explained in large part by this factor alone. In California alone, there are 1.6 million immigrants working today who obtained some form of legal status under IRCA (see Bean, Vernez, and Keely, 1989).[16] Because of what some have termed the "excessive" success of the SAW program, as well as the general amnesty program, a much higher percentage of border crossings are now being made by persons who are no longer at risk of being apprehended.

This significant change in the composition of the migrant flow is reflected in the data from our research communities. As shown in table 8.3, over 60 percent of the U.S.-bound migrants from these communities made their last pre-IRCA trip to the U.S. as undocumented migrants. In the post-IRCA period, only 26 percent entered the U.S. illegally on their most recent rip, while 30 percent migrated as "*Rodinos*"—applicants for legalization under the Simpson-Rodino Act.[17]

SETTLEMENT PATTERNS IN THE UNITED STATES

The long-term trend toward a higher incidence of permanent settlement by Mexican migrants in the United States appears to have been reinforced by IRCA. Although the law did not create this trend, which has been evident at least since the late 1960s, it may end up accelerating it moderately.

Residents of our research communities report that the principal impact of IRCA to date has been to facilitate the movement of individual workers and families back and forth to the United States. Among recent migrants to the United States, the ability to come and go more easily was mentioned most frequently in our interviews as the main benefit accruing thus far from legalization, since most of the newly legalized have not yet experienced any changes in their economic situation as a result of amnesty. "*Rodinos*" can cross the border without having to pay large sums to "coyotes" to be smuggled back into the U.S. clandestinely, and without exposing themselves to the customary risks of illegal entry (e.g., robbery and assault by border bandits and Mexican police).

Amnesty has also given the former "illegals" an important psychological boost: Now that they are able to cross the border at "*la línea*" (the official checkpoints) rather than "*por el cerro*" (over the mountains, clandestinely), they can enter the United States "*con dignidad*" (with dignity). "That's what gives me the greatest satisfaction," one Rodino told us. Large numbers of amnesty applicants returned to the research communities in late 1988 and early 1989— many of them for the first time in five or six years—to celebrate Christmas and the annual town fiesta. They came protected by their newly obtained *permisos*, often accompanied by wives and children; most of them returned to the United States immediately after the hometown fiestas ended.[18]

Table 8.3 LEGAL STATUS OF EMIGRANTS FROM RESEARCH COMMUNITIES, BY PERIOD OF MIGRATION TO UNITED STATES (PRE- AND POST-IRCA)

Legal Status	Last Pre-IRCA Trip (1982–86)		Most Recent Post-IRCA Trip (1987–89)	
	%	(N)	%	(N)
Undocumented migrant	60.7	(233)	26.1	(84)
"Rodino" (amnesty applicant)	3.4	(13)[a]	30.1	(97)
Permanent legal immigrant ("green-carder")	35.9	(138)	43.8	(141)

Source: Center for U.S.-Mexican Studies (University of California, San Diego) survey of three rural communities, 1988–89. Missing data cases are excluded.

Note: Data represent residents of the research communities who migrated to the U.S. at least once during January 1, 1982, to January 31, 1989.

a. These cases represent persons who last pre-IRCA migration to the United States was initiated without documents, but who subsequently applied for amnesty and received their documentation in the post-IRCA period.

Legalized migrants may now spend less time in Mexico than ever before, because they can (at least theoretically) move more easily into urban, nonseasonal U.S. jobs, from which they normally can be absent for only one to three weeks per year.[19] Moreover, in the future those "*Rodinos*" who continue to work in the agricultural sector will no longer need to return to their places of origin at the end of the agricultural cycle. As legal farmworkers, they will have access to unemployment compensation in the United States.

Legalization has also increased the probability of "settling out" in the U.S. by promoting family reunification. Male family heads who secured amnesty for themselves quickly began sending for their wives and children in Mexico, whether or not these dependents themselves could qualify for legalization, using "coyotes" to guide them across the border. There are many different indicators of IRCA-related im-migration for family reunification. Mexican government consultates in San Diego and other U.S. border cities have reported a sharp increase in the number of undocumented children being detained by the U.S. Border Patrol in 1988 and 1989. According to systematic photographic documentation compiled by El Colegio de la Frontera Norte, women account for more than 15 percent of the illegal crossing in the Tijuana-San Diego border area.[20] During the last quarter of 1989, the U.S. consulate in Tijuana experienced an 82 percent in-crease in nonimmigrant visa seekers—most of them dependents of persons who were granted amnesty under IRCA.[21]

Once in the United States, the wives of Mexican migrants often promote "settling out" in this country. Even though their husbands may never abandon the dream of returning some day to live full-time in their home towns, women typically express a preference to remain permanently in the United States (Alarcón, 1989). Even do-mestic work is considerably easier in the U.S., with all its modern conveniences, than in Mexico.

For all these reasons, it is probable that over the medium to long run, the 1986 U.S. immigration law is likely to anchor the legally migrating population more firmly on the U.S. side of the border. IRCA is forcing some Mexicans to choose, finally, between long-term residence in Mexico and long-term residence in the United States (Alejandre, 1989). With the option of more economically secure, year-round residence in the United States now open to them, more emigrants from traditional sending communities view migration to the U.S. as a permanent change in their life situation, instead of just a short-term income-earning strategy. High-emigration communities in central Mexico are thus being transformed increasingly into rest-

and-recreation centers for families whose principal base is now in the United States.

Thus far, IRCA has produced no massive return flow of unamnestied illegals who suddenly found themselves jobless in the United States, as a result of employer sanctions. The undocumented immigrants already here who did not qualify for legalization (or who failed to apply for it, for whatever reason) have not been returning in large numbers to their places of origin, because they have not yet become unemployable in this country. Indeed, at least in the short term, IRCA may have kept more Mexicans in the United States than it has shut out or forced to return to their hometowns. In our research communities, 36 percent of all interviewees claimed to know one or more persons who had returned to their hometown because of IRCA-related problems.[22] But 50 percent knew someone who had decided to *stay* in the U.S. because of IRCA. In 85 percent of these cases, according to our respondents, people stayed to take advantage of the IRCA legalization programs.

For those who remain unauthorized migrants, especially new arrivals without access to well-consolidated social networks, IRCA seems to have increased the average length of stay in the United States. Among our interviewees in the research communities, unauthorized migrants who had gone to the U.S. most recently in the pre-IRCA period spent 16.7 months there; unauthorized migrants who had gone to the United States since IRCA's enactment spent 20.6 months there (the figures are means). This can be attributed, at least in part, to increased job-seeking time and time devoted to acquiring bogus documents. Although newly arriving, unauthorized migrants are still finding work in the United States, it takes them longer to find steady work. Many of them must devote several weeks or even months to poorly paid, highly irregular day-labor before finding steady employment.[23] This lengthens the time needed to accomplish their economic objective, makes it more likely that they will accumulate debts owed to persons in the U.S. that may inhibit their eventual return to Mexico, and increases the probability that they—like their newly legalized counterparts—will eventually settle in the United States.

THE ECONOMIES OF MIGRANT FAMILIES

Advocates and critics of IRCA have postulated a variety of contradictory effects that the law will supposedly have on the economies of migrant families and their home communities. Some have feared that employer sanctions will dry up remittance income, causing serious hardship in areas that had become heavily dependent on this income source. Others have anticipated that legalization will boost the income-earning potential of the "amnestied" workers and thus their contributions to household and community economies. But for the majority of families in the Mexican communities we have studied, IRCA per se has had no dramatic impact on their economic conditions.

The aggregate flow of cash remittances from U.S.-based workers to these communities appears to have been reduced somewhat by IRCA's legalization programs, at least in 1987 and 1988. Our interviewees noted that amnesty applicants spent more time in the United States than usual and sent less money home to their relatives during the application period. This is not surprising, since the costs incurred in applying for legalization reduced migrants' disposable income. Thirty percent of the household heads interviewed reported receiving less money from relatives in the United States in the post-IRCA period (i.e., since January 1987); only 12 percent reported an increase in remittances. But the majority of households (57 percent) had experienced no change in the level of remittance income since the enactment of IRCA.[24] To the extent that legalization reduces shuttle migration and encourages permanent settlement in the United States, however, it is likely to have a negative impact on remittance flows in the longer term.

IRCA may have reduced the financial capacity of some migrants to remit income to Mexico. Some of our interviewees in the research communities complained that wages in agricultural areas of California having heavy concentrations of Mexican workers were being depressed by the arrival of large numbers of SAW-permit holders.[25] Studies of labor-intensive, nonagricultural industries in California conducted by the Center for U.S.-Mexican Studies in 1983–84 and 1987–88 revealed considerable rigidity in wage scales for production workers. However, wages in these sectors of the California economy were being held down mainly by general competitive pressures, the weakness of unions, and other factors essentially unrelated to the size of the immigrant labor supply. Most employers in these industries as well as in California's agricultural sector have not considered raising wages to attract or retain workers in the post-IRCA period; nor have they found it necessary to do so (see Martin and Taylor, 1990).

Among household heads in the communities we have studied in

Mexico, only 15 percent could cite any specific economic benefit to their family resulting from IRCA's legalization programs. Most of those who felt they had benefited mentioned having more stable work in the United States, or not having to pay a "coyote" to guide illegal entries. Clearly, legal access to the U.S. labor market has not translated automatically into increased income for the majority of amnestied workers and their families.

In our research communities, most confirmed "norteños" try to maintain a house in the community that can be occupied during family vacations—sometimes by a spouse or older relative who prefers to remain in the home community. House construction and improvement remain the most common forms of capital investment in the sending communities by persons who migrate to the United States. There is no evidence that IRCA has changed the way in which savings accumulated in the United States are utilized. However, as legalization promotes "settling out" on the U.S. side of the border, more of the houses built or expanded with dollars earned in the United States are destined for use not as primary residences but as vacation or retirement homes.

CONCLUSION

In communities that have long depended on income earned in the United States, our data show that most people continue to have an *essentially* positive view of the U.S. opportunity structure in the post-IRCA period: not as wide open as before, but still accessible to those with determination, perhaps assisted by *papeles chuecos*, and even more importantly, by family contacts. Our interviewees made it clear that having a job prearranged in the United States is far more important to them than any law the U.S. Congress might pass: If they have a solid job prospect, they will migrate, with or without papers. Our field studies suggest that the robust growth in employment opportunities in the United States in the second half of the 1980s has been at least as important in fueling the current wave of emigration as the effects of Mexico's lingering economic crisis.[26]

Except for the legalization components of the law (which caused many first-time migrants to go to the United States, and temporarily kept others in the United States for a longer-than-normal period), IRCA has not proven to be as disruptive to the long-established rhythms of migration to the United States as many had anticipated. There is no evidence that the law has reduced the traditionally heavy flow of workers to the United States from our research communities and similar towns in west-central Mexico. Indeed, IRCA seems to have *augmented* that flow, at least in the short-term, through the legalization programs.

Although IRCA does not seem to have reduced the total pool of workers from our research communities who were employed or seeking jobs in the United States during the 1987–89 period, it did cause a major recomposition of the migrant flow, with a considerably smaller proportion of the total flow now entering the United States illegally. Before IRCA, the U.S.-bound migratory flow from these communities was predominantly undocumented, with a substantial minority of highly experienced, older, "green card"-carrying legal migrants. Primarily through the amnesty programs that it created, IRCA has reduced the relative size of the undocumented component, and it has increased the representation of women and children in the migratory flow. The law also appears to have accelerated the shift from temporary or "shuttle" migration to permanent emigration and settlement in the United States, although there is still a large reservoir of potential short-term migrants in these and other traditional labor-exporting communities.

In short, IRCA has added new dimensions of complexity to the migratory phenomenon; it has not yet altered its fundamental dynamics. Even with employer sanctions increasing the difficulty of finding work—especially steady, full-time employment—in the United States, for many people it is still not worth it to remain in Mexico and try to make ends meet. And through its legalization programs, IRCA may accelerate the evolution of Mexican migration to the United States from a population movement motivated by narrowly economic considerations to one increasingly propelled and sustained by broader social processes, including family reunification and the expansion of transnational social networks linking sending and receiving communities.[27]

Notes

The research reported in this chapter was supported by grants from the Ford Foundation, the University of California Pacific Rim Research Program, the Commission for the Study of International Migration and Cooperative Economic Development, and the Program for Research on Immigration Policy (RAND Corporation/Urban Institute). I am indebted to Jeffrey Weldon, Manuel García y Griego, Delfina Duarte, and Luin Goldring for assistance with the data analysis and for comments on an earlier draft. The first draft of this paper was presented at the XV International Congress of the Latin American Studies Association, Miami, December 4–6, 1989. This chapter is a revised version of an article that appeared in *Population and Development Review*, vol. 15, no. 4 (Dec. 1989).

1. Our selection of the nonmigrant household member deemed most likely to migrate to the United States in the near future was based necessarily on the judgment of the interviewer. Nevertheless, the subsequent behavior of these interviews suggests that we succeeded in tapping a highly migration-prone stratum of the nonmigrant population in these communities. In a follow-up study of residents of one of the three communities who had been interviewed in July or August 1988 as prospective first-time migrants to the United States, we found that about 15 percent had actually migrated between August 1 and December 1, 1988. This rate of emigration is particularly impressive, since these were first trips, occurring during a season when very few people normally leave for the United States; indeed, migration during the August–December period traditionally runs in the opposite direction.

2. The pre-IRCA fieldwork in these three communities has been reported in Castro (1986), Mines (1981), and Cornelius (1976).

3. It would be very valuable to have comparable field studies of sending communities representing the "new undocumented Mexican migration"—that is, from areas that were not heavily involved in labor migration to the United States prior to the 1980s. Appropriate sites could be found in states such as Guerrero, Oaxaca, Puebla, and the Mexico City metropolitan area.

4. For a description of the snowball sampling technique as it has been applied in studies of undocumented immigrants in the United States, see Cornelius (1982).

5. See, for example, Massey et al. (1987), Calvo and López (1988, especially the chapters by Alarcón and Fonseca), and Castro and Galván (1988, especially the chapters by Fernández and Castro).

6. In a survey of 1,835 Mexicans aged 18 or older living in 42 randomly selected towns and cities throughout Mexico, interviewed during August 5–13, 1989, for the *Los Angeles Times*, 60 percent of the respondents felt that it had become harder for Mexicans to get work in the United States during the last year; another 7 percent were unsure (data provided to author by I. A. Lewis, director, *Los Angeles Times* Poll). This survey has a sampling error of plus or minus 3 percentage points, and like all "nationwide" sample surveys done in Mexico, it underrepresents residents of rural communities to some unknown extent.

7. In the *Los Angeles Times* survey in August 1989 (see note 6), 6 percent of the national sample considered it "very likely" that they or someone else in their household would take up residence in the United States within the next 12 months, and another 16 percent said they were "fairly likely" to move to the United States. In response to another question, however, 62 percent said that they had been "discouraged" from going to the United States by recent changes in U.S. immigration laws.

8. The remaining responses were scattered among many different response categories.

9. In a nationwide study of employer sanctions enforcement, Robert Bach and his research associates (Bach and Brill, 1990) have likewise found that use of false documents is pervasive, and that the quality of such documents has improved so much that employers are no longer seeing poorly fabricated ones. The researchers have observed that for unauthorized migrants today, the U.S. labor market experience routinely includes the search for and acquisition of fraudulent documents.

10. The mean price was $87. Among a separate sample of 500 urban, undocumented

immigrant workers employed in southern California who were interviewed by the Center for U.S.-Mexican Studies in 1987–88, 41 percent had got their present jobs using bogus or borrowed documents (see Cornelius, 1990).

11. In the nationwide *Los Angeles Times* survey conducted in Mexico in August 1989 (see note 6), 38 percent of the respondents reported having relatives in the United States.

12. Other recent field studies of high-emigration communities in west-central Mexico have also found high rates of participation in the IRCA legalization programs. For example, among a small sample (*N* = 67) of Jalisco residents—located in 19 different localities of *municipios* (counties) having the highest emigration rates in the state— 79 percent had applied for legalization. Of these, 93 percent had sought SAW permits. The overwhelming majority (83 percent) had initiated the legalization process in the United States rather than in Mexico (i.e., after entering the United States as undocumented workers). See Alejandre (1989).

13. High fraudulent SAW application rates have been reported or estimated by other researchers. For example, Alejandre (1989, table 10, p. 28) found that only 59 percent of the SAW applicants in his sample of Jalisco residents had been employed in U.S. agriculture prior to obtaining a SAW permit. Martin and Taylor (1988) have also assembled statistics suggesting that half or more of the 600,000 SAW applications submitted by California "farmworkers" may have been fraudulent. They point out that the number of SAW applicants in California exceeds the total number of people (not just seasonal workers) believed to be in the state's entire agricultural labor force.

14. Elsewhere in this volume, Douglas Massey and his colleagues (chapter six) also report that IRCA failed to discourage undocumented migration to the United States from the Mexican sending communities that they studied in 1987–88. Another survey, conducted in 1989 among 213 households in a traditionally high-emigration *municipio* (county) in the state of Jalisco, found a significant increase in migration to the United States since 1987 (de la Rocha and Latapí, 1989). The researchers concluded that IRCA's legalization programs (especially the SAW program) and the persistence of Mexico's economic crisis were primarily responsible for the increase.

15. Most RAW permit-seekers are likely to be disappointed. The registration period for this program opened on September 1, 1989, and closed on November 30, 1989. As of January 9, 1990, more than 671,500 RAW application cards had been processed by the U.S. Immigration and Naturalization Service. Additional applications, still being sorted, may bring the final total to 700,000. Among the applicants processed through early January, 86 percent were migrants living in the United States, with or without accompanying immediate family members (data provided by Statistical Division, U.S. Immigration and Naturalization Service, Washington, D.C.). These workers are, in effect, part of the unauthorized immigrant workforce already present in the United States. No Replenishment Agricultural Workers have been authorized for 1990, because the U.S. Department of Labor determined through employer surveys conducted in 1988 and 1989 that no shortage of farm labor was likely to exist in 1990.

16. Within California, general amnesty and SAW applicants were heavily concentrated in the Los Angeles metropolitan area, where 1.1 million applications were submitted (Bean et al., 1989).

17. The overwhelming majority of these legalization applicants seem destined to complete the process successfully. Through November 1989, 95 percent of general amnesty applications were being approved in final form in the U.S. Immigration and Naturalization Service's Western Region, which includes California, Arizona, Nevada, Hawaii, and Guam. Final determinations were still pending on most of the SAW applications in this region, but among the 525,000 applications adjudicated nationally through November 1989, 93.4 percent were approved. INS unpublished documents for 1989.

18. Alejandre (1989, p. 13) also reports that Christmas 1988 brought a much heavier than normal return of migrants from the United States—a phenomenon that was observed in all parts of Jalisco.

19. Our interviews in the research communities suggest that many SAW applicants do not intend to remain in agricultural work—which the 1986 U.S. immigration law does not require them to do. Moreover, most of those who applied for SAW permits using fraudulent documents were never farmworkers in the first place, and are currently working in nonagricultural jobs in the United States.

20. Of course, the increase in female migration reflects a variety of factors in addition to legalization under IRCA, including the changing role of women in the Mexican family and the proliferation of U.S. jobs for which women are the preferred labor source. The trend toward heavier migration of women and children from Mexico to the United States dates from the 1960s, although IRCA seems to have accelerated it. See de la Rocha and Latapí (1989) and Cleeland (1989). This conclusion is consistent with the broader picture revealed by Woodrow and Passel's analysis (chapter two, in this volume) of data from the U.S. Bureau of the Census June 1988 Current Population Survey, which suggest that females may constitute the majority of the post-IRCA undocumented population from Mexico.

21. Experienced observers of the migratory flow from the state of Oaxaca to California have also reported that IRCA's legalization programs stimulated a great deal of first-time migration by women and children in 1988 and 1989. They report that male family heads already in the United States encouraged their dependents to join them there almost immediately after the family heads applied for legalization. Since the vast majority of these family members could not qualify for amnesty themselves, and entered the U.S. illegally, they are now "stuck" in this country, unable to travel back and forth to their home community as easily as the family head (unpublished research reported at a workshop on Oaxacan Migration to California's Agricultural Sector, Center for U.S.-Mexican Studies, University of California–San Diego, and California Institute of Rural Studies, Feb. 15, 1990).

22. The largest group of unsuccessful migrants was in Tlaccuitapa, where more than 35 people had sought entry into the United States under the SAW program, using a single letter of agricultural employment certification that had been obtained by a Tlacuitapeño from a grower in Oregon. Numerous photocopies of the letter were made, the name of the employee whose name appeared on the original was "whited out," and other names were inserted. Most of these crude forgeries were rejected by U.S. immigration authorities at Mexicali, but some Tlacuitapeños were able to cross the border with them.

23. Bach and Brill (1990) report that the job-finding time of newly arriving migrants in the Houston, Texas, labor market has doubled since IRCA's enactment.

24. This finding is consistent with results from another recent survey study of a traditional sending area in Jalisco, which found no significant change in the amount or frequency of remittances received by households during the last three years (see de la Rocha and Latapí (1989).

25. Labor union leaders have reported that in Salinas, the center of one of California's most important agricultural zones, wages for farm workers fell from $7.00 per hour in 1984 to $5.50 per hour in November 1989. The drop was attributed mainly to a massive influx of SAW workers into the region's labor force (Stamp, 1989). Labor organizers in southern California have also observed an IRCA-related excess of migrant labor in that region's agricultural sector, which they blame for increases in unemployment and underemployment among Oaxacan migrants (reported at workshop on Oaxacan Migration to California's Agricultural Sector, Center for U.S.-Mexican Studies, UCSD, University of California–San Diego, and California Institute for Rural Studies, Feb. 15, 1990).

26. For a fuller development of this point, see Alarcón (1989).

27. For syntheses of the empirical evidence documenting this long-term evolution, see Tienda (1990) and Portes and Borocz (1989).

References

Alarcón, Rafael. 1989. " 'Gracias a Dios y al Norte': Tlacuitapa y su relación con los Estados Unidos." Center for U.S.-Mexican Studies, University of California–San Diego, August. Photocopy.

Alarcón, Rafael, Macrina Cárdenas, and Germán Vega. Forthcoming. "Los procesos migratories en los Altos de Jalisco." *Encuentro: Estudios Sociales y Humanidades*, no. 16 (El Colegio de Jalisco, Guadalajara, Mexico).

Alejandre, Jesús Arroyo. 1989. "Algunos impactos de la ley de reforma y control de immigración (IRCA) en una región de Jalisco de fuerte emigración hacia Estados Unidos de Norteamerica." Paper presented at the conference on International Effects of the Immigration Reform and Control Act of 1986, supported by the RAND Corporation, Guadalajara, Mexico, May 3–5, p. 15.

Bach, R. L., and Howard Brill. 1990. "Shifting the Burden: The Impacts of IRCA on U.S. Labor Markets." Interim Report to the Division of Immigration Policy and Research, U.S. Department of Labor, February. Photocopy.

Bean, Frank D., Georges Vernez, and Charles B. Keely. 1989. *Opening and Closing the Doors: Evaluating Immigration Reform and Control*. Santa Monica, Calif., and Washington, D.C.: RAND and Urban Institute.

Calvo, Thomas, and Gustavo Lopez, eds. 1988. *Movimientos de población en el occidente de México*. Mexico, D.F., and Zamora, Mich.: Centre d'Etudes Mexicaines et Centramericaines and El Colegio de Michoacán.

Castro, Gustavo Lopez. 1986. *La casa dividida: Un estudio de caso sobre la migración a Estados Unidos en un pueblo michoacano*. Zamora, Mich.: El Colegio de Michoacán.

Castro, Gustavo López, and Sergio Pardo Galván, eds. 1988. *Migración en el Occidente de México*. Zamora, Mich.: El Colegio de Michoacán.

Cleeland, Nancy. 1989. "Many More Women Decide to Flee Mexico." *San Diego Union*, Aug. 27.

Cornelius, Wayne A. 1976. "Outmigration from Rural Mexican Communities." In *The Dynamics of Migration: International Migration*. Occasional Monograph Series, vol. 2, no. 5, 1–40. Washington, D.C.: Interdisciplinary Communications Program, Smithsonian Institute.

————. 1982. "Interviewing Undocumented Immigrants: Methodological Reflections Based on Fieldwork in Mexico and the United States." *International Migration Review* 16 (2, Summer): 378–411.

————. 1990. "The U.S. Demand for Mexican Labor." In *Mexican Migration to the United States: Process, Consequences, and Policy Options*, edited by Wayne A. Cornelius and Jorge A. Bustamante. La Jolla, Calif.: Center for U.S.-Mexican Studies, University of California–San Diego.

Dagodag, W. Jim. 1984. "Illegal Mexican Immigration to California from Western Mexico." In *Patterns of Undocumented Migration: Mexico and the United States*, edited by Richard C. Jones, 61–73. Totowa, N.J.: Rowman & Allanheld.

de la Rocha, Mercedes González, and Agustin Escobar Latapí. 1989. "Efecto de IRCA en los patrones migratorios de una comunidad en Los Altos de Jalisco." Report submitted to the Commission on the Study of International Migration and Cooperative Economic Development, Washington, D.C. November.

Jones, Richard C. 1984. "Macro-Patterns of Undocumented Migration between Mexico and the United States." In *Patterns of Undocumented Migration: Mexico and the United States*, edited by Richard C. Jones, 33–57. Totowa, N.J.: Rowman & Allanheld.

Martin, Philip L., and J. Edward Taylor. 1988. "Harvest of Confusion: SAWs, RAWs, and Farmworkers." Working Paper PRIP-UI-4. Washington, D.C.: Urban Institute.

————. 1990. "Immigration Reform and California Agriculture a Year Later." *California Agriculture* 44 (1, Jan.–Feb.): 24–27.

Mines, Richard. 1981. *Developing a Community Tradition of Migration: A Field Study in Rural Zacatecas, Mexico, and California Settlement Areas.* Monograph No. 3. La Jolla, Calif.: Center for U.S.-Mexican Studies, University of California–San Diego.

Massey, Douglas, Rafael Alarcón, Jorge Durand, and Humberto González. 1987. *Return to Aztlan: The Social Process of International Migration from Western Mexico.* Berkeley and Los Angeles: University of California Press.

Portes, Alejandro, and Jozsef Borocz. 1989. "Contemporary Immigration: Theoretical Perspectives on Its Determinants and Modes of Incorporation." *International Migration Review* 23 (3, Fall): 606–630.

Stamp, Kathleen. 1989. "For Migrant Workers, Legality Lowers Wages." *New York Times*, Dec. 3, 1989, vol. 139 no. 48,073 sec. F, p. 12.

Tienda, Marta. 1990. "Mexican Immigration: A Sociological Perspective." In *Mexican Migration to the United States: Process, Consequences, and Policy Options*, edited by Wayne A. Cornelius and Jorge A. Bustamante. La Jolla, Calif.: Center for U.S.-Mexican Studies, University of California-San Diego.

Chapter Nine

UNDOCUMENTED MIGRATION SINCE IRCA: AN OVERALL ASSESSMENT

Jeffrey S. Passel, Frank D. Bean, and Barry Edmonston

The chapters in this volume rely on a variety of data sources and methods to address the issue of undocumented immigration to the United States in the post-IRCA era. A thorough synthesis of their results, as well as an understanding of the issues involved in illegal immigration, require further discussion of the nature of undocumented immigration to the United States. Specifically, it is necessary to integrate information on different types of immigrants and their various immigration statuses (both legal and illegal) with the myriad data sources and methods available.

Most of the information in this volume, as well as most previous studies of illegal immigration to the United States, have focused on illegal *Mexican* migration. This focus has generally been warranted because the majority of undocumented immigrants have been from Mexico (Warren and Passel, 1987). Temporary flows of "sojourners" from Mexico, which appear to swamp smaller flows from other countries, have persisted in the post-IRCA period in spite of the legislation's attempts to eliminate them. Among "settlers," too, illegal Mexican immigrants have constituted a majority (Passel, 1986). However, with Mexicans accounting for the bulk of legalizations under IRCA (González Baker and Bean, 1990), the predominance of Mexicans among undocumented settlers may have changed.

The emphasis on Mexican undocumented immigration has also resulted from data and methodological issues. More (and often better) data have been available to address illegal Mexican immigration. In addition, many of the methods used require large samples; residual techniques, especially, perform better with large populations and relatively large residuals. Consequently, estimates of undocumented Mexican stocks and flows have tended to be more frequent and of better quality than estimates for illegal immigrants from other countries.

The non-Mexican component of undocumented immigration is

increasingly important and should not be overlooked, however. With IRCA's two legalization programs reducing the size of the undocumented Mexican population, the relative importance of undocumented immigrants from other countries has increased. Some new data have recently been developed to attempt to measure these stocks and flows. Specifically, data from the INS Nonimmigrant Information System (NIIS), analyzed by Warren in chapter three in this volume, represent a significant improvement in monitoring stocks and flows of non-Mexican undocumented immigrants. However, as is evident from other chapters in this book, the Mexican component still dominates the research agenda.

IRCA aimed to reduce both the stock and the flow of undocumented immigrants. It was designed to deal with sojourner and settler undocumented immigrants. Some provisions apply to both types, but others are specifically designed for one or the other (Bean, Vernez, and Keely, 1989). The general legalization program offered legal status to one particular group of settlers, specifically those who had established illegal residence in the United States before 1982. The requirement of continuous residence in the United States since January 1, 1982, was to ensure that the legalizations went to settlers rather than commuters or temporary migrants. The legalization of special agricultural workers (SAWs) was designed for the segment of the sojourner population working in agriculture.

The IRCA legalization programs did succeed in reducing the size of the illegal immigrant population by legalizing large numbers of formerly illegal migrants. This effect is obvious, but two major questions remain about IRCA's effect on the magnitude of illegal migration to the United States. 1) Has IRCA led to a reduction in the numbers of illegal migrants entering the United States, principally from Mexico? 2) Has the size of the undocumented alien population living in the United States been reduced (beyond just the number who legalized under IRCA)?

FLOW OF MIGRANTS ACROSS THE U.S.-MEXICO BORDER

The largest flow of migrants, temporary and permanent, into the United States occurs across the border with Mexico. The size of this flow back and forth across this border is immense—more than 200 million crossings occur through ports of entry every year. Of course, most of these crossings do not represent net in-migration to (or out-migration from) the United States; rather, they represent shoppers, tourists, and commuters crossing for trips of short duration.

Another large flow across this border consists of temporary labor migrants. This flow, which consists principally of "entries without inspection" (or EWIs), is the one that the U.S. Immigration and Naturalization Service (INS) taps into with border patrol apprehensions. The temporary nature of the labor migration should be apparent from the composition of the flow—about 80 percent to 90 percent of the apprehensions are adult Mexican males. If all the Mexican males apprehended over the last 10–20 years actually represented permanent migrants to the United States, the adult population of Mexico would now be overwhelmingly female and, conversely, the Mexican-born population of the United States would be overwhelmingly male. Neither of these situations has occurred. The close relationship of apprehensions with seasonal labor demands in the United States further reinforces the view that this is a temporary flow of labor (Bean et al., chapter four in this volume).

Relationship between INS Apprehensions and Migration Flows

Most references in the media to INS apprehensions of illegal entrants along the U.S.-Mexico border make the simplistic assumption that there is a direct relationship between the number of illegal immigrants and the number of INS apprehensions. Both the popular and official interpretations of the apprehensions data further assume that there are more illegal immigrants than apprehensions. This assumption is usually stated as "for every one that gets caught, X get away," where "X" most often equals two or three.

These interpretations of the apprehensions data fail on a number of accounts. First, they fail to distinguish clearly between settlers and sojourners. Empirical studies of the size of the undocumented population in the United States do not support the proposition that the INS apprehensions also represent net additions of illegal settlers (i.e., those who "got away") to the U.S. population. Second, they fail to take into account that the count of apprehensions includes many repeaters (i.e., individuals who are apprehended more than once on each trip to the United States plus other individuals who make multiple trips to the United States). Third, they assume that the "got-away ratio" is independent of the level of INS effort put into apprehending aliens and the resources (personnel and materiel) available to the border patrol.

What the apprehensions actually represent, in the most basic terms, is the portion of the migratory flow across the U.S.-Mexico border that is intercepted by the INS. Simply multiplying apprehensions by a "got-away" ratio is inappropriate for estimating flows across the border, because apprehended individuals tend to make additional attempts to enter the United States until they are successful. As a result, if the probability of apprehension increases, apprehensions increase at a faster rate because multiple apprehensions of the same individuals also increase. In other words, there is a relationship between the number of successful border crossers and the number of apprehensions, but it is not necessarily a simple or a one-to-one relationship. (Note also that the same statements hold true for the counts of crossers in the Zapata Canyon photographs [chapter seven, by Bustamante]. Individuals apprehended by the INS on one attempt could appear in photographs on subsequent attempts. Thus, as in the apprehensions data, multiple appearances by the same individual preclude a straightforward interpretation of counts as a one-to-one indicator of crossers.)

As several chapters in this volume indicate, careful attention to the probability of apprehension is necessary to understand the changing relationship between the number of apprehensions and the number of border crossers. Two broad conditions affect the probability of apprehension: INS effort and the "skill" of the crossers. If the INS devotes more personnel to patrolling the border or makes technological improvements in detection technology, the probability of apprehension should increase. On the other hand, if the crossers become more skillful at eluding detection (e.g., by learning from previous apprehensions or by using "coyotes"), the probability of apprehension should decrease. Such changes in the probability of apprehension affect the reported apprehensions.

Review of Research Studies

Two studies in this volume—by Bean et al. (chapter four), and Espenshade (chapter five)—and a recent report by Crane et al. (1990) use time-series methods to analyze apprehensions data as an indicator of illegal migration into the United States across the southern border. The latter two of these studies try to disentangle the relationship between border crossings and apprehensions. To deal with the effect of the probability of apprehension on the level of apprehensions, they use two different approaches.

The Bean et al. and Espenshade studies are companion pieces and thus use virtually identical models. Both conceptualize apprehensions as a product of the size of the population at risk of being apprehended (i.e., the people crossing the border illegally) times the probability of apprehension. They further model the number of border crossers as a function of the size of the Mexican population likely to migrate and the propensity to migrate. The propensity to migrate is modeled with economic factors, seasonal factors, and factors related to IRCA. Bean et al. do not directly estimate the probability of apprehension. Rather, they include INS effort in terms of linewatch, or non-linewatch hours (depending upon which type of apprehension is being modeled) and U.S. Border Patrol resources (budget) in their model as indicators of the probability of apprehension. The economic variables included in the model use national ratios of wages and unemployment rates; ratios specific to certain areas in Mexico and the southwestern United States might be better indicators of the factors affecting migration, but such ratios are not generally available. The final result of their analysis is an estimate of the number of apprehensions averted as a result of IRCA, that is, the number of additional apprehensions that would have occurred in the absence of IRCA. This modeling effort represents a significant advance in understanding the nature of the flows across the U.S.-Mexico border and their response to IRCA.

Crane et al. (1990) use simpler models in their time-series analysis of migratory flows across the border. They include only linewatch hours (as a measure of INS effort) and seasonal effects. In one of their models, they also include a time trend to represent the increasing size of the population of potential migrants in Mexico. By ignoring economic and social factors, Crane et al. risk some misspecification of their models. In fact, the apparent serial correlation of their annual residuals (especially for the pre-IRCA period) and the large standard errors of their residuals suggest that their model could be improved by including such variables. It is nonetheless useful for their purposes, and from their time-series analyses, Crane et al. derive estimates of apprehensions averted after the passage of IRCA.

Espenshade's research extends the work of Bean et al. His model includes the same variables to represent the population at risk of migrating and the propensity to migrate. The contribution of Espenshade's research is that it explicitly converts apprehensions into estimated border crossings using an estimate of the probability of apprehension derived from the proportion of all apprehensions that are multiple apprehensions. The result is an estimate of the reduction in border crossings brought about by IRCA, rather than the reduction in apprehensions.

Crane et al. (1990) also convert the estimate of reduction in apprehensions into an estimate of the number and proportion of border crossings averted by IRCA. Their approach is to supply educated guesses (or a range of guesses) for various populations and proportions in a logical model of the border crossing and apprehension process. They also estimate the probability of apprehension from data on multiple apprehensions and derive essentially the same formula as Espenshade, based on slightly different assumptions.

The basic issue for both Espenshade and Crane et al. concerning the translation of apprehensions into flows is that of estimating the probability of apprehension. The crucial piece of data they use to estimate this probability is the proportion of apprehendees reported to have been apprehended previously. These data, collected by the Border Patrol, are neither verified for accuracy nor subject to cross-checking, and are hand-tallied for administrative reports. Further, the administrative definition of a repeater does not correspond to that used by Espenshade or Crane et al. The INS defines a repeat apprehendee as someone "previously required to depart" and generally requires an oral admission or recognition by the Border Patrol officer. This could mean a previous apprehension on attempt to enter this month, this year, or ever. In addition, the difficult field environment in which the data are obtained does not facilitate accuracy. Indeed, the INS has found that much of the information is invented, and feels the data are so inaccurate as to be useless. It stopped collecting such data in fiscal year 1990 because of data quality concerns (Michael Hoefer, personal communication, August 1990).

Accurate measurement of multiple apprehensions is essential to estimates in all three papers. Furthermore, the time frame defining the multiple apprehensions affects the interpretation of the resulting estimates. Crane et al. contend that the probability of apprehension has remained virtually constant over a long period of time. They also argue that the data are probably accurate, since potential biases offset one another. Other indicators suggest that a relatively constant probability of apprehension is illogical. In the nearly 12 years since 1978, linewatch hours devoted to enforcement have more than doubled. Yet, there have been variations of more than two to one in the number of apprehensions per linewatch hour, even at similar levels of enforcement. In addition, the Border Patrol has upgraded its equipment substantially over this period, including the adoption of some high-tech innovations for detecting and apprehending potential EWIs. Moreover, the highly seasonal pattern of apprehensions suggests that there may be monthly variation in apprehension probabilities (to maintain a constant probability of apprehension, the INS would have to match staffing levels to flow levels). All of this suggests that the probability of apprehension has not remained constant over time. Espenshade does, in fact, find substantial monthly variation in the probability, but the pattern is not so strong as the seasonal pattern of apprehensions. In light of these results, apprehension probabilities must have varied substantially over time.

The models derived by Espenshade and Crane et al. (1990) further assume that the probability of apprehension does not vary across individuals, nor does it change for subsequent trips after an individual has been apprehended one or more times. Data to address this issue are negligible, although these are strong statistical assumptions about the probability process. Some results from a survey in Mexico covering migration to the United States during the 1974–78 period contradict these assumptions and suggest that the probability of apprehension is much higher for individuals who have been previously apprehended than for those who have not (Kossoudji, 1990). The various problems with the data on multiple apprehensions and other assumptions underlying the models suggest that caution should be exercised in interpreting estimates of border crossings based on apprehensions data.

Research Findings

In spite of the problems of apprehensions data and of modeling them, two consistent findings emerge from the research. *First and foremost, there has been a clear reduction in the flow of undocumented immigrants across the U.S.-Mexico border in the post-IRCA period.* Furthermore, this reduction has occurred in the presence of expanded INS effort, indicated by more linewatch hours and upgraded equipment—factors that should lead to an increase in apprehensions, not a decrease. The current research suggests that a portion, and possibly a significant portion, of the reduction in apprehensions is attributable to the legalization of large numbers of Mexicans in the general legalization and SAWs programs.

Second, studies are broadly consistent regarding how much of the reduction can be attributed to IRCA. Espenshade estimates reductions of 30 percent and 44 percent in border crossings for fiscal years 1987 and 1988, respectively, that can be attributed to IRCA. Bean et al. estimate a 47 percent decline in apprehensions between November 1986 and September 1989 below the level that would be anticipated in the absence of IRCA. For the same period, the models used by Crane et al. (1990) lead to estimates of 21 percent to 32 percent in the decline in apprehensions.

Bean et al. further attempt to partition the decline into the component due to removal of the SAWs from the illegal labor migration stream and other IRCA effects, which would include any deterrent effect of employer sanctions. They find that about half of the decrease in apprehensions was attributable to SAW legalizations and half to other IRCA effects. They found no significant impact of the general legalization program on apprehensions. Indeed, none should be expected, since this group is made up of settlers who would contribute very little to the apprehensions. This latter point was corroborated by John Bjerke, of the INS (personal communication, May 1990), who stated that about two-thirds of a sample of legalized aliens interviewed reported that they had made no trips out of the United States since 1982. Although not directly comparable, the work of Crane et al. points in the same direction.

Other Evidence

Other studies in this volume address IRCA's effect on the magnitude of immigration across the U.S.-Mexico border less directly than the apprehensions studies. Bustamante's Zapata Canyon study, in chapter seven, suffers from some of the same limitations as the apprehensions data—for example, the lack of any measure of successful entry to the United States, the inclusion of the same individual more than once (crossings versus entries), and the failure to distinguish settlers from sojourners. In addition, the Zapata Canyon data do not have a pre-IRCA baseline for comparison. Nonetheless, Bustamante's data show a clear decline in the post-IRCA period, with the numbers of crossers in late 1988 falling significantly below the corresponding figures for 1986.

Cornelius's survey, in chapter eight, finds some evidence of a small deterrent effect of IRCA on undocumented immigration. About 83 percent of undocumented immigrants and would-be immigrants think that IRCA has made getting a job in the United States harder. Furthermore, about 20 percent of potential immigrants who considered going to the United States gave an IRCA-related reason for not making the trip. Cornelius does note, however, that this small effect may be more than offset by new undocumented immigrants, notably wives and children of newly legalized aliens, leaving Mexico to join the family member in the United States.

There is some contradictory evidence of no deterrent effect from

IRCA. Massey et al., in chapter six, find no evidence in their study communities that IRCA has lowered the probability of first-time undocumented migration to the United States. Nor do they find that the costs or difficulty of illegal entry have increased. However, Massey et al. characterize their results as "preliminary" because of the small number of communities involved, the very small number of cases, and the necessity of extrapolating from the past.

The report by Crane et al. also attempts to find evidence of a decline in the stock and flow of undocumented workers resulting from employer sanctions, by examining the change over time in wages of car washers and dishwashers in cities with significant undocumented populations and those without. Their analysis requires a number of assumptions about the relationship of wages to labor supply, plus many assumptions about the nature of their data and their statistical model. Overall, they find little evidence of an IRCA-related effect on undocumented workers in these occupations. Given the small number of observations, any effect would have to be quite large to be apparent, so their finding is not surprising. In addition, the economic model does not fully take into account the possibility of a pre-existing oversupply of labor with wage levels being supported by a minimum wage. If such a situation existed, even if IRCA did reduce the labor supply in these occupations no effect on wages would be found.

STOCK OF UNDOCUMENTED IMMIGRANTS IN THE UNITED STATES AND ADDITIONS TO THE PERMANENT RESIDENT POPULATION

Woodrow and Passel, in chapter two, examine directly the effect of IRCA on the number of undocumented immigrants living in the United States. They find that IRCA has definitely reduced the undocumented population of the United States to the point where the total number may be smaller than the number in the country in 1980. However, the evidence from their analysis of Current Population Survey (CPS) and census data is that the reduction is due entirely to the legalization of formerly illegal residents; that is, they do not find evidence consistent with the idea that IRCA's employer sanctions have led to out-migration of undocumented residents. Nor do they find evidence for a decrease in the overall flow of illegal migrants, although some of their results suggest the possibility of a decline in the flow of migrants from Mexico (thus supporting the evidence reported earlier from the apprehensions data regarding flows across the U.S.-Mexico border). This result leaves open the question of differential effects of IRCA on Mexican flows because of the high level of Mexican participation in the legalization programs, the effects of Southwest regional economies in the United States and their labor demands, the geographic concentration of Mexican immigrants, and other factors that affect non-Mexican undocumented immigrants differently from Mexicans.

The CPS data show a definite shift in the composition of the undocumented population living in the United States. As a result of the legalization programs, the proportion of the undocumented population that is Mexican has declined, possibly to the point where a majority of undocumented residents in 1988 may be from countries other than Mexico. More than three-quarters of the Mexican-born population living in the United States consists of legal residents, according to the CPS. Before the passage of IRCA, less than 40 percent were legal residents. This shift is one of the most significant changes wrought by IRCA and is likely to have long-term ramifications for the composition and magnitude of future legal immigration flows, because of the delayed effects of family reunification policies.

Another change found in the CPS-based estimates of the undocumented population is the greatly increased proportion of women in this population. Apparently only 20 percent to 40 percent of the undocumented population included in the 1988 CPS are men. In the 1980 census estimates, the corresponding figure was 55 percent. The decreased proportion of men is the result of the disproportionately male population that legalized, particularly in the SAW program. In addition, there is some evidence to suggest that post-IRCA flows of undocumented female immigrants are increasing. Bean et al. report that apprehensions of Mexican women and children (and of non-Mexicans) increased in 1988 and 1989, a time when apprehensions of Mexican males were decreasing dramatically. Cornelius also finds some evidence for augmented undocumented flows of families (i.e., women and children) who are leaving Mexico to join the newly legalized aliens in the United States. Finally, Bustamante's photographs from the Zapata Canyon show higher percentages of women in the flows for 1987 and 1988 than for 1986.

Visa Overstayers

The research reported by Warren represents the first successful attempt to quantify the number of visa overstayers, an important but unstudied component of illegal migration to the United States. For fiscal years 1985–88, Warren estimates 217,000 to 255,000 estimated visa overstayers per year. These figures *do not* represent a net addition to the U.S. population each year; rather, they represent the number of *new* overstayers each year. To estimate net additions to the population from visa overstayers in one year, it is necessary to deduct the number of existing visa overstayers who depart the country or become legal residents. For 1988, Warren generates provisional estimates of *net* overstayers and finds that the net visa overstayers of 174,000 are almost one-third below the total estimated overstayers of 255,000. Although Warren labels the estimates of net overstayers as "provisional," they should represent an upper bound on net overstayers for 1988 because they fail to take into account several categories of persons adjusting status from temporary to permanent residence. The relationship of net to gross overstayers that Warren finds for 1988 should be typical of earlier years, however.

The estimates of net visa overstayers are broadly consistent with the CPS and census-based estimates of undocumented immigration. Warren finds less than 200,000 (174,000) net visa overstayers per year, with about 48,000 per year from Mexico. The vast majority of Mexican illegal immigrants are assumed to be EWIs, not visa overstayers. However, most non-Mexican undocumented immigrants are probably visa overstayers. Thus, an appropriate comparison group for Warren's estimates is CPS-based estimates of change in the number of non-Mexican illegal residents. The studies of undocumented immigration for the 1980s that are based solely on CPS data yield estimates of average annual changes in the undocumented population of roughly 100,000 to 180,000 for countries other than Mexico. Warren's estimates for 1988 fall in the middle of this range. In addition, tabulations of overstayers by region of origin are also broadly consistent with the CPS data—Europe and Canada show lower levels in both datasets and Latin America, higher levels. Exact agreement between the two datasets should not be expected, given the sampling variability of the CPS estimates and the residual nature of both sets of estimates.

Warren finds a slight increase between 1985 and 1988 in the number of annual apparent overstayers. On its face, this finding suggests no impact of IRCA on the flow of illegal immigrants who enter through this route. However, to some extent, this finding is derived from the increases in the number of nonimmigrant visa grants during the same time period. When examined in terms of the number of overstayers per nonimmigrant entry, the same data show a decline in the *rate* of overstayers. However, this trend information must be considered in light of the assumptions underlying the estimates. The estimates of visa overstayers are residual estimates, derived by taking the difference of two numbers that are relatively large compared with the number of apparent overstayers. Thus, the resulting estimates are sensitive to rather small errors in the assumptions. (The CPS-based estimates of the undocumented population have this same property.) Trend information, derived by differencing the annual estimates, is even more sensitive to possible errors in the assumptions. Thus, although the annual estimates appear to be robust in terms of their overall magnitude and geographic composition, year-to-year differences are particularly sensitive to the assumptions. As a result, the trend over time could differ from what is shown in Warren's paper.

CONCLUSION

The authors of this book have attempted to assess the impact of IRCA on the stock and flow of illegal immigrants to the United States during the three-year period after the legislation was passed. Full implementation of the employer sanctions provisions of IRCA were delayed by the INS for more than a year following passage of the law. Thus, the full force of the deterrent effects of the act may not yet have emerged. Several of the studies reported here are based on data collected before or just after the beginning of INS enforcement of employer sanctions. Consequently, only very large and immediate effects are likely to be detectable.

The studies are generally consistent in suggesting a decrease in the flow of illegal migrants across the U.S.-Mexico border, notwithstanding the difficulties of detecting an effect. A large proportion of the decrease is due to the effects of the legalization programs. The SAW legalization, to a great extent, and the general legalization program, to a lesser extent, removed individuals from the illegal flow in two ways: first, by making them part of the legal flow of labor and other migrants across the border; and, second, by allowing them to settle permanently in the United States. The effect of removing legalized migrants from the illegal flow across the border does not appear to account for all of the estimated decline in flows across the U.S.-Mexico border, however. Thus, IRCA may have had some deterrent effect.

As a result of IRCA, the proportion of the undocumented population and undocumented flow from Mexico is smaller than before IRCA. In addition, a larger proportion of the post-IRCA undocumented population is female, especially for Mexican migrants. This compositional shift has occurred because IRCA legalized a very large segment of the undocumented Mexican and undocumented male labor force. There is also some evidence that the composition of the undocumented flow has changed because families of formerly undocumented immigrants are migrating to join the legalized men in the United States. In addition, IRCA's employer sanctions provisions may have brought about some of this compositional shift, since female illegal migrants may find it easier than males to locate jobs less subject to the enforcement of employer sanctions. One consequence of these patterns and of other IRCA provisions may be an alteration of the migration process, so that there may now be more settlers and fewer sojourners than before the enactment of IRCA. More data are needed, however, before this can be confirmed.

The INS has instituted a policy of not deporting illegal aliens who are immediate relatives of aliens legalized under IRCA (González Baker, forthcoming). Although the number of such relatives is not known, they may constitute a significant fraction of the remaining undocumented population. If so, the number of *deportable* aliens actually residing in the United States may now be even smaller than the estimates from the CPS and other sources suggest.

Whether these changes continue into the future is a key question in determining IRCA's success in controlling illegal immigration. Ultimately, an important factor will be the ability of the INS to obtain sufficient budgetary resources to enforce the act's provisions (Fix and Hill, 1990). Some recent data suggest that undocumented migrant flows continue to evolve in the post-IRCA period. INS apprehensions are higher in fiscal 1990 than they were a year earlier, but the evidence pointing to higher flows remains contradictory after taking INS effort into account. For the last three months of 1989, Mexican border apprehensions were 40 percent higher than the corresponding period in 1988. However, linewatch hours, the most direct measure of INS effort, were up about 38 percent. This evidence, then, suggests hardly any increase in flow. For the first three months of 1990, however, apprehensions were 52 percent higher than one year earlier, whereas INS effort was up only 17 percent. The majority of the increase in apprehensions was accounted for by a 73 percent increase in apprehensions in the San Diego sector, which had a roughly constant number of enforcement hours (Michael Hoefer, personal communication, May 1990). Thus, there may have been a turn-around in the flow in early 1990.

It is important to continue to assess IRCA's effects on illegal immigration and the U.S. labor force. Data from the 1990 Census should shed additional light on these issues by providing the first detailed look at the foreign-born population since the enactment of IRCA. As the legalized aliens progress through the process of attaining permanent resident status and, eventually, citizenship, more information on their settlement patterns and adaptation to American society will become available; such information has been particularly lacking on the SAWs population to this point. As IRCA continues to be implemented and its employer sanctions enforced, its success or failure at reducing the stock and flow of undocumented immigrants should become more measurable. At this point, however, we can conclude that IRCA has had an impact, but to a large extent because it legalized a large proportion of the formerly undocumented population. Whether the effects will persist can only be answered with the passage of time. Ultimately, measurement of IRCA's full effects will require verification with new data and new research.

References

Baker, Susan González. Forthcoming. *The Cautious Welcome: The Legalization Programs of the Immigration Reform and Control Act.* Washington, D.C.: Program for Research on Immigration Policy, Urban Institute.

Baker, Susan González, and Frank D. Bean. 1990. "The Legalization Programs of the 1986 Immigration Reform and Control Act: Moving Beyond the First Phase." In *In Defense of the Alien,* edited by Lydio F. Tomasi, 3–11. New York: Center for Migration Studies.

Bean, Frank D., Georges Vernez, and Charles B. Keely. 1989. *Opening and Closing the Doors: Evaluating Immigration Reform and Control.* Santa Monica, Calif., and Washington, D.C.: RAND and Urban Institute.

Crane, Keith, et al. 1990. "The Effect of Employer Sanctions on the Flow of Undocumented Immigrants to the United States." Program for Research on Immigration Policy JRI-03, Urban Institute Report 90-8. Washington, D.C.: Urban Institute.

Fix, Michael and Paul Hill. 1990. "Enforcing Employer Sanctions: Challenges and Strategies." Program for Research on Immigration Policy JRI-04, Urban Institute Report 90-6. Washington, D.C.: Urban Institute, March.

Kossoudji, Sherrie A. 1990. "Playing Cat and Mouse at the Border: Does the INS Alien Apprehension Strategy Alter the Aggregate Supply of Illegal Labor?" Paper presented at the annual meeting of the Population Association of America, Toronto, May 2–5.

Passel, Jeffrey S. 1986. "Undocumented Immigration." *Annals, American Academy for Political and Social Sciences* 186 (Sept.): 181–221.

Warren, Robert, and Jeffrey S. Passel. 1987. "A Count of the Uncountable: Estimates of Undocumented Aliens Counted in the 1980 U.S. Census." *Demography* 24: 375–96.

ABOUT THE EDITORS

Frank D. Bean is Ashbel Smith Professor of Sociology and Research Associate at the Population Research Center at the University of Texas at Austin. From 1988 to 1990, he was at The Urban Institute where he served as Co-Director of the Program for Research on Immigration Policy and Director of the Population Studies Center. A demographer with specializations in international migration, fertility, the demography of racial and ethnic groups, and population policy, his recent books include *Opening and Closing the Doors: Evaluating Immigration Reform and Control*, (with Georges Vernez and Charles B. Keely), *Mexican and Central American Population and U.S. Immigration Policy* (edited with S. Weintraub and J. Schmandt), and *The Hispanic Population of the United States* (with Marta Tienda).

Barry Edmonston is Senior Research Associate in the Population Studies Center of The Urban Institute. He was previously Associate Professor of Demography and Epidemiology at Cornell University's International Population Center. He has studied population change in Canada and the United States, fertility variations among immigrant groups, and demographic models of the family in recent years, authoring *Population Distribution in American Cities*, and *The Impact of Immigration on Canada's Future Population Growth* (with Roger Avery), and editing *Infant and Child Mortality in Bangladesh* (with Rahdeshyam Bairagi).

Jeffrey S. Passel recently joined The Urban Institute's Population Studies Center as a Senior Research Associate. Prior to this he served as Assistant Division Chief for Estimates and Projections and Chief of the Population Analysis Staff in the Population Division of the U.S. Bureau of the Census. He was the agency's principal technical expert on demographic techniques for measuring census undercount and developed many of the techniques for measuring legal immigration, undocumented immigration, and emigration; his work also includes measuring and defining the Hispanic population, the American Indian population, and other racial/ethnic groups in the United States. Recent publications include *The Coverage of Population in the 1980 Census* (with Robert E. Fay and J. Gregory Robinson), "Change in the Undocumented Population in the United States: 1979–1983" (with Karen A. Woodrow), and "A Count of the Uncountable: Estimates of Undocumented Aliens Counted in the 1980 United States Census" (with Robert Warren).

ABOUT THE CONTRIBUTORS

Jorge A. Bustamante is Eugene Conly Professor of Sociology at the University of Notre Dame. He received the highest award given by the Mexican government to national scholars from the President of Mexico in November of 1988 for his studies on Mexican immigration to the United States. He commutes between South Bend and Tijuana, Baja California where he heads El Colegio de la Frontera Norte, a leading research institution dedicated to the study of U.S.-Mexico border problems. He has coauthored books and has published numerousa articles in scientific journals of the United States, Mexico, France, Germany, Switzerland, Japan and Venezuela.

Wayne A. Cornelius is Gildred Professor of Political Science and Founding Director of the Center for U.S.-Mexican Studies at the University of California, San Diego. He has conducted field research in Mexico since 1962, and has published extensively on rural-to-urban migration in Mexico, Mexican labor migration to the United States, and the Mexican political system. His most recent books are *Mexico's Alternative Political Futures* (coeditor), *Mexican Migration to the United States: Process, Consequences, and Policy Options* (coeditor), and *The Changing Role of Mexican Labor in the U.S. Economy: Sectoral Perspectives* (editor). He is currently writing a book on Mexican migration and U.S. immigration reform.

Katharine M. Donato is Assistant Professor of Sociology at Louisiana State University. She is also the principal investigator for the "Effects of the Immigration Reform and Control Act of 1986: Mexican Immigration to the United States," a project funded by the Sloan Foundation.

Robert F. Dymowski graduated from George Washington University in 1988 with bachelor of science degrees in statistics and computer science. He was the recipient of the Kullback Memorial Prize for Excellence in Statistics in 1988. While at The Urban Institute from 1988 to 1990, he worked on several social and demographic issues including immigration policy, hiring discrimination, and mobility variations by ethnicity. Currently employed with

Westat, Inc. in Rockville, Maryland, an independent research corporation, he is working on an Urban Institute study of the District of Columbia Courthouse Multi-Door Dispute Resolution system.

Thomas J. Espenshade is Professor of Sociology and Faculty Associate of the Office of Population Research at Princeton University. From 1985-87 he headed The Urban Institute's Study of the Impacts of Immigration to California. This project produced several books and numerous articles and reports on the effects of immigration to the United States, including *The Fourth Wave; California's Newest Immigrants*, coauthored by Espenshade. He has written widely on contemporary U.S. immigration and immigrant policy. His current research is related to developing models of undocumented migration to the United States, the role of undocumented migrants in California agriculture, determinants of public attitudes towards undocumented migrants and illegal migration, and proposed reforms of U.S. policy towards legal immigration.

Zai Liang is a doctoral candidate in sociology at the University of Chicago. His research interests are human migration, stratification, and sociology methodology. Currently he is working on his dissertation, which concerns the naturalization process of immigrants in the U.S.

Douglas S. Massey is Professor of Sociology and Public Policy Studies at the University of Chicago. He has written numerous scholarly articles on the general topic of international migration and is coauthor of *Return to Aztlan*, an in-depth study of U.S. migration from four Mexican communities. In collaboration with his colleague Jorge Durand, he has just published a book in Mexico on the depiction of U.S. migration in Mexican folk art, entitled *Doy Gracias: An Iconography of Mexican Migration to the United States*.

Robert Warren has worked with the federal government since 1969, conducting analyses of U.S. immigration statistics with an emphasis on developing methodology for estimating emigration and illegal immigration. He is currently director of the Statistics Division of the Immigration and Naturalization Service. He is coauthor (with Jeffrey S. Passel) of "A Count of the Uncountable: Estimates of Undocumented Aliens Counted in the 1980 United States Census."

Michael J. White is Associate Professor of Sociology at Brown University. He was previously a Senior Research Associate and Acting Director of the Program in Demographic Studies at The Urban Institute. He has held teaching and research appointments at the University of Chicago and Princeton University. His research includes work on internal migration, population distribution, and immigration. Previous research includes use of censuses to trace social, economic, and demographic developments in residential patterns and neighborhoods. He plans to explore several aspects of this research further, such as neighborhood changes in ethnicity, life cycle stages, and socio-economic status.

Karen A. Woodrow has worked at the Census Bureau since 1983 as a demographic statistician on the Population Analysis and Evaluation Staff of the Population Division. Her work involves a number of immigration topics, especially estimation of undocumented immigration and emigration from the United States to other countries. She has published several articles on undocumented immigrants as well as articles applying demographic methods to model labor force status and marital status transitions.